FROM FEMINISM TO LIBERATION

Collected by Edith Hoshino Altbach

SCHENKMAN PUBLISHING CO., INC.

Cambridge, Massachusetts
London, England

Acknowledgements

As much as this book is the work of the women whose articles and poems appear here, the editorial chores sometimes seemed to take on mammoth proportions. These people helped along the way: Thanks go to Enid Eckstein and Ann Gorden, who on a number of occasions read and edited manuscripts; to Dagmar Schultz, who deciphered and translated a German article—a thankless task, since we eventually decided not to use the article; to Don McKelvey, who type-set the original *Radical America* Women's Issue; to the editors at the Schenkman Publishing Co., Cynthia McClintock and Page Hinton for their attention and guidance; and, for service above and beyond the call of duty, thanks go to Mari Jo and Paul Buhle, and my husband, Philip G. Altbach.

Contents

NOTES ON A MOVEMENT
Edith Hoshino Altbach

*Edith Hoshino Altbach is a graduate student
at the University of Wisconsin. She edited
the* Radical America *(Feb. 1970) issue on
Women's Liberation.*

A vigorous and determined social movement has recently gathered supporters and adherents from among America's largest 'silent majority'—
women. Not only are many young women—to date mainly within the
radical movement, in the universities and in the professions—becoming
active in Women's Liberation groups, but women at *all* levels of society are
perceiving that the 'woman problem' was not solved by the suffragists in
the 1920's. The 'new' women's movement has tremendous potential as an
intellectual force and as a social movement with a mass base.

Women's Liberation has actually become fashionable as a topic of conversation, possibly at times among people who are themselves blind to the
explosive significance of the movement's power. Its literature, some of which
was consciously directed to women already in the movement, has filtered
its way into the most respectable places—women's magazines, of course,
but also *Time*, The New York *Times*, various highbrow journals, TV talk
shows. All this attention does not, needless to say, mean that the issues
raised by the movement are now common knowledge throughout this land;
the mass media have merely been quick to recognize and exploit an exciting,
current subject for all its headline and selling power. Moreover, the coverage
the movement has received in such places is often ridiculously superficial.
However, it will not be the purpose of this volume to combat such misinformed and distorted journalism.

In contrast, this book (which grew out of the February, 1970 Special
Issue on Women's Liberation of the journal *Radical America*, published in
Madison, Wisconsin) aims at thoughtful analysis. It hopes particularly to
further critical analysis of the Women's Liberation Movement and its revolutionary potential, as well as of the many functions of women's subjugation in pre-capitalist as well as in our neo-capitalist society. It is too early
to say anything conclusive on the directions the Women's Liberation

1

Movement will take. We can, however, see its strength and potential for human liberation, and there is reason to believe that the movement has a good chance of drawing a mass base and avoiding the errors of past women's movements. As for a thorough structural analysis of the position of women in past and present societies, however, the work has just begun. Thus, this collection of articles might best be viewed as documents of a segment of the Movement in the process of clarifying its goals and strategy, while at the same time mobilizing and organizing its forces.

Certain perspectives also bind together the women who have contributed to this book. Although their specific ideological positions and life-style preferences are quite divergent, most of these women work from a socialist perspective. Generally, Mari-Jo Buhle's statement in "Women and the Socialist Party" that "The Socialist who is not a Feminist lacks breadth, and the Feminist who is not a Socialist is lacking in strategy," would also be endorsed by the people who developed this book. This statement was also the slogan of people who supported the women's cause in the early Socialist Party; however, in contrast to the ideas of the Socialists at the beginning of the century, our conviction is that the condition of women in our society is a very *basic* instance of oppression and not merely a symptomatic one. Further, the women editing and contributing to this book also share a critical attitude, a willingness to do their own groundwork in the process of rendering more than just rhetorical service to their sisters.

The Condition of Women in the late 1960's

Why did the Women's Liberation Movement arise at the end of the 1960's? In "Women: The Longest Revolution," Juliet Mitchell defines woman's condition as determined by her relation to production, reproduction, sexuality, and the socialization of children. Mitchell's hypothesis is that as long as each of these separate "structures" reinforces the others, as long as woman's complex roles do not, in a sense, cancel each other out, then woman's oppressed condition will not change. If this "unity" of structures "ruptures" (in the words of Louis Althusser, the French Marxist theoretician, whose concept Juliet Mitchell uses) then there is some chance of real social change and ultimately for revolution. However, in her article, only one of the structures—sexuality—is seen as in a sufficiently rapid state of flux to have any potential for upsetting the accepted condition of women. In fact, all the evidence picked up by Women's Liberation groups and other interested observers indicates there are radical changes underway in each of the roles which fall to women.

It might be useful to note briefly, in a general way, the specific changes in women's condition the U.S., according to the categories set down by Juliet Mitchell. In the sphere of *production* the number of women in the labor force has risen spectacularly. True, most of the jobs open to women are dull, demeaning and badly paid, but at least on the latter point some pressure has been building for equal pay for equal work. Yet, the fact cannot be ignored that in 1968 two-fifths of all women sixteen years and over were in the labor force, as opposed to one-fourth in 1940. Today close to 31 million women are in the labor force as opposed to 23 million in 1960 and 18 million in 1940. The projected figure for 1985 is 39.4 million women in the labor force. Further, more and more working women are also mothers. Today, two in five mothers work. Many of these working mothers have pre-school children. Specifically, of the 11.6 million working mothers with children under eighteen, about 4 million have children six years or younger. These figures represent a sizeable increase from earlier eras, an increase which is continuing: it is expected that by 1980 6.6 million mothers with children six years or younger will be working.

In *reproduction*, there has been a general trend spurred by new possibilities for birth control and by the fear of over-population, towards smaller families, thus reducing the child-bearing years.

In *sexuality*, the double-standard which allows freedom and initiative for the male but not for the female becomes ever more difficult to uphold. Attitudes toward pre-marital and, in some groups, extra-marital sex have grown more tolerant. This turn of events should not, of course, be confused with a true liberation of sexuality for which basic changes in society would first have to occur.

Lastly, even the *socialization* of children no longer seems to be as predictable and satisfactory as the general public would like. High school dropout rates, high rates of youth drug addiction, a high incidence of runaways, and youthful political radicalism alarm the elders, who ask why American families are failing to "produce" good all-American citizens. Some right-wingers who see the permissive "subversion" of Dr. Benjamin Spock as the sole cause for the crisis in the family are surely close to the lunatic fringe. But it is true that woman is a central figure in the crisis. Statistics on alcoholism and drug addiction among middle-aged married women attest to their central role. So do the statistics on the changes in woman's role in other areas. Would millions of women read women's magazine articles on the problems of their condition over and over, as they reappear with minor disguises month after month, if they did not harbor major doubts and confusion as to their proper relationship to work outside the home, to sex, to making and raising babies? Interestingly enough, public and official concern for the white middle-class family and its child-rearing patterns resembles the infamous Moynihan Report of a few years ago, which saw disruption of the poor black family as a major contributing factor to crime and other "deviant behavior" in the black ghettos.

Taken together, these changes in each of the four spheres have had dynamic repercussions on one another. In the resulting uncertainties and changing expectations a new women's movement has formed. It becomes possible once again for age-old inequities to be challenged.

As in the past, the women's movement is almost totally middle-class and *mostly* white, but what is new and startling is the strong active support among young women in their 20's and early 30's, many married and mothers of young children. Some high school girls have also joined. The membership of previous women's movements was made up of spinsters, divorced women or exceptional married women over forty-five whose years of child-raising and housekeeping had passed and left them with sufficient good health and energy to join such a movement. Without a doubt the Women's Liberation Movement must now grow beyond the younger groups of women; yet the commitment of these women is already encouraging because these women look for changes in their own lifetimes. Thus we hope they can be counted on to be more uncompromising, more persistent.

No one is surprised that Women's Liberation began as a rebellious middle-class movement. Many observers have said that the middle-class woman is in a better condition than her working-class sister to see through the true worth of an affluent society, of the "higher standard of living" philosophy. On the other hand, as must be said time and time again, black women and all the women who have to worry about making ends meet know a truth that is perhaps more important: that renouncing housework responsibilities or cosmetics is not liberation. Selma James, in "The American Family: Decay and Rebirth," explains that the working-class woman does not have the opportunity to make principled intellectual decisions about her role as a woman, simply because the real conditions of her life and her family's life do not allow much room for choice. The young college-educated middle-class woman in Women's Liberation is naive if she assumes that she must make black women or working-class women or welfare mothers *aware* of their oppression as women. It has perhaps become rhetorical to call for a Women's Movement led and dominated by black and working-class women; however, this American movement will go no further than previous ones unless it discovers ways of dealing with the different grievances of women from all classes, and of channeling these grievances into lasting social change.

The Women's Liberation Movement

The Women's Liberation Movement originated among women working in or around New Left organizations. Gradually, from 1964 on, these women began to discover in a concrete, day-to-day way the facts of male supremacy. They saw that the movement was dominated by males who had no intention of letting women make any decisions, of letting them do much more than office work. As G.P. Kelly discusses in "Women's Liberation and the Cultural Revolution," the women, like the blacks before them, finally (or once again) wanted a movement that would fight their own oppression.

Why and how did the consciousness of women gradually shift in this way, at the time that it did? Men try to explain the shift by claiming (falsely) that in the early days of the New Left (late 1950's) the movement was so small that each person, man or woman, was evaluated by his or her skills and talents, and everyone worked together. Others claim that the radical movement merely began to apply what is was advocating in other areas of society, i.e., the New Left eventually got around to the women. Gail Paradise Kelly goes beyond these explanations to concentrate on how the movement was able to ignore for so long (9 years?) something as corrupting and pervasive as male chauvinism. Her point is that the "Old New Left," with a more traditional view of revolution and oppression, saw itself as "spokesman" for the oppressed groups in society, in whose name it "protested."

However, as America's genocidal war in Vietnam escalated and the black movement developed, the radical student movement became more activist and militant, and its support grew dramatically. Increased militance drew increased repression from the authorities. Young radicals began to see themselves as an oppressed class — "Student as Nigger," etc. In a recent article (*The New Left Reader*, Grove Press, New York, 1969, p. 15.), Carl Oglesby writes:

"The new activists acquired their radical anti-authoritarianism at the end of police sticks. . . . The policeman's riot club functions like a magic wand under whose hard caress the banal soul grows vivid and the nameless recover their authenticity — a bestower, this wand, of the lost charisma of the modern self: I bleed, therefore I am."

This male "charisma" and the set of attitudes and behavior it implied had become questionable, if not unacceptable, to many radical women by 1968. These women did not need to be hit over the head to become aware of themselves as oppressed beings.

Because of its origin in the New Left — as well as its recognition of the inadequacies of previous feminist movements that failed to move beyond isolated middle-class demands of a "Right to Vote" or "Right to Work" nature — the Women's Liberation Movement has generally developed in a "Set us free" and not a "Let us in" spirit. But this is merely a general tendency. Perhaps the Women's Liberation Movement contains within itself almost the whole spectrum of strategy and ideology that earlier movements — the peace movement, the civil rights movement, the black power movement, the revolutionary youth movement — tried and, to some extent, discarded in the 1960's. Perhaps, too, the Women's Movement believes that as it reconsiders these strategies it will be able to develop one of them in a new and more effective way, or create a new and more effective synthesis. In "Where Are We Going?" Marlene Dixon discusses the Movement's struggle towards this end, stressing the difficulties of departing from the strategies of male leaders who had for so long been role models for the women.

Actually, the Women's Liberation Movement seems unique in that it has been able to sustain a whole spectrum of groups, differing, even conflicting, in organization and ideology. Each political grouping left of the New Democratic Coalition, including some Weathermen collectives, seem to have a women's caucus, and, significantly, many autonomous Women's Liberation groups have sprung up, some calling themselves "revolutionary socialist," others known as the "radical feminists," and still others shunning a political designation and centered around abortion, day-care, or welfare organizing. In addition to these overtly political and activist groups, there are countless intimate introspective consciousness-raising groups.

The organizational boundaries within the Women's Movement are at present fluid enough to allow considerable innovation and interchanging of membership; many women belong to several groups simultaneously. Further, the dissolution of one group and the formation of new ones are very common events, approved by the Movement. The Women's Liberation Movement itself has no organizational structure, thus doing away with the liabilities of a national office bureaucracy and insuring the autonomy and optimum development of the capacities of local groups *and* individual women. The Movement as a whole, Marlene Dixon suggests, gets its business done through the regional conference system.

Despite this flexibility and openness, hostilities between groups of incompatible political positions do arise. In "Where Are We Going?" Marlene Dixon indicates that the scenario of mutual suspicions and power fights, several of which she describes, are all too common in Women's Liberation, and in fact have been present from the beginning. Dixon points out that such hostilities are characteristic of the early stages of "most rebellious movements." The warm sense of sisterhood that bound us together regardless of our politics or life styles — and proved a shocking joy to most of us — to some extent remains, but it becomes increasingly elusive.

The coexistence of such a diversity of tendencies within Women's Liberation has raised the question of "repressive tolerance" in the minds of some women and probably many radical men. The question arises as to whether the revolutionary potential of Women's Liberation as a mass movement is being blunted or even sabotaged by the presence of middle-class liberals such as the women in N. O. W. or the anti-Marxist women in the proliferation of groups which concentrate on "consciousness-raising." The question is an old one, the old specter of many a radical movement. Perhaps this Movement might best preserve its revolutionary promise by broadening its base and truly serving women wherever their oppression is most acute. There is a strong feeling that no group of women should exclude or ostracize another group because of supposed differences in ideological sophistication or radicalism; that does not mean the groups accept all points of view willy nilly but that, in their relations within Women's Liberation, the groups seek to convince by word and example — a kind of internal education.

The Women's Liberation Movement also accepts the existence of so many different groups with differing commitments because it hopes the less demanding groups will be able to reach the more timid and conservative women and stir them with a deeper consciousness, not only of the oppression of women in the United States but of the essentially related oppression of workers and the non-white peoples.

There are other compelling reasons why an organization such as N. O. W. (The National Organization of Women), the radical feminist New York Redstockings or other consciousness-raising groups serve a function in Women's Liberation *at this point*. The radical feminists believe that they often have more in common with a bourgeois group such as N. O. W. than they do with the male-dominated radical movement. Another point of view (ours) is that even the moderate, "Let us in" demands of a group of professional women, which is what N. O. W. is, are in fact still resisted with great tenacity by the system. Because of its liberalism, its pre-occupation with bureaucratic and legalistic channels, N. O. W. is a fairly marginal group in Women's Liberation; yet, if they can help some women and raise the issue of women's oppression, that will be of benefit — but only if the Women's Movement does not stop with moderate successes. What the Movement must do is to surpass such moderate groups by reaching out to those women with the will to work for changes which go far beyond the repeal and reform of existing legislation regarding women.

A similar modification must be made of criticisms of the small "Personal Liberation" groups. Women in these groups try to work out the personal pains they share from years of trying to understand their men, of putting men first, and of accepting the bad times as proof of their own failures as women. The groups have proliferated, and critics charge that the groups have little value because they never get beyond the personal level. These critics forget that often the small group is the only way to reach some women long intimidated by competitive and exploitative personal relations in organizations dominated by men. Further, these groups are not necessarily isolated from the rest of the Movement, but are often brought to a level of greater social and political awareness at regional conferences or through their contacts with the more activist, less introspective groups in their area. Hopefully we will learn, collectively, that the oppression that a woman experiences in her private life is present throughout the institutions of American society, and that if she is to remedy her own life, she will have to try to remedy society; that an individual solution — such as living in a commune — will remain just that: individual.

Women's Liberation is the last and possibly one of the most culturally and politically radical trends in the 1960's. It is the culmination of the deepening struggle against war and oppression witnessed in the United States during the decade, from the peace and civil rights movements to the black power and revolutionary youth movements. In "Bread and Roses," McAfee and Wood put forth the conclusion that prior to the Women's Liberation Movement the "American liberation movement" had reached an impasse in part because of the elitism, coerciveness, aggressive individualism and class chauvinism it had inherited from capitalist society.

Racism and Sexism

The analogy between blacks' oppression and women's oppression has been of unabashed inspiration to the Women's Movement. A number of the terms used in Women's Liberation were patterned after those in the black liberation movement: "Woman Power," "sexism," "male supremacy," and "Aunt Thomasina." Recently, there has been some justified criticism of the tendency in Women's Liberation to coast in on the coat-tails of the black movement; in response, the Movement has decreased its use of and reliance on the blacks-women analogy.

Yet, analyzing the process by which they themselves became conscious of their own condition and decided to build a Women's Movement, many radical women do perceive relevant comparisons between their Movement and that of the blacks'. The women were working in a male-dominated movement which saw women as part of the rank and file; however, the movement was very engrossed in bringing the revolution to other con-stituencies. Likewise, the black power movement arose from the peace/civil rights movement and brought or coincided with an upsurge in militancy and political consciousness among blacks. As G. P. Kelly discusses briefly in "Women's Liberation and the New Left," women, as blacks before them, finally (or once again) wanted a movement which would fight their own specific oppression.

In her historical essay on black women, "A Historical and Critical Essay for Black Women," Patricia Robinson and her sisters view the question of women's oppression from within the black movement. The problem of male supremacy in the black movement has been aggravated by the compelling way in which black women, by force of circumstances traditionally more assertive and independent than white women, have been called upon to re-store the manhood of their black brothers, emasculated by a racist society. The black man's need is the context in which to understand the cry of "Pussy Power" which was heard in some Panther circles a year ago. Robin-son does not specifically discuss the development of female consciousness within the black movement or of black women in Women's Liberation; rather, she shows how Africa's feudal period was a time during which black women were cruelly oppressed by black men. The disenchanted his-tory, pieced together by a group of black women, expresses their commonly felt need to purify the dialectic of oppression in order to perfect their own movement with their brothers.

The absence in the book of an article on black women in Women's Liber-ation corresponds to the difficulty many black women have at this point in identifying with the white, middle-class Women's Movement. These black women experience oppression first as blacks and then as women, and, therefore, they identify with other blacks before they identify with other women. Robinson discusses how this suppression by black women of their identity as women among many sisters weakens and corrupts the black movement. On the other hand, the absence of black women in Women's Liberation does point to a weak spot in our Movement. McAfee and Wood define this weakness as the "stagnation in New Left women's groups caused by the lack of the *need to fight*."

Class Chauvinism and Male Chauvinism

Many of the articles in this book have been written by women whose politi-cal experience is defined by the radical movement in which they have been involved. In their articles they try to examine the forms and content of that movement in view of their relatively new commitment to Women's Liberation. Through a structural analysis of women's place in society under capitalism they assess the revolutionary potential of Women's Liberation. Finally, and most urgently, quite a few of the articles speak tentatively of leaving the confines of the radical student and youth movement, which form Women's Liberation's most standard milieu, and of going out among other groups of women, not necessarily with specific organizing or agitational projects in mind but with a desire to learn through associating with other women.

These new groups of radical women see in Women's Liberation greater potential for a revolutionary movement than they saw in the radical organizations in which they once functioned. Before leaving the male-dominated organizations the women had gone through a period of trying to educate the men on their male chauvinism; next, they usually tried forming a women's caucus and then, finally the conscious women made their exodus and began to build an autonomous women's group. In the process, many radical women have developed deep and constructive criticisms of the "Male-Movement."

In her article in this book, Mari Jo Buhle documents the earlier struggle of women in the Socialist Party to force their male and female comrades to move beyond rhetoric and organize women around their own oppression. She describes the conflicts which arose when the Party's inertia on women's oppression was confronted with the successes in rallying women of the feminist-suffrage movement. Within a few years, however, feminist impulses in the Party had subsided to the familiar level of rhetoric.

At the same time, the militant socialist women who left the Party never found the alternate organizational form which they sought in order to be able to combine socialism and feminism. This failure weighs heavily upon some radical women and persuades them to stay within the larger movement. When these radicals (both men and women) analyze their opposition critically, they base their arguments on a Marxist class analysis. They perceive, in the words of Kathy McAfee and Myrna Wood, a "dichotomy between the 'bourgeois,' personal and psychological forms of oppression on the one hand, and the . . . material forms on the other hand," and argue that only the material forms are "real." In "Bread and Roses," McAfee and Wood stress that this mentality misses the truth: both psychological and material aspects reinforce and support each other. Further, McAfee and Wood emphasize that the oppression of women and the oppression of the working class both stem from the same attitudes — elitism and authoritarianism. Unless radicals understand this fact, they do not understand oppression, and they do not understand the lives of the working people — the sector of the population to whom at least many of them fervently wish to "bring" the revolution. If the male "charismatic theoreticians" cannot break out of their elitist attitude toward women in the movement, will they not adopt an elitist attitude toward working people, if and when working class people join the movement? After all, both women and working class people seem inferior to radical men because they suffer the same cultural deprivations and oppressive socialization. Thus, male chauvinism and class chauvinism are parts of the more general problem of elitism that plague radical movements, past and present. Radicals would quickly perceive their authoriatarian, coercive, and competitive ways of dealing with people if they were observing them in a business context, but they fail to observe them in their own radical movement.

Also, ultimately, as Marlene Dixon writes in "Where Are We Going?," the male chauvinism of radical movements weakens the total movement. The women, "Welcomed to the barricades . . . sent back to the kitchens," fail to develop their potential strengths. The women continue to be socialized away from thinking and acting with political wisdom. Thus, in the end, the movement loses a great deal of strength and power that it badly needs.

Both "Where Are We Going?" and "Bread and Roses" show how the traits rewarded in the movement — the traits of the "aggressive 'guerilla'," "street fighter and organizer," "charismatic theoretician," or "intellectual male heavy" — are traits society encourages in men and discourages in women. An extreme example of how women are treated by one group whose ideal is the "aggressive 'guerilla,'" the Weathermen, was given by the Boston Women's Liberation group, Bread and Roses, one of the largest groups in the country. Weathermen expect women in their collectives to make a break with monogamy by an act of will. But Weathermen collectives have apparently not made it a similar prerequisite that men share child rearing. Consequently, few women with children could ever remain or become members of the Weathermen collectives unless willing to assume full responsibility for the children. In their "machismo" and "militarism," the Weathermen (and women) remain trapped in the values reinforced by the very capitalist, imperialist totality which they oppose.

The position paper from the Boston Women's Liberation group goes on to say that because the Women's Movement has not yet settled on a strategy for what is "correct work," "many women in the radical movement find themselves accepting a political position that does not stem from their own understanding or experience." There are many political and stylistic differences separating the women whose articles appear in this book, but they are united by their common wish to do their own groundwork — both theoretical and practical — always addressing themselves to women and not to an "invisible audience" of men.

The Family

Not since the beginning of the century has the institution of the family been exposed to such a total and critical reappraisal. Charlotte Perkins Gilman's book, *Women and Economics*, which appeared in 1898, found the nuclear family unhealthy, inefficient and unjust, with especially crippling effects on women and children; even earlier, in the 19th century a few radical feminists had attacked the family as an institution of bondage and enslavement which produced parasitic women, brutal men and damaged children. Yet except for the Utopian Socialists, no movement was willing to maintain that the nuclear family was *not* the most natural unit of society. The feminists were very sensitive about charges that they were destroying the family; they countered by trying to show women could combine work, suffrage and other activities *with* their traditional roles as wife and mother.

Even the student movement of the past decade has not generated such concentrated criticism of the family as Women's Liberation has. Since about 1964 and the Free Speech Movement in Berkeley, young people have increasingly rejected the life styles of their parents and elders, but they tended to submerge any general criticism of the family in the slogan: "Don't trust anyone over thirty."

Today, however, the Women's Liberation Movement is subjecting the family to much more sophisticated criticism. As in earlier centuries, there is a feeling that the closed family unit is not the hallowed home of happy motherhood, childhood and marital togetherness that it is supposed to be. The articles by Juliet Mitchell, Selma James, Margaret Benston and Peggy Morton in this book concentrate on women and the family. Juliet Mitchell sets the present Movement's tone on the subject of the family with her widely quoted statement, "The 'true' woman and the 'true' family are images of peace and plenty: in actuality they may both be sites of violence and despair." Selma James analyzes the dilemma of the woman (and her family) when the *ideology* of the family as a natural unit comes into ever increasing conflict with the realities of its changed functions and conditions. She draws the conclusion that the family, already bereft of its economic rationale, is less and less able to provide even an emotional refuge from the pressures of capitalist society. Margaret Benston and Peggy Morton suggest ways in which these contradictions in the many spheres of woman's life might be heightened to an intolerable degree. In thinking along these lines, they are drawing from the concepts on possibilities for a break in the controls on woman's condition which Juliet Mitchell discusses in "Woman: the Longest Revolution," concepts which are discussed earlier in the section of this article on "The condition of women in the late 1960's." Benston suggests that the shift of household labor from the private to the public sphere may be the decisive change which would begin the chain of events necessary to dissolve the family and, eventually, other institutions. The stress Benston places on women as a precapitalist class by virtue of their position as unpaid household laborers is counter-balanced by Peggy Morton, who correctly shows that women may be exploited as workers outside the home, but they are by no means peripheral to the labor force or the system. None of these authors would support a call for the abolition of the family; each would doubtless agree that working to meet the needs of women — equal pay, equal work, day-care centers, socialization of housework — holds the best chance for creating the conditions which will transform the family, the "lynch-pin" we all agree is so integrally connected to the oppression of women.

Women's Liberation has also been concerned with the process by which a woman begins to assert her rights with her family or with a man. In "The American Family: Decay and Rebirth," Selma James describes one syndrome that the woman goes through once she adopts a women's Liberation stance as the *unending need to decide*. This syndrome need not be restricted to the middle-class woman as it is by James. In the syndrome things a woman might earlier have done for or with husband or friend, for example, and done with pleasure, are spoiled for her because she must first "decide" whether the thing is part of the old sex-role patterns, and would hinder her restructuring the relationship with her man. It is an undeniably painful process on both sides, but one that almost every woman in Women's Liberation has persisted in completing. The extent to which she changes her relationship to men varies, according to what the individual woman needs in order to live with dignity and some happiness as a person, sufficiently in keeping with her new beliefs. For some women this means paying their own way when out with men and doing without the aid of standard gentlemanly etiquette, for many it means dividing up housework and child care responsibility; for others (not as many) it means communal marriage, and for a few it means living apart from men, with their sisters, and calling a moratorium on exhausting and in many cases destructive man-woman relationships.

Yet, although the Movement recognizes that these decisions are personal, it also recognizes that this Movement will go no further than previous ones unless it reaches women of all classes. Thus, most women in the Movement feel that a demand for immediate and unilateral abolition of the family is flamboyant and elitist, in the sense expressed in the section "Class Chauvinism and Male Chauvinsm." The article "Bread and Roses" says, in effect, that although the family perverts the human potential of all its members and is oppressive to women, still it is the only way we now have of raising children *and* it must *appear* to serve as a decent refuge socially, economically and even psychologically and sexually, given the bleak alternatives. We must look at the situation honestly and not through old-feminist-rugged-individualist glasses.

Theoretical Contributions of Women's Liberation

Many in Women's Liberation who came from the radical movement are very conscious of the fact that women's political work may be motivated by a desire for self-assertion: by a desire to prove to men that women can be good Marxist ideologues. But such women are putting these fears aside and beginning to work at taking Marxism through more permutations, if necessary, in order to understand better the historical situation of women. All are adamant that the time has come to stop analyzing woman on a single dimension — be that biologic, psychologic, technologic, economic, or legalistic.

In this effort, Women's Liberation has borrowed some concepts and ideas from Marxist writers such as Herbert Marcuse, Theodor W. Adorno, Wilhelm Reich, Norman O. Brown, and Louis Althusser, to name the most prominent. Actually Women's Liberation's rediscovery of these writers parallels their rediscovery by the New Left, from about 1966 on. The influence of Marcuse on Women's Liberation is strongest in his ideas on consumerism and the deceptive nature of our so-called sexual revolution. Wilhelm Reich's work on the history of the patriarchal family, describing it as the product of authoritarian societies and *not* of nature, is extremely useful now. So too are his warnings on the possible weaknesses in reformist campaigns such as abortion and sex education.

Contributors to this book have found several concepts of these writers particularly valuable. Juliet Mitchel makes excellent use of Althusser's concept of "overdetermination." Pat Robinson has written that she now finds many parallels of her own work in Norman O. Brown's *Life Against Death.* Her article, "A Historical and Critical Essay for Black Women," is theoretically controversial because she interweaves Marxist, Freudian, and mythologic themes with concrete black history. One critic of her essay wrote that it had great "poetic vitality" but could not be considered as "serious social analysis" because, for one thing, it used the work of Robert Briffault.

His work traced the existence of matriarchal societies, but is now discounted. Matriarchal societies form an episode in anthropologic history important to us because previous Women's Movements have relied heavily on theories about them; however, these are now surrounded by controversy, which I discuss in my bibliographic essay. However, the main thesis proposed by Pat Robinson and her sisters is somewhat different, though very important. As they write in the article, "The Western world was built on much more than colonialism and imperialism. It was built on a split in the minds of men that thoroughly separated male from female as well as the body from the mind."

The level of theoretical confidence which Women's Liberation has attained is gratifying. However, the possession of these tools has made many women impatient to go out among their sisters and build the Women's Movement which they envision.

Future Directions

During the past year, Women's Liberation groups of all persuasions have multiplied. They have begun work in many different areas: abortion reform and abortion counselling, organization of neighborhood women's centers, and day-care centers — industrial, institutional, and parent-cooperative. They also work among welfare mothers, working women (both union and non-union), professional women, and high school women.

This diversity of groups has almost forced the Movement to think in a comprehensive way about Women's Liberation and to avoid a single-issue mentality. The single-issue mentality was that short-sighted perspective which, among other things, led the women's rights movements of earlier periods to concentrate their efforts on such things as property rights or the vote. Yet, tolerance of diversity does not mean an uncritical stance. Consequently, many groups in Women's Liberation have warned against the tendency of a few women to demand — for all women now — what only a small elite of women can partake of at this point in time. The demand for the abolition of the family, for example, one we have already considered at some length, simply goes beyond the level of possibility for the vast majority of women in the Movement today, and more importantly perhaps for the vast majority of women the Movement hopes to reach, whether for reasons of material circumstances or level of consciousness.

This erroneous reliance on demands such as the vote or the abolition of the family are summarized by Juliet Mitchell in "Women: the Longest Revolution" under the terms *Reformism* and *Voluntarism*. As *Voluntarism* she designates "maximalist" demands, such as the call for the abolition of the family or the separation of parents from children, "which have no chance of winning any wide support . . ." But more reprehensible is the fact that *Voluntarism* is an abdication of our responsibility regarding "theoretical analysis or practical persuasion." *Reformism*, which entails a more familiar set of problems, carries the liability of doing without a "fundamental critique of woman's condition or any vision of their real liberation . . ." Juliet Mitchell proposes instead an approach which encompasses both "immediate and fundamental" demands.

Perhaps we can see more vividly what the Movement means by the acceptance of diversity and a multi-issue perspective if we examine a specific issue. Take, for example, abortion. It is estimated that between 5 and 10,000* women are murdered yearly at the hands of abortionists. Women's Liberation groups are working to protect women from this slaughter in their drives for free abortions upon demand, administered by doctors or para-medical personnel, for information and counselling services for women in need, and in tentative moves towards establishing liberated clinics for women.

Yet, the campaign on the abortion issue has raised many criticisms. First, Women's Liberation groups, especially the socialist groups, charge reform-ism. It is true that reforms tend to bring too little change too late and usually reflect long standing social and economic changes. It is doubtless the case that much of the public readiness for abortion reform stems only from a wish to salve the conscience, in view of the high rate of maternal deaths from abortion. Further, there is recognition that abortion reform may only be coming to be accepted because of the current threats to the family as a stable institution. Perhaps, then, abortion reform will only go towards saving an institution which is imperfect if not repressive in nature?

The criticism of abortion work as reformist, however, comes dangerously close to elitism. Women who criticize the work are usually not in a position where an unwanted pregnancy presents them with an option between an un-wanted child or abortion and the risk of death. They have the money and contacts to find themselves a competent abortionist. Thus, they forget the needs of other women without their advantages. They forget that thousands of women will continue to suffer death, injury, and anguish when caught with an unwanted pregnancy. They forget that the inhuman attitude toward abortion is part of a specific bias held by the medical profession against women, as well as part of a public health service problem of massive pro-

---

* These figures are not accepted by all "experts"—many of whom place the U.S. maternal death rate at a mere 4-600 annually from abortions.

portions. Further, the fact that thousands of women are driven to accept the risk of death rather than bear an unwanted child is an instance of the oppression that exists in every other sphere of women's lives.

There is a second criticism of abortion work, however, which is more valid. Many women working on abortion campaigns rely on abortion as a single issue. They seek to raise the decision *not* to have a child to an individual and personal level. This type of organizing stirs the criticism that this means offering women, and society as a whole, an individual solution to problems which are based in the very structure of society — in the inhuman conditions in the work sphere, in the male chauvinistic sexual morality. The approach of these women reinforces in an insidiously negative way the psychological oppression inflicted on and accepted by women concerning illegitimate children and female inadequacies on the job or in a career. "Unwed mothers" must submit to social ostracism, and pregnant women are discriminated against and victimized by many employers. The critics of this approach fear, in short, that organizing around the right to abortions would fall short of building a strong Women's Movement for all women because it gives in to the values and practices of a repressive society. As Janet Tenney expresses it:

"Children — all children — are the social wealth of this country. They [women] should not be oppressed for bearing them. But to get an abortion for fear of this oppression is to accept the state as legitimate and to side with the state against yourself and your child." [1]

A related position which a person doing abortion work among black women will encounter is the one which calls birth control and abortion genocidal. While there are surely white racists who may have such fantasies, it seems cruel to allow a paranoia of genocide to delude us into opposing the right each woman must have to control her body.

These criticisms of abortion reform must be answered by a new effort to make free abortion only one demand among others. In other words, abortion should always be seen as a link in a chain of demands. We always hope, furthermore, that such specific 'liberation' from oppression will have unforseen effects which may help to break down the old order of woman's condition and make possible new and more totally liberating developments in society.

Viewed from this perspective, each proposal or suggestion for future directions in Women's Liberation, many of which are made in this book,

---

[1] Janet Tenney, "Economics of the Family and Abortion," *Something Else!*, Vol. II, No. 5. (Jan.-Feb. 1970), p. 5.

can be interpreted as a tentative step toward a cohesive and comprehensive collection of demands, aims, and goals for the Movement. Each demand — whether it be Margaret Benston's call for changes in 'household production,' Helke Sander's plea for non-repressive day-care centers, or Patricia Robinson's introduction to the history of black women — will reinforce and support the others. From its very diversity, the Movement will gain strength.

The Vow
for Anne Hutchinson

sister,

your name is not a household word.
maybe you had a 2 line description
in 8th grade history.
more likely you were left out,
as i am when men converse in my presence.
Anne Hutchinson:
"a woman of haughty and fierce carriage."
my shoulders straighten.
you are dead, but not as dead as you
have been, we will avenge you.
you and all the nameless brave spirits.
my mother, my grandmothers,
great grandmothers (Breen Northcott, butcher's wife,
the others forgotten.) who bore me?
generations of denial and misuse
who bore those years of waste? sisters and mothers
it is too late for all of you. waste
and waste again, life after life,
shot to hell, it will take more
than a husband with a nation behind him
to stop me now.

— Alta

SECTION I:

THE WOMEN'S LIBERATION MOVEMENT

BREAD & ROSES
Kathy McAfee and Myrna Wood

*Kathy McAfee was on the New York editor-
ial staff of Leviathan. She now plans on
working full time for Women's Liberation.
Myrna Wood is active in Toronto Women's
Liberation.*

BREAD & ROSES song

As we come marching, marching in the beauty of the day,
A million darkened kitchens, a thousand mill lofts gray,
Are touched with all the radiance that a sudden sun discloses,
For the people hear us singing: "Bread and roses! Bread and roses!"

As we come marching, marching, we battle too for men,
For they are women's children, and we mother them again.
Our lives shall not be sweated from birth until life closes;
Hearts starve as well as bodies; give us bread,but give us roses!

As we come marching, marching, unnumbered women dead
Go crying through our singing their ancient cry for bread.
Small art and love and beauty their drudging spirits knew.
Yes, it is bread we fight for—but we fight for roses, too.

As we come marching, marching, we bring the greater days.
The rising of the women means the rising of the race.
No more the drudge and idler—ten that toil where one reposes,
But a sharing of life's glories: Bread and roses! Bread and roses!

—*By James Oppenheim, inspired by banners carried by young mill girls in
the 1912 Lawrence textile strike.*

A great deal of confusion exists today about the role of women's liberation
in a revolutionary movement. Hundreds of women's groups have sprung up
within the past year or two, but among them, a number of very different
and often conflicting ideologies have developed. The growth of these movements has demonstrated the desperate need that many women feel to escape
their own oppression, but it has also shown that organization around
women's issues need not lead to revolutionary consciousness, or even to an
identification with the left. (Some groups mobilize middle class women to

Reprinted from *Leviathan*, vol. 1, no. 3. June, 1969, pp. 8-11 and 43-44, by permission of the authors and *Leviathan*. Copyright, 1969, *Leviathan*.

21

fight for equal privileges as businesswomen and academics; others maintain that the overthrow of capitalism is irrelevant for women.)

Many movement women have experienced the initial exhiliration of discovering women's liberation as an issue, of realizing that the frustration, anger, and fear we feel are not a result of individual failure but are shared by all our sisters, and of sensing—if not fully understanding—that these feelings stem from the same oppressive conditions that give rise to racism, chauvinism and the barbarity of American culture. But many movement women, too, have become disillusioned after a time by their experiences with women's liberation groups. More often than not these groups never get beyond the level of therapy sessions; rather than aiding the political development of women and building a revolutionary women's movement, they often encourage escape from political struggle.

The existence of this tendency among women's liberation groups is one reason why many movement activists (including some women) have come out against a women's liberation movement that distinguishes itself from the general movement, even if it considers itself part of the left. A movement organized by women around the oppression of women, they say, is bound to emphasize the bourgeois and personal aspects of oppression and to obscure the material oppression of working class women *and men*. At best, such a movement "lacks revolutionary potential" (Bernadine Dohrn, *New Left Notes*, V.4, No. 9). In SDS, where this attitude is very strong, questions about the oppression and liberation of women are raised only within the context of current SDS ideology and strategy; the question of women's liberation is raised only as an incidental, subordinate aspect of programs around "*the* primary struggle," anti-racism. (Although most people in SDS now understand the extent of black people's oppression, they are not aware of the fact that the median wage of working women, (black and white) is lower than that of black males.) The male domination of the organization has not been affected by occasional rhetorical attacks on male chauvinism and most important, very little organizing of women is being done.

Although understandable, this attitude toward women's liberation is mistaken and dangerous. By discouraging the development of a revolutionary women's liberation movement, it avoids a serious challenge to what, along with racism, is the deepest source of division and false consciousness among workers. By setting up (in the name of Marxist class analysis) a dichotomy between the "bourgeois," personal and psychological forms of oppression on the one hand, and the "real" material forms on the other, it substitutes a mechanistic model of class relations for a more profound understanding of how these two aspects of oppression depend upon and reinforce each other.

Finally, this anti-women's liberation attitude makes it easier for us to bypass a confrontation of male chauvinism and the closely related values of elitism and authoritarianism which are weakening our movement.

Before we can discuss the potential of a women's liberation movement, we need a more precise description of the way the oppression of women functions in a capitalist society. This will also help us understand the relation of psychological to material oppression.

(1) *Male Chauvinism—the attitude that women are the passive and inferior servants of society and of men—sets women apart from the rest of the working class.* Even when they do the same work as men, women are not considered workers in the same sense, with the need and right to work to provide for their families or to support themselves independently. They are expected to accept work at lower wages and without job security. Thus they can be used as a marginal or reserve labor force when profits depend on extra low costs or when men are needed for war.

Women are not supposed to be independent, so they are not supposed to have any "right to work." This means, in effect, that although they do work, they are denied the right to organize and fight for better wages and conditions. Thus the role of women in the labor force undermines the struggles of male workers as well. The boss can break a union drive by threatening to hire lower paid women or blacks. In many cases, where women are organized, the union contract reinforces their inferior position, making women the least loyal and militant union members. (Standard Oil workers in San Francisco recently paid the price of male supremacy. Women at Standard Oil have the least chance for advancement and decent pay, and the union has done little to fight this. Not suprisingly, women formed the core of the back to work move that eventually broke the strike).[1]

In general, because women are defined as docile, helpless, and inferior, they are forced into the most demeaning and mindrotting jobs—from scrubbing floors to filing cards—under the most oppressive conditions where they are treated like children or slaves. Their very position reinforces the idea, even among the women themselves, that they are fit for and should be satisfied with this kind of work.

(2) *Apart from the direct, material exploitation of women, male supremacy acts in more subtle ways to undermine class consciousness.* The tendency of male workers to think of themselves primarily as men (i.e., powerful) rather that as workers (i.e., members of an oppressed group) promotes a false sense of privilege and power, and an identification with the world of

---

[1] *See Movement*, May 1969, p. 6-7.

men, including the boss. The petty dictatorship which most men exercise over their wives and families enables them to vent their anger and frustration in a way which poses no challenge to the system. The role of the man in the family reinforces aggressive individualism, authoritarianism, and a hierarchical view of social relations—values which are fundamental to the perpetuation of capitalism. In this system we are taught to relieve our fears and frustrations by brutalizing those weaker than we are: a man in uniform turns into a pig; the foreman intimidates the man on the line; the husband beats his wife, child, and dog.

(3) *Women are futher exploited in their roles as housewives and mothers, through which they reduce the costs (social and economic) of maintaining the labor force.* All of us will admit that inadequate as it may be American workers have a relatively decent standard of living, in a strictly material sense, when compared to workers of other countries or periods of history. But American workers are exploited and harassed in other ways than through the size of the weekly paycheck. They are made into robots on the job; they are denied security; they are forced to pay for expensive insurance and can rarely save enough to protect them from sudden loss of job or emergency. They are denied decent medical care and a livable environment. They are cheated by inflation. They are "given" a regimented education that prepares them for a narrow slot or for nothing. And they are taxed heavily to pay for these "benefits."

In all these areas, it is a woman's responsibility to make up for the failures of the system. In countless working class families, it is mother's job that bridges the gap between week to week subsistence and relative security. It is her wages that enable the family to eat better food, to escape their oppressive surroundings through a trip, an occasional movie, or new clothes. It is her responsibility to keep her family healthy despite the cost of decent medical care; to make a comfortable home in an unsafe and unlivable neighborhood; to provide a refuge from the alienation of work and to keep the male ego in good repair. It is she who must struggle daily to make ends meet despite inflation. She must make up for the fact that her children do not receive a decent education and she must salvage their damaged personalities.

A woman is judged as a wife and mother—the only role she is allowed— according to her ability to maintain stability in her family and to help her family "adjust" to harsh realities. She therefore transmits the values of hard work and conformity to each generation of workers. It is she who forces her children to stay in school and "behave" or who urges her husband not to risk his job by standing up to the boss or going on strike.

Thus the role of wife and mother is one of social mediator and pacifier. She shields her family from the direct impact of class oppression. She is the true opiate of the masses.

(4) *Working class women and other women as well are exploited as consumers.* They are forced to buy products which are necessities, but which have waste built into them, like the soap powder the price of which includes fancy packaging and advertising. They also buy products which are wasteful in themselves because they are told that a new car or TV will add to their families' status and satisfaction, or that cosmetics will increase their desirability as sex objects. Among "middle class" women, of course, the second type of wasteful consumption is more important than it is among working class women, but all women are victims of both types to a greater or lesser extent, and the values which support wasteful consumption are part of our general culture.

(5) *All women, too, are oppressed and exploited sexually.* For working class women this oppression is more direct and brutal. They are denied control of their own bodies, when as girls they are refused information about sex and birth control, and when as women they are denied any right to decide whether and when to have children. Their confinement to the role of sex partner and mother, and their passive submission to a single man are often maintained by physical force. The relative sexual freedom of middle-class or college-educated women, however, does not bring *them* real independence. Their sexual role is still primarily a passive one; their value as individuals still determined by their ability to attract, please, and hold onto a man. The definition of women as docile and dependent, inferior in intellect and weak in character cuts across class lines.

A woman of any class is expected to sell herself—not just her body but her entire life, her talents, interests, and dreams—to a man. She is expected to give up friendships, ambitions, pleasures, and moments of time to herself in order to serve his career or his family. In return, she receives not only her livelihood but her identity, her very right to existence, for unless she is the wife of someone or the mother of someone, a woman is nothing.

In this summary of the forms of oppression of women in this society, the rigid dichotomy between material oppression and psychological oppression fails to hold, for it can be seen that these two aspects of oppression reinforce each other at every level. A woman may seek a job out of absolute necessity, or in order to escape repression and dependence at home. In either case, on the job she will be persuaded or forced to accept low pay, indignity and a prison-like atmosphere because a woman isn't supposed to need money or respect. Then, after working all week turning tiny wires, or typing endless forms, she finds that cooking and cleaning, dressing up and making up, becoming submissive and childlike in order to please a man is her only relief, so she gladly falls back into her "proper" role.

All women, even including those of the ruling class, are oppressed as women in the sense that their real fulfillment is linked to their role as girl-friend, wife or mother. This definition of women is part of bourgeois culture —the whole superstructure of ideas that serves to explain and reinforce the social relations of capitalism. It is applied to all women, but it has very different consequences for women of different classes. For a ruling-class woman, it means she is denied real independence, dignity, and sexual freedom. For a working-class woman it means this too, but it also justifies her material super-exploitation and physical coercion. Her oppression is a total one.[2]

It is true, as the movement critics assert, that the present women's liberation groups are almost entirely based among "middle class" women, that is, college and career women; and the issues of psychological and sexual exploitation and, to a lesser extent, exploitation through consumption, have been the most prominent ones.

It is not suprising that the women's liberation movement should begin among bourgeois women, and should be dominated in the beginning by their consciousness and their particular concerns. Radical women are generally the post-war middle-class generation that grew up with the right to vote, the chance at higher education and training for supportive roles in the professions and business. Most of them are young and sophisticated enough to have not yet had children and do not have to marry to support themselves.

---

[2] We referred above to "middle class" forms of oppression, contrasting the opportunity for wasteful consumption among relatively affluent women, and superficial sexual freedom of college women to the conditions of poor and uneducated working women. Here "middle class" refers more to a life style, a bourgeois cultural ideal, than to a social category. Strictly speaking, a middle class person is one who does not employ other people but also does not have to sell his labor for wages to live, e.g., a doctor or owner of a small family business. Many people who think of themselves as "middle class," and who can afford more than they need to live on are, strictly speaking, working class people because they must sell their labor, e.g., high school teachers and most white collar workers. There is, of course, a real difference in living conditions as well as consciousness between these people and most industrial workers. But because of the middle class myth, a tremendous gap in consciousness can exist even where conditions are essentially the same. There are literally millions of female clerical workers, telephone operators, etc., who work under the most proletarianized conditions, doing the most tedious female-type labor, and making the same wages, or even less, as sewing machine factory workers, who nevertheless think of themselves as in a very different "class" from those factory women.

In comparison with most women, they are capable of a certain amount of control over their lives.

The higher development of bourgeois democratic society allows the women who benefit from education and relative equality to see the contradictions between its rhetoric (every boy can become president) and their actual place in that society. The working class woman might believe that education could have made her financially independent but the educated career woman finds that this is not so. In fact, because she has been allowed to progress halfway on the upward-mobility ladder she can see the rest of the distance that is denied her only because she is a woman. She can see the similarity between her oppression and that of other sections of the population. Thus, from their own experience, radical women in the movement are aware of more faults in the society than racism and imperialism. Because they have pushed the democratic myth to its limits, they know concretely how it limits them.

At the same time that radical women were learning about American society, they were also becoming aware of the male chauvinism in the movement. In fact, that is usually the cause of their first conscious verbalization of the prejudice they feel; it is more disillusioning to know that the same contradiction exists between the movement's rhetoric of equality and its reality, for we expect more of our comrades.

This realization of the deep-seated prejudice against themselves in the movement produces two common reactions among its women: 1) a preoccupation with this immediate barrier (and perhaps a resultant hopelessness), and 2) a tendency to retreat inward, to buy the fool's gold of creating a personally liberated life style.

However, our concept of liberation represents a consciousness that conditions have forced on us while most of our sisters are chained by other conditions, biological and economic, that overwhelm their humanity and desires for self fulfillment. Our background accounts for our ignorance about the stark oppression of women's daily lives.

Few radical women really know the worst of women's condition. They do not understand the anxious struggle of an uneducated girl to find the best available man for financial security and escape from a crowded and repressive home. They have not suffered years of fear from ignorance and helplessness about pregnancies. Few have experienced constant violence and drunkeness of a brutalized husband or father. They do not know the day-to-day reality of being chained to a house and family, with little money and lots of bills, and no diversions but TV.

Not many radical women have experienced 9-11 hours a day of hard labor, carrying trays on aching legs for rude customers who may leave no tip, but leave a feeling of degradation from their sexual or racist remarks— and all of this for $80-$90 a week. Most movement women have not learned to blank out their thoughts for 7 hours in order to type faster or file endless numbers. They have not felt their own creativity deadened by this work, while watching men who were not trained to be typists move on to higher level jobs requiring "brain-work."

In summary: because male supremacy (assumption of female inferiority, regulation of women to service roles, and sexual objectification) crosses class lines, radical women are conscious of women's oppression, but because of their background, they lack consciousness of most women's class oppression.

The development of the movement has produced different trends within the broad women's liberation movement. Most existing women's groups fall into one of the four following categories:

(1) *Personal Liberation Groups.* This type of group has been the first manifestation of consciousness of their own oppression among movement women. By talking about their frustrations with their role in the movement, they have moved from feelings of personal inadequacy to the realization that male supremacy is one of the foundations of the society that must be destroyed. Because it is at the level of the direct oppression in our daily lives that most people become conscious, it is not surprising that this is true of women in the movement. Lenin once complained about this phenomenon to Clara Zetklin, leader of the German women's socialist movement: "I have been told that at the evening meetings arranged for reading and discussion with working women, sex and marriage problems come first."

But once women have discovered the full extent of the prejudice against them they cannot ignore it, whether Lenin approves or not, and they have found women's discussions helpful in dealing with their problems. These groups have continued to grow and split into smaller, more viable groups, showing just how widespread is women's dissatisfaction.

However, the level of politicization of these groups has been kept low by the very conditions that keep women underdeveloped in this society; and alienation from the male dominated movement has prolonged the politicization process. These groups still see the source of their oppression in "chauvinist attitudes," rather than in the social relations of capitalism that produce those attitudes. Therefore, they don't confront male chauvinism collectively or politically. They become involved solely in "personal liberation" attempts to create free life styles and define new criteria for personal relations in the hoped for system of the future. Bernadine Dohrn's criticism of these groups was a just one: "Their program is only a cycle that produces more women's groups, mostly devoted to a personal liberation/ therapy function and promises of study which are an evasion of practice" (*N.L.N.*, *V.4, No. 9*).

(2) *Anti-Left Groups.* Many women have separated from the movement out of bitterness and disillusionment with the left's ability to alter its built-in chauvinism. Some are now vociferously anti-left; others simply see the movement as irrelevant. In view of the fate of the ideal of women's equality in most socialist countries, their skepticism is not suprising. Nor is it surprising that individuals with leadership abilities who are constantly thwarted in the movement turn to new avenues.

These women advocate a radical feminist movement totally separate from any other political movement. Their program involves female counter-institutions, such as communes and political parties, and attacks upon those aspects of women's oppression that affect all classes (abortion laws, marriage, lack of child care facilities, job discrimination, images of women in the media).

The first premise of the theory with which these radical feminists justify their movement is that women have always been exploited. They admit that women's oppression has a social basis—*men as a group oppress women as a group*—therefore, women must organize to confront male supremacy collectively. But they say that since women were exploited before capitalism, as well as in capitalist and "socialist" societies, the overthrow of capitalism is irrelevant to the equality of women. Male supremacy is a phenomenon outside the left-right political spectrum and must be fought separately.

But if one admits that female oppression has a social basis, it is necessary to specify the social relations on which this condition is based, and then to change those relations. (We maintain that the oppression of women is based on class divisions; these in turn are derived from the division of labor which developed between the stronger and weaker, the owner and the owned; e.g, women, under conditions of scarcity in primitive society.) Defining those relations as "men as a group *vs.* women as a group," as the anti-left groups seem to do, is ultimately reducible only to some form of biological determinism (women are inherently oppress-able) and leads to no solution in practice other than the elimination of one group or the other.

(3) *Movement Activists.* Many radical women who have become full time activists accept the attitude of most men in the movement that women's liberation is bourgeois and "personalist." They look at most of the present women's liberation groups and conclude that a movement based on women's issues is bound to emphasize the relatively mild forms of oppression experienced by students and "middle class" women while obscuring the funda-

mental importance of class oppression. "Sure middle class women are oppressed," they say, "but how can we concentrate on making our own lives more comfortable when working class women and men are so much more oppressed." Others point out that "women cannot be free in an unfree society; their liberation will come with that of the rest of us." These people maintain that organizing around women's issues is reformist because it is an attempt to ameliorate conditions within bourgeois society. Most movement activists agree that we should talk about women's oppression, but say we should do so only in terms of the super-exploitation of working women, especially black and brown working women, and not in terms of personal, psychological, and sexual oppression, which they see as a very different (and bourgeois) thing. They also say we should organize around women's oppression, but only as an aspect of our struggles against racism and imperialism. In other words, there should not be a separate revolutionary women's organization.

Yet strangely enough, demands for the liberation of women seldom find their way into movement programs, and very little organizing of women, within or apart from other struggles, is actually going on:

—In student organizing, no agitation for birth control for high school and college girls; no recognition of the other special restrictions that keep them from controlling their own lives; no propaganda about how women are still barred from many courses, especially those that would enable them to demand equality in employment.

—In open admissions fights, no propaganda about the channeling of girls into low-paying, deadend service occupations.

—In struggles against racism, talk about the black man's loss of manhood, but none about the sexual objectification and astounding exploitation of black women.

—In anti-repression campaigns, no fights against abortion laws; no defense of those "guilty" of abortion.

—In analysis of unions, no realization that women make less than black men and that most women aren't even organized yet. The demands for equal wages were recently raised in the Women's Resolution (at the December, 1968 SDS, National Convention), but there are as yet no demands for free child care and equal work by husbands that would make the demand for equal wages more than an empty gesture.

It is clear that radical women activists have not been able to educate the movement about its own chauvinism or bring the issue of male supremacy to an active presence in the movement's program any more than have the personal liberation groups.

The failure of the movement to deal with male supremacy is less the result of a conscious evaluation of the issue's impact than a product of the male chauvinism that remains deeply rooted in the movement itself. Most full-time women organizers work in an atmosphere dominated by aggressive "guerilla" street fighters and organizers (who usually have a silent female appendage), of charismatic theoreticians (whose ability to lay out an analysis is not hampered by the casual stroking of their girl's hair while everyone listens raptly), of decision-making meetings in which the strong voices of men in "ideological struggle" are only rarely punctuated by the voice of one of the girls more skilled in debate, and of movement offices in which the women are still the most reliable (after all, the men are busy speaking and organizing).

"Bad politics" and "sloppy thinking" baiting is particularly effective against women who have been socialized to fear being aggressive, who tend to lack experience in articulating abstract concepts. And at the same time, a woman's acceptance in the movement still depends on her attractiveness, and men do not find women attractive when they are strong-minded and argue like men. Many of the characteristics which one needs in order to become respected in the movement—like the ability to argue loud and fast and aggressively and to excell in the "I'm more revolutionary than you" style of debate—are traits which in our society consistently cultivates in men and discourages in women from childhood. But these traits are neither inherently male nor universally human; rather they are particularly appropriate to a brutally competitive capitalist society.

That most movement women fail to realize this, that their ideal is still the arrogant and coercive leader-organizer, that they continue to work at all in an atmosphere where women are consistently scorned, and where chauvinism and elitism are attacked in rhetoric only—all this suggests that most movement women are not really aware of their *own* oppression. They continue to assume that the reason they haven't "made it" in the movement is that they are not dedicated enough or that their politics are not developed enough. At the same time, most of these women are becoming acutely aware, along with the rest of the movement, of their own comfortable and privileged backgrounds compared with those of workers (and feel guilty about them). It is this situation that causes them to regard women's liberation as a sort of counter-revolutionary self-indulgence.

There is a further reason for this; in the movement we have all become aware of the central importance of working people in a revolutionary movement and of the gap between their lives and most of our own. But at this point our understanding is largely an abstract one; we remain distant from and grossly ignorant of the real conditions working people face day to day. Thus our concept of working class oppression tends to be a one-sided and mechanistic one, contrasting "real" economic oppression to our "bourgeois hang-ups" with cultural and psychological oppression. We don't understand that the oppression of working people is a total one, in which the "psychological" aspects—the humiliation of being poor, uneducated, and powerless, the alienation of work, and the brutalization of family life—are not only real forms of oppression in themselves, but reinforce material oppression by draining people of their energy and will to fight. Similarly, the "psychological" forms of oppression that affect all women—sexual objectification and the definition of women as docile and serving—keep working class women in a position where they are super-exploited as workers and as housewives.

But because of our one-sided view of class oppression, most movement women do not see the relationship of their own oppression to that of working class women. This is why they conclude that a women's liberation movement cannot lead to class consciousness and does not have revolutionary potential.

(4) *Advocates of a Women's Liberation Movement.* A growing number of radical women see the need for an organized women's movement because: (a) they see revolutionary potential in women organizing against their direct oppression, that is, against male supremacy as well as their exploitation as workers; and (b) they believe that a significant movement for women's equality will develop within any socialist movement only through the conscious efforts of organized women, and they have seen that such consciousness does not develop in a male chauvinist movement born of a male supremacist society.

These women believe that radical women must agitate among young working class girls, rank and file women workers, and workers' wives, around a double front; against their direct oppression by male supremacist institutions, and against their exploitation as workers. They maintain that the cultural conditions of people's lives is as important as the economic basis of their oppression in determining consciousness. If the movement cannot incorporate such a program, these women say, then an organized women's liberation movement distinguished from the general movement must be formed, for only through such a movement will radical women gain the consciousness to develop and carry through this program.

The question of "separation" from the movement is a thorny one, particularly if it is discussed only in the abstract. Concretely, the problem at the present time is simply: should a women's liberation movement be a caucus within SDS, or should it be more than that? The radical women's liberationists say the latter; their movement should have its own structure and program, although it should work closely with SDS, and most of its members would probably be active in SDS (or other movement projects and organizations) as individuals. It would be "separate" *within* the movement in the same sense that say, NOC* is separate, or in the way that the organized women who call themselves "half of China" are separate within the Chinese revolution.

The reason for this is not simply that women need a separate organization in order to develop themselves. The radical women's liberationists believe that the true extent of women's oppression can be revealed and fought only if the women's liberation movement is dominated by working class women. This puts the question of "separation" from SDS in a different light. Most of us in the movement would agree that a revolutionary class movement cannot be built within the present structure of the student movement, so that if we are serious about our own rhetoric, SDS itself will have to be totally transformed, or we will have to move beyond it, within the coming years.

The radical women's liberationists further believe that the American liberation movement will fail before it has barely begun if it does not recognize and deal with the elitism, coerciveness, aggressive individualism, and class chauvinism it has inherited from capitalist society. Since it is women who always bear the brunt of these forms of oppression, it is they who are most aware of them. Elitism, for example, affects many people in the movement to the detriment of the movement as a whole, but women are always on the very bottom rung of participation in decision-making. The more they are shut out, the less they develop the necessary skills, and elitism in the movement mirrors the vicious circle of bourgeois society.

The same characteristics in the movement that produce male chauvinism also lead to class chauvinism. Because women are politically under-developed —their education and socialization have not given them analytic and organizational skills—they are assumed to be politically inferior. But as long as we continue to evaluate people according to this criterion, our movement will automatically consider itself superior to working class people, who suffer a similar kind of oppression.

We cannot develop a truly liberating form of socialism unless we are consciously fighting these tendencies in our movement. This consciousness can come from the organized efforts of those who are most aware of these

---

* National Organizing Committee, a group active mainly in Detroit in 1968.

faults because they are most oppressed by them, i.e. women. But in order to politicize their consicousness of their own oppression, and to make effective their criticisms of the movement, women need the solidarity and self-value they could gain from a revolutionary women's liberation movement involved in meaningful struggle.

The potential for revolutionary thought and action lies in the masses of super-oppressed and super-exploited working class women. We have seen the stagnation in New Left women's groups caused by the lack of the *need to fight* that class oppression produces. Unlike most radical women, working class women have no freedom of alternatives, no chance of achieving some slight degree of individual liberation. It is these women, through their struggle, who will develop a revolutionary women's liberation movement.

A women's liberation movement will be necessary if unity of the working class is ever to be achieved. Until working men see their female co-workers and their own wives as equal in their movement, and until those women see that it is in their own interests and that of their families to "dare to win," the position of women will continue to undermine every working class struggle.

The attitude of unions, and of the workers themselves, that women should not work, and that they do not do difficult or necessary work, helps to maintain a situation in which (1) many women who need income or independence cannot work, (2) women who do work are usually not organized, (3) union contracts reinforce the inferior position of women who are organized, and (4) women are further penalized with the costs of child care. As a result, most women workers do not see much value in organizing. They have little to gain from militant fights for better wages and conditions, and they have the most to risk in organizing in the first place.

The position of worker's wives outside their husbands' union often places them in antagonism to it. They know how little it does about safety and working conditions, grievances, and layoffs. The unions demand complete loyalty to strikes—which means weeks without income—and then sign contracts which bring little improvement in wages or conditions.

Thus on the simple trade union level, the oppression of women weakens the position of the workers as a whole. But any working class movement that does not deal with the vulnerable position of totally powerless women will have to deal with the false consciousness of those women.

The importance of a working class women's liberation movement goes beyond the need for unity. A liberation movement of the "slaves of the slave" tends to raise broader issues of peoples' oppression in all its forms, so that it is inherently wider than the economism of most trade union movements. For example, last year 187 women struck British Ford demanding equal wages (and shutting down 40,000 other jobs in the process). They won their specific demand, but Ford insisted that the women work all three rotating shifts, as the men do. The women objected that this would create great difficulty for them in their work as house-keepers and mothers, and that their husbands would not like it.

A militant women's liberation movement must go on from this point to demand (1) that mothers must also be free in the home, (2) that management must pay for child care facilities so that women can do equal work with men, and that (3) equal work *with* men must mean equal work *by* men. In this way, the winning of a simple demand for equality on the job raises much broader issues of the extent of inequality, the degree of exploitation, and the totality of the oppression of all the workers. It can show how women workers are forced to hold extra full time job without pay or recognition that this is necessary work, how male chauvinism allows the capitalist class to exploit workers in this way, how people are treated like machines owned by the boss, and how the most basic conditions of workers lives are controlled in the interests of capitalism.

The workplace is not the only area in which the fight against women's oppression can raise the consciousness of everybody about the real functions of bourgeois institutions. Propaganda against sexual objectification and the demeaning of women in the media can help make people understand how advertising manipulates our desires and frustrations, and how the media sets up models of human relationships and values which we all unconsciously accept. A fight against the tracking of girls in school into low-level, deadend services jobs helps show how the education system channels and divides us all, playing upon the false self-images we have been given in school and by the media (women are best as secretaries and nurses; blacks aren't cut out for responsible positions; workers' sons aren't smart enough for college) .

Struggles to free women from domestic slavery which may begin around demands for a neighborhood or factory child care center can lead to consciousness of the crippling effects of relations of domination and exploitation in the home, and to an understanding of how the institutions of marriage and the family embody those relations and destroy human potential.

In short, because the material oppression of women is integrally related to their psychological and sexual oppression, the women's liberation movement must necessarily raise these issues. In doing so it can make us all aware of how capitalism oppresses us, not only by drafting us, taxing us, and exploiting us on the job, but by determining the way we think, feel, and relate to each other.

In order to form a women's liberation movement based on the oppression of working class women we must begin to agitate on issues of "equal rights" and specific rights. Equal rights means all those "rights" that men are supposed to have: the right to work, to organize for equal pay, promotions, better conditions, equal (and *not* separate) education. Specific rights mean those rights women must have if they are to be equal in the other areas: free, adequate child care, abortions, birth control for young women from puberty, training in self defense, desegregation of all institutions (schools, unions, jobs). It is not so much an academic question of what is correct theory as an inescapable empirical fact; women must fight their conditions just to participate in the movement.

The first reason why we need to fight on these issues is that we must serve the people. That slogan is not just rhetoric with the Black Panthers but reflects their determination to end the exploitation of their people. Similarly, the women's liberation movement will grow and be effective only to the extent that it abominates and fights the conditions of misery that so many women suffer every day. It will gain support only if it speaks to the immediate needs of women. For instance:

(1) We must begin to disseminate birth control information in high schools and fight the tracking of girls into inferior eduaction. We must do this not only to raise the consciousness of these girls to their condition but because control of their bodies is the key to their participation in the future. Otherwise, their natural sexuality will be indirectly used to repress them from struggles for better jobs and organizing, because they will be encumbered with children and economically tied to the family structure for basic security.

(2) We must raise demands for maternity leave and child-care facilities provided (paid for, but not controlled) by management as a rightful side benefit of women workers. This is important not only for what those issues say about women's right to work but so that women who choose to have children have more freedom to participate in the movement.

(3) We must agitate for rank and file revolt against the male supremacist hierarchy of the unions and for demands for equal wages. Only through winning such struggles for equality can the rank and file *be* united and see their common enemies—management and union hierarchy. Wives of workers must fight the chauvinist attitudes of their husbands simply to be able to attend meetings.

(4) We must organize among store clerks, waitresses, office workers, and hospitals where vast numbers of women have no bargaining rights or security. In doing so we will have to confront the question of a radical strategy towards established unions and the viability of independent unions.

(5) We must add to the liberal demands for abortion reform by fighting against the hospital and doctors' boards that such reforms consist of. They will in no way make abortions more available for the majority of non-middle class women or young girls who will still be forced to home remedies and butchers. We must insist at all times on the right of every woman to control her own body.

(6) We must demand the right of women to protect themselves. Because the pigs protect property and not people, because the violence created by the brutalization of many men in our society is often directed at women, and because not all women are willing or able to sell themselves (or to limit their lives) for the protection of a male, women have a right to self-protection.

This is where the struggle must begin, although it cannot end here. In the course of the fight we will have to raise the issues of the human relationships in which the special oppression of women is rooted: sexual objectification, the division of labor in the home, and the institutions of marriage and the nuclear family. But organizing "against the family" cannot be the basis of a program. An uneducated working class wife with five kids is perfectly capable of understanding that marriage has destroyed most of her potential as a human being—probably she already understands this—but she is hardly in a position to repudiate her source of livelihood and free herself of those children. If we expect that of her, we will never build a movement.

As the women's liberation movement gains strength, the development of cooperative child care centers and living arrangements, and the provision of birth control may allow more working class women to free themselves from slavery of sex objects and housewives. But at the present time, the insistence by some women's liberation groups that we must "organize against sexual objectification," and that only women who repudiate the family can really be part of the movement, reflects the class chauvinism and lack of seriousness of women who were privileged enough to avoid economic dependence and sexual slavery in the first place.

In no socialist country have women yet achieved equality or full liberation, but in the most recent revolutions (Vietnam, Cuba, and China's cultural revolution) the women's struggle has intensified. It may be that in an advanced society such as our own, where women have had relatively more freedom, a revolutionary movement may not be able to avoid a militant women's movement developing within it. But the examples of previous attempts at socialist revolutions prove that the struggle must be instigated *by* militant women; liberation is not handed down from above.

Women's Liberation and the New Left

Gail Paradise Kelly

Gail Paradise Kelly is a graduate student in Education at the University of Wisconsin. She has been active in Women's Liberation since its beginning.

The past several years have seen the growth of a radical Women's Movement. It is widely accepted that this movement has its origins in the New Left. Beginning with a brief discussion of the transition from Old to New Left, this article will show how changes in the Left during the 1960's led to the alienation of women from the Left as a whole and helped to convince them of the need for an autonomous Women's Movement.

Developments on the Left

The American Left is said to fall into two phases — "Old" and "New." These terms are often used as simple chronological distinctions. However, the distinctions are ideological; the interplay of Old and New Left ideologies was much in evidence during the course of the Movement in the 1960's, and this process has continued on into the Women's Liberation Movement.

Most of the Old Left, from Trotskyites to members of the Communist Party, to Maoists, conceives of revolution as institutional change and the process of revolution as the process of one *class obtaining power.* Put another way, revolution has to do with political power relationships that will bring about institutional change. Old Leftists as a whole perceive that their first task is organizing a group capable of exerting power — e.g., the working class. They know intellectually, if not emotionally, that this is a long process and that, therefore, revolution in the foreseeable future is highly unlikely. Finally, to organize the working class, personal fulfillment had to be put aside as Leftists from a bourgeois background attempted to get jobs on the line, in auto plants, and in steel mills.

Reprinted from *Radical America*, vol. IV, no. 2, February, 1970, pp. 19-25, by permission of the author and *Radical America.*

The Left in the late Fifties and early Sixties was still concerned primarily with changing power relationships, *and* it was helpless, isolated and irrelevant. The Old Left had just emerged from a period of justifiable paranoia — McCarthyism. The Movement, the traditional left sectarian parties and the newer organizations concerning themselves with liberal causes such as the arms race or civil rights were caught in an almost paralyzing dilemma: Should they work for liberal causes which would not destroy capitalism but which might at best raise some consciousness of the need for change, or should they withdraw from these activities because of the risk of cooption (which was real) and participating in only "true" pure revolutionary activity such as only those things "guaranteed" to bring the system down. The major activities of the Old Left usually consisted of interminable meetings, debates, and study sessions. In the early 1960's many leftists knew more about Russia, Hungary, and China than they did about the United States, more about the Paris Commune than the ghettos, poverty, the nature of American capitalism, *or* women's oppression.

At the same time, the New Left received a strong infusion of people upset with their own perceived oppression. They did not share the Old Left's perspective on the working class. In fact, they developed a decidedly anti-working class bias. The working class, they argued, was racist and reactionary; capitalism had taken away its revolutionary potential. The constituency for revolution was composed of the dispossessed, the unemployed, the Blacks, the alienated middle class. Whoever felt oppression was potentially a revolutionary. The early SDS JOIN and Newark Projects, the SCEF projects in Kentucky and Appalachia, the Mississippi Voter Registration Projects were based on this new conception of a revolutionary class. So, the first element introduced was activism which believed that change was possible, which rejected the exclusive role assigned to the working class, and which, finally, saw elements of the middle class as one of the constituencies for revolution.

Moreover, in another reaction against the Old Left, the New Left seemingly rejected not only Marxist ideology, but *all* ideology on the grounds that (a) capitalism, rather than Leftists with different ideological casts, is the enemy; (b) ideology is irrelevant, especially since so much of it is grounded on non-American (e.g., Russian, Chinese, Cuban,) experiences and conditions and not on the American context; (c) ideology in-fighting leads to a de-emphasis on activism and an over-emphasis on faction-fighting and ideology construction. (Actually, one can question whether the distinction is valid today, especially given recent SDS fractionalizing and other instances of hostile confrontation between groups — now all the factions are highly ideological, rigidly Marxist, and strongly sectarian. Likewise, the "back to the worker" movement is still much in evidence among the Trotskyist SWP (Socialist Workers Party) and the Maoist PL (Progressive Labor) — facts which show, again, that the distinction between Old and New Left is more ideological than chronological.)

The second factor that accounts for changes in the Left is the subsequent disillusionment of the Left with the activism directed toward working within the framework of institutions traditionally used by the Left — e.g., politics, organizing, demonstrating. Whites soon learned they could neither organize Blacks nor poor whites. Despite a nuclear test ban treaty the U.S. had begun a bloody war in Asia, and while Cuba still survived, all of Latin America was in fact occupied. The war in Vietnam, more than anything else, helped shape the new movement. By the time the 1964 presidential campaign rolled around, it had become obvious to some that nothing short of armed revolution could end American imperialism, racism, and capitalism. So corrupt had the ruling class become that many Leftists no longer attempted to relate to what they considered "establishment groups" — defined often as labor unions, liberals, petit bourgeois, the poor — since most of them either supported the war or were racist, or voted Democratic.

Instead, large segments of the Left started to withdraw from political activism and rationalize that withdrawal as a form of revolution — e.g., the lifestyle revolution. The focus shifted to how revolutionaries lived, what their hang-ups were, how a new revolutionary man could be developed, how *individual* forms of oppression could be dealt with. Freud replaced Marx. Much of the lifestyle revolution was accompanied by the increasing use of drugs and by the development of a rock-blues counter-culture.

Among New Leftists (more specifically, elements of the Weathermen, some members of the New University Conference (NUC), New Mobe types), revolution has taken on a cultural, almost existentialist character. First there is emphasis on adopting a revolutionary life style here and now, which is considered possible without institutional changes in capitalism. A good example of such thought is an article written by Bob Klawitter in the NUC newsletter last Fall. Revolution, Klawitter proclaims is "swiss pink-a-dots," or whatever else you personally groove. The formation of communes and collectives are steps in this direction. There are some who think that the adaptation of a new lifestyle in and of itself is the revolution, especially in the "green" communes that have taken up farming. The great majority see the lifestyle changes as fundamental to the creation of a revolutionary *man*. The change in lifestyles is supposed to serve the following functions: (a) to detach the individual from the comfort of capitalism (although often the lifestyle is supported by rich parents clipping coupons); (b) to rid individuals of hang-ups carried over from bourgeois upbringings; (c) to provide financial support for members of the commune so that only a few might work and the rest might be engaged in revolutionary action of some sort or another; (d) to develop a group capable of taking part in terrorist-disruptive activities; (e) to provide a ready-made "cell" when their actions bring repression into full swing. These goals tend to stress elements totally foreign to the Old Left and at first appears Narodnik rather than socialist. But it lacks a crucial Narodnik element: the Narodniks attempted to *go among the people and organize them*, while to some extent the New Left has abandoned organizing.

The cult of the lifestyle revolution has led to another emphasis on the Left which is by no means new, but which came to the fore with the New Left's politics — ego-tripping. The emphasis on lifestyle in the New Left, while it has established an *easy* role that revolutionaries from the middle-class can play, also tends to bring out romantic egotistical tendencies among its participants. The prime role is that of the individual revolutionary — his (or her) life, his or her act of revolution. It tends to stress revolution as an individual act rather than a class act; as a psychological purging rather than a change in political power relationships. To paraphrase a speech made by Mark Rudd at Indiana University in Fall 1969, middle-class revolutionaries have to show they have the balls to make revolution (the psychological dress rehearsal for the real thing? or an existentialist final act or meaning like Hugo's in Sartre's "Dirty Hands"?)

The foregoing was not intended as a definitive discussion of the Old versus the New Left. Rather, it presents the perspective from which the relationship of Women's Liberation to New Left will be analyzed in the next section. The next section will comment on ways in which New Leftism influenced the growth of Women's Liberation as a separate movement and, at the same time, increased the alienation of women from Old and New Left alike.

Women's Liberation and the Cultural Revolution

Once the Left had taken the turn toward *living* the revolution, examining individual hang-ups, developing alternative institutions in the present, it was inevitable that the sisters in the movement would gain greater consciousness of the oppression inherent in not only traditional relationships between men and women, but also in the so-called "revolutionary" relationships in which the women typed, cleaned, and were fucked and the men did "political work." Women began to understand how little the movement offered them. They began to understand some of the experience of the Blacks, that the only effective work for Blacks was done by exclusively Black groups. In order to deal with women's oppression, women had to form a distinct group.

Women in the Old Left did not form their own group, not because there was no oppression, but because they were not conscious of it. The ideology of the Old Left militated against such a consciousness with its emphasis on economic and political analysis of capitalism almost, if not entirely, to the exclusion of the psychological dimensions of oppression. It was, so to speak, Marxism devoid of human content. Male chauvinism was just as rampant in the movement ten years ago as it is today; Those sisters who were active in the Old Left know all too well the remarks about "horizontal recruitment," the almost exclusively male leadership and the almost exclusively female office staff.

Those political groups today which have an Old Left orientation — PL, SWP, YSA, (Young Socialist Alliance) — have an ambivalent position on Women's Liberation. They think that the oppression of women is a phenomonon restricted to capitalism and that, therefore, if one wants to fight for Women's Liberation, one should not necessarily form a separate group, unless, of course, it is either to organize working class women to join the Left or recruit middle-class women *out* of Women's Liberation into the Left. Such a view appears condescending to most women who are not willing to sacrifice ameliorating their own lives to working for some amorphous "revolution" that only promises to put the working class (male only?) in control.

Like the New Left movement from which it broke away, Women's Liberation has a similar affinity for the "psychological" and "cultural" sides of revolution. This is apparent in the amount of time which Women's Liberation devotes to support groups. The purpose of these groups is to heighten the consciousness of women to their own hang-ups and the oppression which confronts them in day-to-day existence — from TV ads to job discrimination. Women in the group receive support in dealing with their jobs, their husbands or lovers, men on the Left, etc. The emphasis here is on personal oppression, not on class oppression, unless women are considered a class (which is the case with many theorists in Women's Liberation — to wit, Kate Millett in her book, *Sexual Politics*). The influence of the lifestyle revolution is apparent in the development of a women's counter-culture complete with women's communes, the destruction of symbols of oppression on an individual basis, the development of a body of prose and poetry about women written by women.

Although the Women's Liberation movement has a good reason to be hostile to both the Old and New Left, it has not yet been able to solve the dilemmas of the Left as a whole. Women's Liberation has vacillated between the psychological and social aspects of revolution and the political aspects. We have seen how political orthodoxy made the Old Left sterile and isolated. Yet, we have also seen that an exclusive preoccupation with the cultural revolution has led the New Left to a stalemate — changing psyches and individual lifestyles in and of themselves is not likely to bring about revolution. This approach has already created a sub-culture that can survive in peaceful harmony with male chauvinism, with capitalism, with imperialism, and with every other form of oppression. It can even give profits to capitalism, as the Woodstock rock festival has shown. The expansion of the Minnie Pearl Chicken Chain into day-care centers has shown Women's Liberation how easily one of its central demands can be turned into a profit making business. Women's Liberation must rather seek to form a synthesis of the diverging sides to revolution.

As the Women's Movement tries to solve this dilemma it must decide whether to organize constituencies for revolution or make revolution now. While this dilemma is not put in the language of Women's Liberation, it might well be — whether to seek to organize new constituences of women for bread and butter, concrete political, economic, and social demands which may "radicalize" women for further actions — or whether to take the present constituency and further "steel it" for immediate direct attacks on capitalism. But immediate guerilla tactics assume an elitist small group character. At this stage, the Weatherwoman"ish" tendencies are in a minority, but their influence is strong and very capable of destroying Women's Liberation just by virtue of their secretiveness and their efforts to turn the movement into an underground elite.

There is a strong element of compassion for the condition of their sisters which has thus far protected Women's Liberation from being satisfied to remain within its own subculture. It was not only the ego-tripping, the chauvinism, and the refusal to take female oppression seriously that led to hostility between Women's Liberation and the Left. Much of the hostility was and is in reaction to the New Left's increasing refusal to engage in activities that might fall short of immediate revolution — i.e., its withdrawal out of community organizing, its withdrawal (at the insistance of the Blacks) out of the Black movement, the withdrawal out of student politics, etc. The New Left seemingly was trapped in its own sub-culture. Women, as Blacks, understood on a gut level that something *had to be done* about female oppression. They also understood that something short of revolution could be done that would make women's lives more bearable e.g., abortion law repeal, formation of day care centers, inroads against job discrimination and work conditions. Women wanted a movement for themselves that would not sluff off their oppression as something to be dealt with after the revolution.

The majority of Women's Liberation which has begun to move toward *organizing* has bogged down on the question of whom to organize, on what basis to organize them, and for what purpose. Only organizing working class women, some maintain, is revolutionary; organizing middle-class women is not. Many have gotten so hung up in this discussion that *no organizing* at all has taken place, even among middle-class college women whose destiny unhappily appears to be that of sex kitten in suburbia. Even if the decision is made toward organizing, the problem then arises of how a group of middle-class women can relate to them. One possible way is through the establishment of day care centers. But even this has been limited by Women's Liberation itself over the insistence that any day care center that be established be run cooperatively by both parents regardless of whether both have to work from 8 to 5, five days a week. The purpose of the day care centers becomes confused — is their purpose to develop "revolutionary" children or are they a means of helping people realize that control of their own lives is a right? The insistance on "purity" may unfortunately tie us to the sub-culture rather than organize us for revolution. The same kind of problem is evident in the current ambivalence toward abortion law repeal. Many in Women's Liberation are opposed to the reforms now because legislators are voting to repeal the laws for the "wrong" reasons — i.e., because of over-population, especially among poor people, because middle-class women want abortions — rather than because they believe that abortion is a woman's right. One can only wonder if this represents a tendency on the part of the sisters to be right, regardless of relevancy or effectiveness. This position is also indicative of another problem besetting the "organizers" — how to accept minor victories. There is a fear of "winning" anything based on the idea that: (a) if one's demands are accepted and capitalism does not fall, the demands were not revolutionary in the first place; and (b) if one's demands are accepted, then one is coopted and ends up supporting sexism and capitalism. A comprehensive program could put small victories into perspective and could explain why it is worth fighting for legalized abortions even though sexism would still remain afterwards. Women's Liberation has accepted the political implications of its movement on an intellectual basis. However, the movement has not yet fully understood emotionally what such a comprehensive program would entail. Ultimately this means deferred fulfillment of individual desires; it means we must make demands that *will* be accepted. Ours should be a long-term program that encompasses the full range of psychological, social, economic, and political aspects of the revolution against capitalism and sexism.

What this article has tried to stress is the need of Women's Liberation to develop a program. It is no longer enough to know what we are against, we have to know what we are for. Only then can we engage in action, only then can we organize, impatient as we are, for a revolution that avoids the weaknesses of both Old and New Left ideologies.

MEN & WOMEN LIVING TOGETHER

Diagrams of some women's liberation discussions

by a Bread + Roses member

When we were little, this is how we thought about marriage:

little, inside
safe, final

and divorce:

knives. power
outside   (1)

cut, hammered
exposed

later we had a period of free sex:

then we tried: yoga, shrinks, clothes, politics, poetry, diets, bitterness, drinking, money, revenge   (2)

By the time we settled down with one man we had learned that a woman has to do her own thing as well. Our ideas and lives varied, but in general it felt like this:

(3)

sometimes we noticed this happening:

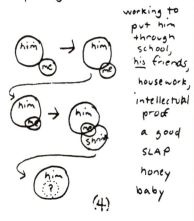

working to put him through school, his friends, housework, intellectual prod a good SLAP honey baby

(4)

Sometimes we had babies to reassert ourselves:

but really:

him
him
me
baby

(5)

When people talked about "smashing monogamy" we remembered the period of "free sex" and got scared. when we tried to put it into practice, things often worked out like this:

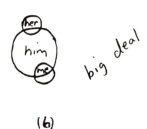

big deal

(6)

A man described what it would be like after monogamy was smashed:

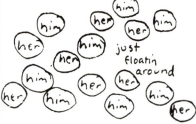

just floatin around

I thought that was scary but I was afraid to say so because I didn't want to sound like the clinging type (7)

At some point we all brought
whatever we had to a
woman's collective. The
first meeting was like this:

We had a hard time
and a lot of things
happened (8)

While I was tripping once
I thought about being
together and separate
sort of like this:

(but the picture
is too static
because really
the image was
vibrating
back + forth)

thoughts
looks
experiences
memories
work
sex
laughs
climbing mountains
trips
etc
etc

(9)

I feel like we're moving
toward this:

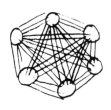

I mean not there yet

(10)

Many of us felt this
beginning to happen:

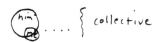

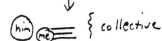

Even some of us who were not with
men felt this. Because it was
happening to us, our heads
(11)

It made us afraid of this:

or this:

or this:

(12)

(but the whole point of it all is to achieve this:

and every once in a while we felt like this:

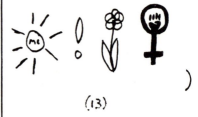

)

(13)

It was scary for the men. We began to see that a lot of them felt like this:

him?

where?

(14)

Some men seemed to want to do this:

but we are too small and that would make us an awfully wierd shape

(15)

But the men seemed mainly
afraid of this:

"castrating,
rejecting, cold,
    bitter"

"taking it all out
    on me"   (16)

Those of us who are with
men are trying to do
something like this:

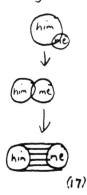

(17)

It could work like this:

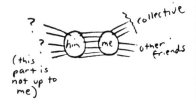

(this
part is
not up to
me)

or maybe even this:

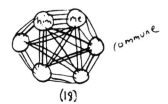

(18)

But nobody can figure out
all that in theory.
It has to be worked out
according to how we feel.
It doesn't have much to do
with rules about who sleeps
with who, or how many
people, or what sex they
are.

That also depends on
what we want, and
what feels right

(19)

But remember
we started out like this:

me   (20)

But for all of us
the most important
thing is that for
the first time, we
are beginning to
feel like this:

(21)

There's a lot of pain
and risk and fear in the
changes we want. If you
think there's not, you don't
understand yet.
The best hope for our
relationships with men
is that we keep this in
our minds:

That means love ourselves
and each other
From choice this time (22)

many relationships will not
survive these changes -
often men's fears will make
them fight against us,
often women will decide the
whole thing is too painful, or
impossible, or not worth it.

more and more women will
choose not to relate
to men at all.

many will continue to
live with men and try
to work through it (23)

Where are We Going?

Marlene Dixon

Marlene Dixon has taught Sociology at the University of Chicago and McGill University. She now devotes most of her time to the Women's Liberation Movement.

Psychology Hides As Ideology

The first national gathering of militant women's groups since Seneca Falls met during Thanksgiving 1968 at a YMCA summer camp outside Chicago. The conference began in an atmosphere of organizational chaos. The clash of political interests, groups vying for ideological influence, proselytizing for one or the other's vision of truth and the overriding suspicion of 'heavies' and 'elitists' marked it as a Movement gathering. The ideology of sisterly unity was often invoked verbally but one saw little of it in practice. As the conference continued, however, the surface resemblance to a typical conference began to show itself illusory.

What marked the significant conference workshops was not the rhetoric, but the intensity of the participants, the electric current of anger and outrage that coursed beneath the surface of the driest discussions of 'women and capitalism' or 'marriage and new life-styles'. As the conference progressed, old rhetoric gave way to originality in language and politics. The charismatic quality of the WITCH group with its wild and inspired poetic imagery of Kings and Fairies, Witches and Powers invoked a litany of oppression and rebellion. There was also the impassioned messianic prophecy of the New York women committed to 'consciousness raising', a form of organizing that calls upon women to recognize at the deepest emotional level their own contained resentment flowing from frustrated aspirations, their loneliness as the givers of understanding who are themselves not understood. Many of the consciousness-raising groups drew upon women's suppressed rage, refusing to utter the ritualistic 'we don't hate men', preferring to proclaim that they

Reprinted from Radical America, vol. IV, no. 2, February, 1970, pp. 26-35, by permission of the author and *Radical America*.

not only hated men, but that these oppressors of women *should* be hated.

The character of Women's Liberation as a powerful and politically original movement appeared in workshops, while the defensive, Movement-trained quality of women's liberation dominated plenary sessions. The workshops often left one elated, while the plenary sessions left one depressed. The conference ended in the atmosphere in which it had begun: suspicion, envy, arrogance bred from the sure knowledge that one's consciousness raising or one's socialist ideology was the single truth. No national organization, no journal or newsletter, no communication network, nothing of the structural framework for a movement did or could have emerged from the Chicago conference. What many participants had learned was the nature and condition of the national radical women's movement. One left the conference with a sense of strengths and weaknesses, as well as future promise, of rebellious American women.

The strength of the women's movement is rooted in the real oppression of women, while its future potentiality as a mass movement clearly depends upon the quality of the consciousness that women develop. Both the socialist and the consciousness-raising groups were in this sense correct. Ultimately, the strength of the movement will rest upon the depth of women's understanding of the nature and origins of their oppression and upon the honesty with which they are able to face the psychological terrors of open rebellion. It is a fearful thing for a woman to be a rebel, as much for the Movement 'wife' as for the average housewife.

Indeed, much of what passed for 'ideological struggle' at the women's conference was in fact a disguised struggle between totally rebellious 'independent' women and radical women who work primarily within women's caucuses. The tension that surrounded the unspoken fears of women concerning the consequences of open rebellion often took the form that women, and other oppressed groups, are most familiar with: turning upon each other. Much of the pathology of the conference, particularly in terms of personal animosity and suspicion, could be directly traced to the degree to which each woman was still dependent upon men for her evaluation of herself. The boldest and most fearless women were clearly those who had bolted from, or never belonged to, established leftist organizations; they were followed by those women still in such organizations, but active in women's auxiliaries. The unattached and curious women, newcomers to the movement, were the most timid and confused.

The defensiveness that characterized the workshops and plenary sessions was the expression of an overriding anxiety about being able to justify the existence of a women's movement. The Invisible Audience present at the

Chicago conference were the very 'male heavies' who had done so much to bring about the existence of a radical women's female liberation movement. The radical women had a prior history engraved upon their foreheads: Ruby Doris Smith Robinson presenting "The Position of Women in SNCC" (1964) provoking Stokley Carmichael's famous reply: 'The only position for women in SNCC is prone'; Casey Hayden and Mary King rousing a storm of controversy for their articles in *Studies on the Left* and *Liberation;* and the December 1965 SDS conference greeting a discussion and floor demonstration on the issue of women with catcalls, storms of ridicule and verbal abuse, 'She just needs a good screw,' or (the all-time favorite) 'She's a castrating female.'

Women had learned from 1964 to 1968 that to fight for or even to sympathize with women's liberation was to pay a terrible price: what little credit a woman might have earned in one of the Left organizations was wiped out in a storm of contempt and personal abuse.

The strategy that the leftist woman had adopted for the Chicago conference was to develop a 'politics' with sufficient analytical merit to force the men to recognize the legitimacy of the women's movement, a tactic which has paid off in the Movement by 1969. Socialism, Revolution, Capitalism were thick in discussion. WITCH, Consciousness Raising and Radicals met head-on in debate, amid many hard feelings. The trouble was that none of these analyses, and this unfortunately especially applied to radical women, seriously linked theory and practice in such a way as to lead to strategies for action. For instance, the radical women had not yet begun to push for day care centers in working class organizing, although when they at last found an action, they were to become as fanatical and sectarian in rejecting all those whose minds remained unblasted by Truth as the non-Movement women.

The 'ideology' of the radical women was, by and large, an academic exercise in the art of the 'intellectual male heavy' in the Movement. The radical women were decimated by the invisible male audience. Thus, the real split among the women hinged upon the significant audience that women addressed: other women, or Movement men. The audience determined not only ideology, but the role women took in workshops and debate. Also, most crucially, the choice of audience determined the ability of one woman to understand another. Yet, irrespective of the origin of stressing political analysis above all other elements of the women's movement, or even the rather vulgar Marxist-Leninist character of early attempts, the long range effect has had tremendous importance to furthering the intellectual maturity of the women's movement.

At the conference, and in later controversies, the basic division between women is usually referred to as 'consciousness raising' vs. 'radical' or 'bourgeois' vs. 'revolutionary'. The names are very misleading for understanding the division, but highly indicative of the nature of the misunderstanding between women.

Women are trained to nuances, to listening for the subtle cues which carry the message hidden under the words. It is part of that special skill called 'intuition' or 'empathy' which all female children must learn if they are to be successful in manipulating others to get what they want and to be successful in providing 'sympathy and understanding' to their husbands and lovers. The skill is so central to communication between women and all others—women to women, women to men, women to children—that it is not surprising to note that intuition is also central to political communication among women. There are no words for communication which occurs on many complex levels, so that it is quite possible to have two complete communication processes going on at once — the articulated and the implicit levels. At the women's conference the overt process was all in a man's vocabulary of political rhetoric and analysis, while the covert level was altogether different.

The 'wildcat' women—those who had bolted leftist movements or never belonged to them—were communicating that their chief point of honor was militance on behalf of women and their complete contempt for women incapable of dismissing the 'invisible' audience. They were also picking up the defensive vibrations of the 'intellectual' movement women, for the wildcat women knew, although they did not overtly articulate it, that the invisible male audience was always present. Their recognition of this reality led them, in the name of militance as they understood it, i.e. as independent women with women's liberation as first priority, to scorn Movement women as 'unliberated,' and permitted them to express their suspicion and resentment in the form of a rampant anti-intellectualism.

The Movement women, in turn, picked up the hostile and contemptuous vibrations of the wildcat women with equal clarity. More damaging, the very recklessness and originality of the wildcats terrified Movement women who were observing the very woman-ness (irrationality, expressiveness, emotionality, anti-intellectualism) that the leftists knew provoked the most brutal reactions from the Movement men they would have to live and work with in the future. The Movement women counter-attacked by rejecting 'consciousness-raising' as 'bourgeois counter-revolutionism' and even less flattering descriptions.

Thus the battle was waged in a political vocabulary, but the issues had really to do with basic orientations toward women. The wildcat groups took woman (as mystical, rebellious, expressive and mysterious, or as enragés) as their ideal, while the leftist women were using leader-intellectual (the role from which all rewards flow in the Movement) as theirs. The tragedy of this misunderstanding was that political polarization — needless polarization — was the result. The wildcat women, many of whom hate the Movement bitterly because of the chauvinism they experienced in it, dismissed the leftists as unliberated spokeswomen for the submersion of the women's struggle in the 'revolutionary struggle'; while the leftist women dismissed the wildcats as hopelessly a-political and counter-revolutionary. That each might have learned from the other, that all shared real conditions of oppression, was obscured.

Another battle was waged on the level of sentiments, in the suspicion of leaders. The resentment against women who seemed in charge (such as experienced by Marilyn Webb and others who had worked hard, and thanklessly, to bring the conference about) was real, a product of all of the participants' experience with established organizations. Women had suffered so much from the oppression of 'males heavies,' whether from a boss on the job or a boss in the Movement or the boss at home, suffered from being forced to be camp followers, ignored in decision making and treated generally with contempt for their intellectual and moral qualities. Their resentment, therefore, of any woman who even appeared to be playing a typical male leadership role, whether true or not, bordered on the pathological.

The women's movement, like the black movement before it (and most rebellious movements in their early stages of development), is torn by suspicion and rivalry: everyone wants to be a leader, or to be in a position to achieve recognition for which they are starved. But no one wants to admit it. Years of second class citizenship breeds in people an enormous hunger to be recognized. If one's hunger is to be once again frustrated, then, damn it!, no one else is going to enjoy the pleasures of recognition either. The result was that 'leaders' 'led' by virtue of doing hard, ugly work and then bent over backwards trying to appear to be 'non-leaders.' This, of course, fooled no one. The long nurtured, secret hunger for recognition has been hidden for so long it had taken on a magical, fearful meaning — no one could talk about it. It remained, at the conference, unexpressed and sour, a slow acid eating at the women's movement, guaranteeing that it will remain segmentalized, split into tiny groups in every major city and region, unaware of its potential size and power. Thus the issue of leadership, of democratizing the structure of the movement, of fighting against the manifold corruptions of elitism is not only a major problem in political theory for women, which must be solved before the movement can reach its maturity. The alternative is death through factionalism and disintegration.

A Case Study In Useless Virulence

Hostility and misunderstanding have only grown more acute with time, and hostility and misunderstanding mean that women spend more energy fighting each other, or merely fighting male chauvinism, than they do organizing the Movement. The possibilities of the situation were made depressingly clear at the Black Panther Party's recent United Front Against Fascism conference held in Oakland. A brief account of events will serve to set the stage: the Panthers had arranged a woman's panel for the first evening's meeting, to follow upon key-note speeches by the conference leadership. Security precautions and other difficulties had necessitated the conference getting off to a late start. As a result, there was, among many of the women, a flurry of rumors that the women's panel would be cancelled at the last moment. The atmosphere among the women was one of suspicion and a sense of determination that the women should have their opportunity to participate along with the men. A spontaneous floor demonstration during the lengthy speech by Herbert Aptheker was sparked by calls from the audience to 'let the women speak,' and a large number of women stood up to protest silently the cancellation of the woman's panel. The Panthers, concerned about provocateurs, police, federals, SDS-PL confrontations and all the other machinery of ruthless repression, denounced the demonstration as the action of 'pig-provocateurs,' issuing threats if the disruptive demonstration were continued. It was unclear whether the Panther leadership understood that the demonstration of the women was for the women's panel, and not against either the Panthers or Herbert Aptheker. In any event, the women's panel was held. It was true that there had been discussion of the possibility of cancellation, but the women did get to participate. It is also crucially important that the majority of the women present who engaged in the floor demonstration were long-term supporters of the Panthers and were some of the best radical women in the country. It may be regrettable that long-repressed frustration was spontaneously expressed at a Panther conference, but at the same time respect must be given to those who had decided to fight oppression wherever they found it.

All might have been smoothed over, as the Panthers attempted to spread oil on the waters of female discontent and the women to make clear that they had no desire whatsoever to disrupt or in any way 'take over' the Panther conference. However, on the following day a group of women, identified with various leftist sects, came to defend the Panthers. Their idea of defense was to attack the other women as counter-revolutionary lackeys of Capitalism, objectively racist, etc. etc., and to insist that there had never been any intention of cancelling the women's panel. The women under attack became in turn enraged, for they were being accused, misrepresented, and generally subjected to absurd abuse. What on the surface was represented as a 'class' battle between the 'baddies' — all women who had taken part in the demonstration — and the 'goodies,' was in fact a battle between women who were primarily committed to a struggle for women and those who were primarily committed to whatever line was dominant in their sect at the time. The confrontation, surely one of the ugliest exchanges between women to date, brought near disaster, for the non-sectarian women were so enraged that they considered denouncing male chauvinism at the conference.

An evening meeting followed the afternoon confrontation, which had been broken up by the sectarian women chanting HO HO HO CHI MINH (the irony of that I leave to the reader). Here, Berkeley women, socialist women from Seattle, anarchist women from Boston, radical women from New York and other equally seasoned and politically wise women's liberation types debated all of the issues that had been raised, and voted overwhelmingly to let the issue of male chauvinism at UFAF drop (denunciations were circulated, but they were not prepared nor endorsed by Women's Liberation).

The bungling interference of the sectarian leftist women not only provoked a far more serious threat to UFAF than had been represented by the floor demonstration, but also served to bring into being a deeper rift between leftist women, intensifying an increasing atmosphere of suspicion and distrust between those who were still members of established organizations rather than independent, radical women's liberation groups. It was tragic that the arrogance and ignorance of the sectarian women had created such hostility. The vote not to create additional problems for the Panthers, who needed support and not contention, was interpreted by some, needlessly, as a failure of nerve and a sellout of women's liberation.

Bourgeois Male Supremacy is Counter-Revolutionary

The underlying issue was not in fact the Panthers. It was the confrontation between sectarian women and other radical women. The sectarian women apparently had approached the meeting with a stereotype so grotesque, and so typically male, that communication was impossible. Charges of being 'petty bourgeois,' 'men-haters,' 'objectively racist,' and so on, contained all of the men's invective against the women's movement. The non-sectarian women reacted defensively, over-reacted in fact, to their attackers. There was little if any truth in the accusations, but the women were pushed almost to a frenzy by the fact that other women were using the men's line to attack them. Rather than being able to dismiss the attack as nonsensical (since communication with the sectarian women was unfortunately hopeless), they felt a struggle had to be engaged in before they could once again feel secure in their own Movement and their socialist or revolutionary commitments.

The root of such confrontation as occurred at UFAF remains the presence of the Invisible Audience and all the defensiveness and insecurity it generates. Equally, such confrontations grow out of the fact that increasingly for one segment of the women's movement, the significant audience remains Movement men, while for another the significant audience is militant women. The consequences of this division are very serious, for potentially the lack of recognition of the real causes of such confrontations can destroy the infant movement. A brief example from a much maligned student struggle serves to make the point.

Women's Liberation as part of the student movement achieved national notoriety during the University of Chicago sit-in of January 1969. The Women's Caucus, formed in the building by Women's Radical Action Project (the SDS caucus) had from the earliest days of the battle pushed for demands based on the university's oppression of women. Indeed, they engaged in the first direct action, by placing a hex on Morris Janowitz. Once the students had occupied the building, women presented a statement and a set of demands to the plenary within the administration building. The women's proposals were passed without debate. The women concluded, quite rightly, that this process was a 'white liberal' response, a token answer to the moral correctness of the women's insistence on recognition of their oppressed position in society, in the university and in the Movement. As the men continued to dominate as spokesmen for the sit-in, the women demanded and got an all-women's press conference. All men with the exception of photographers were barred from the press conference, to show the support women's liberation felt for the oppression of women reporters, and while the men reporters howled about civil rights and racist women, the female reporters experienced a change of consciousness. The women's press conference brought women's liberation as a radical movement to national attention.

The women believed the next step should be to initiate a women's action.

The response to the suggestion that they occupy their own building, leaving the men to hold the administration building, was that such action would be divisive — the great rallying call to suppress women's action. The negative response to the women's idea of their own action was a classic example of the radical male supremist response. The tactical facts were that President Levi had assumed he could outwait the students: the university had all the resources, the students none. He would simply starve and wear them out of the building. And that was precisely what he did. On the other hand, President Levi was under pressure from many senior faculty (playing their usual reactionary role), who were demanding that the police be called to deal with the situation. The women believed that if they had taken their own building, the entire student struggle might have had a very different end than the purges that followed. The women's action, by starting a whole new phase of the occupation, might have prolonged the student's battle far past sixteen days, and thus made a difference that might have forced the university to negotiate with the students.

The Chicago women, irrespective of their organizing for a day-care center for workers at the university for nearly a year, were alone in actively trying to organize workers, and yet were attacked for being 'bourgeois' and 'counter-revolutionary' because their demands included proportionate representation of women in the student body and in the faculty. The sectarianism of this kind of male supremicist attack, spearheaded by an Aunt Jane, was made abundantly clear when the Billings Hospital wild-cat strike followed upon the work that women had done. No strikes, or anything other than a great deal of hot air, had been produced by those who were busy attacking the women for being 'anti-working class.'

The University of Chicago sit-in is a contemporary example of the fact that male supremacy weakens the entire Movement. History is repeating itself. From the Abolitionists to the Labor movement, women have been exploited: welcomed to the barricades when needed, sent back to the kitchen when no longer required to fight the men's battles.

Token recognition continues, with a few women selected to grace the upper echelons, in finest liberal style, while the men declare their astonished admiration for the hidden talents of the women. Yet, the issue of the oppression of women remains peripheral and well-controlled.

Exploitation of women is indeed practiced by radicals, by working and middle class men, no less than by capitalist relations of production. There remains the massive exploitation of women, producing an unorganized mass base for a social movement. Such a mass base must, if it understands correctly the nature of its exploitation, be radical. In practical terms, women who organize women know how quickly radicalization occurs, when they are appealed to in terms of their own interests and with respect to actions and organizations that address the oppression of women. Working women and trapped housewives alike are too aware of their own exploitation and oppression to be exploited in turn by the student movement, or any other movement.

A Race Against Time

Yet the radical women, even in the face of a large, well-funded liberal or left-liberal organization such as the National Organization of Women, remain tied to a male audience, defining themselves in terms of men's organizations exclusively and continuing to regard women opportunistically, as another group to further the struggle. So long as women remain tied to the men's 'line,' and blind to their own exploitation by white middle-class male radicals, it will not be radical women who do the organizing. The organizing will be done by politically unsophisticated, profoundly liberal women who address women's oppression directly. Unless the radical women get themselves together, in the interests of their own oppression and the oppression of all their sisters, a mass movement dominated by an ideology of 'let us in' (and not 'set us free') will develop in the next few years.

Women must face facts. Men will never, until forced by circumstances, place first, or even urgent, priority upon a struggle against the oppression of women. Witness the fact that there is not one male dominated organization, from the left-liberal New University Conference to the radical youth movement, that has been willing to place top priority upon the women's struggle. Indeed the idea is so repugnant to many men that they cannot tolerate a woman who refuses male leadership in order to address her energies primarily to the liberation of her sisters. Men must carry the burden of 'white middle class guilt'; they cannot live with the growing recognition that in their daily lives they exploit and oppress; and so, they struggle against women and against the almost intolerable process of self-recognition women are now demanding they undergo.

For example, it is not an accident that radical women have not been organizing. The energies of radical women have too long been deflected into arguing-pleading-justifying their cause, i.e., to fighting male chauvinism, male supremacy, in the Movement. Theirs has been a profoundly a-political personalized struggle, one devoted to personal liberation. It is ironic that radical women, so wrapped up in their sex lives and Movement careers, so obsessed with personal liberation, have been unable to see the contradiction in turning to attack (as utopian, a-political and bourgeois) women who are doing no more than the same thing, only with more boldness, originalty and courage: women refusing to marry, women setting up liberated communes, women concerned with raising children collectively, women who have tried to show the possibilities of experimentation with free lives.

Male supremacy is a man's problem, and they are either with us or part of the problem — the solution is their responsibility. What is important is building an army that will attack the brutal inhumanity and injustice of a capitalist society at every weak point of its abusive exploitation of the powerless, that will spread the idea of liberation through all the web of contradiction and oppression that destroys human beings before they are half begun in life. The arrogance, duplicity and culpability of men who will not admit the power and authenticity of a mass movement based upon the oppression of women — all women — is to be condemned, in the name of revolutionary discipline, for they weaken and abort the liberation of a people. These men are dupes and victims of their own society, containing within themselves the image of a ruling class, for they exhibit contempt for human beings, opposition to the freedom of human beings, an absolute refusal to stop benefiting from the exploitation of human beings. Let them come along or get out of the way.

Women and the Socialist Party, 1901-1914

Mari Jo Buhle

Mari Jo Buhle is a graduate student in History at the University of Wisconsin.

Introduction

The basic problems facing women within American capitalism have undergone little qualitative change. The mechanical innovations of a century of technological progress, while lightening the burdens of household drudgery, have contributed to the reification, or "professionalization," of woman's role as housewife. Modern Capitalism staved off the disintegration of the family, a horror predicted by the first generations who grappled with the implications of the transformation of American economy after the Civil War. The family remained as a vestige of economic production of a by-gone era, but through certain technical and social ramifications, lingered as the basic social unit of American society, perpetuated with new rationales for strapping women to the institution. The protests of women against the oppression inherent in such a system are transhistorical, but the contradictions become most explicit during periods of intense social crisis, for example, the linkage of the women's rights movement with ante-bellum reform. Similarly, as the Progressive Era marked the first social confrontation with modern corporate capitalism, tensions heightened as institutions outgrew their usefulness in industrial society. Women took active roles in the various reform movements of the turn of the century, from agitation for factory safety legislation, pure food laws, Temperance, and conservation to their long-standing demand for the right to vote. The entry of masses of women and girls into industrial labor once more dramatized the inequalities; as they saw the possibility of economic independence, the standards which demanded their submission seemed without justification. The most outspoken protest against their irrational inferiority took form in the wave of Femin-

Reprinted from *Radical America*, vol. IV, no. 2, February, 1970, pp. 36-58 by permission of the author and *Radical America*.

ism, which sought to shatter the myths of the Victorian Woman. The most radical sector of the women's struggle worked not only for absolute equality but also for the ultimate abolition of capitalism.

Socialist women in the Progressive Era reacted to the tensions in much the same way as radical women today react: they demanded day-care centers, discarded bourgeois clothes fashions, kept their maiden names or joined them to their husbands' with a hyphen, and sometimes rejected marriage entirely to carry on a career in a social movement. But the historical situation which faced them implied a different set of relationships. The Socialist Party itself occupied a unique position in the reform movements of American society. It was the *only* Party that allowed women's participation, and until 1912 it carried within and around it the bulk of all progressive forces in the nation. Therefore, the Party naturally provided the women with the organizational experience and expertise which they could utilize in all their political activities.

Within the Socialist Party the women's interests and functions varied greatly. Especially during the Party's early years, prominent women were socialists foremost and interested in the Woman Question only secondarily, if at all. The famed labor agitator Mother Jones, her younger counterpart Elizabeth Gurley Flynn, the popularizer of Marxian ideas May Wood Simons and several outstanding public lecturers were notable examples. Thousands of lesser-known women provided organizational aid in auxiliaries in every part of the country while relinquishing political decision-making and participation to their husbands. Increasingly numerous but always present were the women of a third type, militant socialists who insisted that the struggle for sexual equality was essential to their agitation for the socialist cause.

Like the women's liberation activists of today, the militant socialist women emanated from several political sources. Some, like the tremendously popular public speaker Kate Richards O'Hare, came to see the necessity of a self-conscious women's movement through long participation in the party's agitational work. Others took their struggle for women's liberation into the socialist movement. In many cases their lives were shaped and transformed by their political activities within the party. Josephine Conger-Kaneko devoted her life's work to the publication of the only mass-circulation radical women's magazine in American history, known for most of its seven-year span as the *Progressive Woman*. Margaret Sanger, who later became the leader of the world-wide birth control movement, had her political beginnings in the socialist movement and press. For many prominent woman socialists, marriage became a burden which had to be cast off. The first woman elected to the party's national executive committee, Lena Morrow

Lewis, revealed in 1911 that, due to her lecturing, for fifteen years she had not spent more that a week in the same town. By 1912, she was embroiled in a National Office scandal for her relationship with the (married) National Secretary, J. Mahlon Barnes. Although prestigious in the Party, she was savagely attacked in much of the socialist press, above all in the *Christian Socialist.* Like many of her sister-comrades, Lena Morrow Lewis had tied her personal fate to her political beliefs.

In the study that follows, two principle categories of socialist women have been brought together chronologically. First, there were the women who formed themselves into autonomous, socialist-oriented groups. The Socialist Party was forced to recognize these separate organizations because it feared they would be drained off into reformist movements and would subsequently expose the party's failure to stand as the vanguard of all progressive social forces. The suffrage movement which supported thousands of semi-radical women was correctly deemed a particular threat to the integrity and leadership of socialists. Second, there were women within the Party who were *reacting* to the insurgency of the spontaneous women's groups. They often played a mediating role, organizationally successful, between the autonomous women's organizations and the Party structure. For a brief period, between 1908 and 1912, the aspirations of the two categories of women were complemented by their shared functions within the Party's framework. But as tensions grew within the socialist movement after 1912 and during the war, the question of primary goals was tragically sharpened. Ultimately the women parted ranks. While the die-hard socialists stayed on to fight internal Party battles, the majority of militant women left the Socialist Party and sought a new organizational form which they were never to find.

I. Beginnings, 1901-1907

At the founding convention of the Socialist Party of America, eight women served as regularly-elected delegates. The one hundred seventeen men who attended the historic unity meeting of 1901 took little note of the women and extended no special privileges, while the women participated with the usual vigor of socialist agitators, reflecting past experiences in Party work which set them off from other members of their sex. The female delegates were active in formulating the policies of the new organization, but their influence was and would remain that of individuals, neither representatives of women as a group nor of other women in the Socialist Party. The convention itself offered only a formal declaration demanding "equal civil and political rights for men and women." Yet, the future proponents of sex equality within the Party would look back to this minor motion as an initial stimulus to women's rights in the Party framework.[1]

The women, who sensed a special need for a social organization compatible with their husbands' political aspirations, organized themselves in social clubs and discussion groups on the periphery of the party. Their associations greatly resembled non-socialist women's literary societies and church groups and drew membership from among the wives of regular party members. The women, rarely dues-paying members of the Socialist Party, provided an auxiliary or supplement to regular party activities while giving formal homage — albeit abstractly — to the great struggle for Socialism among the working peoples of the world.

The most impressive display of energy in women's activities centered around the Socialist fund-raising bazaars, where the women handled entertainment, served the ice cream, and made the craft items sold for Party benefit. Occasionally the meeting of a party local would be devoted to a special "Women's Night" with a low-level political program. The few women concerned with politics in an on-going fashion expressed themselves outside the male-dominated meetings of the local, sharing the methods of their non-socialist "woman's rights" sisters, described by a male member as "pink tea-party propaganda; nice little lady-like salon meetings and scented notes to legislators begging their votes."[2] But the majority of socialist wives clung to the traditional woman's role of providing a social auxiliary and served the Party as they thought themselves best able. Perhaps their most autonomous activity was taking charge of children's education in the Socialist Sunday Schools. For the most aggressive women not directly agitating for socialism, the days of temperance agitation were not far behind, and their concerns continued to focus on essentially ethical questions.

As the Socialist Party began to organize locals across the United States, wives usually followed the example of women in New York and San Francisco, setting themselves apart in small auxiliaries of a few comrades. By 1904, the Party membership had grown in three years from scarcely four thousand to over twenty thousand. Such success in recruiting was not reflected by a proportionate increase of women members in the regular Party aparatus. At the national convention of 1904 the number of women delegates had not increased, and there remained neither acknowledgement of women's special needs nor any particular stress upon

---

[1] *Proceedings* of the National Convention of the Socialist Party, 1912, Appendix I (Report of the Woman's Department).

[2] John Spargo, "Woman and the Socialist Movement," *International Socialist Review*, VIII (February 1908), 449-55.

reaching them and enrolling them into the Party. The only self-conscious activity of women at the convention was that of the German Women's Socialist Club, which extended an invitation to the delegates to attend a reception prepared for them at the Trade Union Hall.[3]

Yet despite the Party's official disregard, the growth of the socialist movement and woman's rights agitation had a combined effect upon the more independent-minded socialist wives and single women. While the regular delegates met in convention, a small group held several sessions in a separate hall for the purpose of organizing a Woman's National Socialist Union. The impetus for this move came from the California women, the most forward sector of the women's socialist battle and of suffrage agitation. Among women of the "less-informed" locals the idea of a woman's national movement remained unpopular at the time, thus the Union had little influence outside of California.

Between 1904 and 1908, the Woman's National Socialist Union movement proved only precocious, for separate women's branches of the Party sprang up spontaneously across the country, in every major city and in the rural areas like Kansas and Colorado where the Party was growing most rapidly. As the feminist movement and above all its suffragist component began to reach beyond the middle class to the rapidly increasing body of working-class women, male socialists began to recognize the social implications of masses of women entering into social and political activities. And if the Socialist Party was to speak for the most progressive forces in the nation, it could not easily stand aside when women, conscious of their new political and economic roles, were organized into non-socialist reform movements. Most embarrassing personally, perhaps, was the continual lack of interest the Party members own wives displayed toward the Party organization and function. Thus the reassessment which marked the period indicated a development of intent among socialists toward the neglected problem of women's liberty.

In defense of this belated realization, the men repeatedly referred to the nominal plank in the 1901 constitution as evidence of their prevision and idealism in the struggle for "perfect equality of women with men in political and social matters." One socialist man commented," all of us believe that this is one of the proudest features the Socialist Party has in its program," but admitted afterward that "when we come to practice, we are not always in accord with this highly respectable principle of ours." The men

---

[3] Josephine C. Kaneko, "The Activity of Socialist Women," *The Socialist Woman.* I (January 1908), 6.

searched out their own contributions to the indifference of their wives. Since the women were burdened by household cares which prevented them from thinking of the questions of the day, the men concluded that the great responsibility was on the part of the husbands to converse with them, to encourage their wives to study at home, so that the typical plight of an intelligent woman discussing her husband's socialism should not be repeated: "In the six years in which my husband has been a Socialist," one wife related, "he has a good deal of the time been interested in the local and in public meetings; and he has never yet asked me to attend any of them with him!"[4]

The active women in the party complained similarly of the apathy shown by the majority of wives toward political questions. The wives were even accused of willfully discouraging their husbands' devotion to his local or committee work. The women agitators pleaded, "if we cannot lead the columns in the battle for rights, let us be good followers. If we cannot teach our men, we can learn from them, we can cheer their efforts, we can give them God."[5] The role assigned to Party wives continued to reflect socially orthodox attitudes toward family life; the woman was at the side of her Socialist husband to offer him "courage of his spirit" in the struggles ahead. Socialism was man's struggle and women were to be educated primarily because an uneducated woman was assumed to be a naturally conservative influence. Moreover, since woman's suffrage was considered inevitable, the Party had a responsibility to educate at least its members' wives not to follow their intuitions and vote against socialism. Thus, while more real than before, the emphasis seemed to remain primarily negative, to prevent advanced women from being siphoned off into reform groups and ordinary wives from dragging their socialist husbands into inactivity.

* * *

But the separate socialist women's organizations on the fringes of the Party continued to grow. They were greatly aided by the foundation of the *Socialist Woman*, in July 1907, which was both a popular magazine and a co-ordinator of news from the various women's branches. Serving as a sounding-board for national activities, the *Socialist Woman* made it clear to male Socialists that women engaged in their separate branches were not only housewives in search for an education in socialism but were in many cases articulate spokesmen of woman's rights who seemed to draw most heavily from a volatile Feminism. These latter women, especially, saw hope for the

---

[4] As told to Kiichi Kaneko, "Where is Your Wife?" *ibid.*, I (August 1907), 5.
[5] Anna A. Maley, "Do You Help, or Do You Hinder?" *ibid.*, I (October 1907), 5.

future in the Socialist Party but believed the nominal "equal rights" plank
was insufficient" so long as the rights stay in the program in cold, printed
words and do not . . . manifest themselves in real pulsating life."[6] A woman,
they declared, could never gain freedom and equality as long as she
was satisfied being in the "dishwashing contingency," even to the Socialist
Party. Holding that even under socialism, women could not be free until
they had developed the power of freedom *within themselves,* the organizers
stressed the significance of separate women's clubs. The women identified
equally with socialism and with sex equality, recognizing their "special
needs" and combining the appeal for immediate suffrage demands with the
promise of socialism. Still, they remained indifferent to their role in the
structure of the Socialist Party. As the editor of the *Socialist Woman,*
Josephine C. Kaneko, wrote,

> We have said, half-heartedly, that women would come to our locals in
> these dreary places. But they haven't cared to come in any great extent,
> any more than the men would have cared to meet in the women's par-
> lors. It has been plainly a discrimination in favor of one sex above
> another. But it has always seemed a matter of expediency.
>
> As we have chosen our meeting places in favor of men, we have also
> directed our speeches and our published matter to mankind. His wrongs
> and his needs have filled our mouths and our newspaper columns, with
> the exceptional moment when we have given publicity to the oppression
> and needs of women. This, too, has seemed a matter of expediency; we
> have always had male audiences and male readers, and naturally have
> made our principal appeal to them. . . . But that belonged to the cruder
> days of our movement.[7]

II. The Woman's National Committee

In 1907 at the International Congress of Socialists at Stuttgart, the woman
contingency met separately and urged a world-wide coordination of women's
activities. The demands for equal suffrage in many European countries
drew from a more advanced and militant movement than in the United
States, and the strength of the women's influence was shown by the International's inclusion of a special woman's rights plank in their constitution.

---

[6] Eleanor Hayes, "Socialist Women in the United States," *ibid.,* I (November 1907),
10.
[7] Josephine C. Kaneko, "Are the Interests of Men and Women Identical?" *ibid.,*
I (May 1908), 5.

Socialist Parties throughout the world were urged to make definite provisions for women in their platforms and to work more explicitly in every way in support of the suffrage movement. Confronting the difficulty of their locals easily assimilating these principles into their programs, the American delegates realized that sincere efforts would have to be made among the majority of male members, who gave only pious expression to the abstract commitment to the emancipation of women. But the most candid Socialists admitted that until special organization of women became more than theoretical, more than a resolution in favor of equal suffrage, the men in the locals would not regard it very seriously.

In February of 1908, the Party's neglect of its women became a vital topic of discussion, noteworthy because one of the most respected male spokesmen publicly shamed the organization for its failure to appeal to the sister comrades. John Spargo, writing in the leading theoretical journal, the *International Socialist Review*, chided the male members for their indifference. The women, he declared, had taken matters into their own hands, had correctly chosen their own methods, and despite his personal urging to remain in the Party and fight for recognition from the inside, had formed their own separate organizations. Spargo urged the Party to pay more serious attention to women's stake in the movement; to provide for full cooperation and support, he proposed the establishment *within* the Party of a National Committee of Women devoted to specialized propaganda among their sex.[8]

During the months prior to the National Convention in May, 1908, both the Party and the women's organizations voiced their opinions on Spargo's proposition. Spargo apparently represented a small minority among the men, the majority of whom resented both Feminism and its implications and refused to acknowledge the women's branches as a potential strength for the socialist movement. For those women who identified themselves more with their own organizations than with the Party, the creation of a Woman's Committee seemed possible only if it existed as an autonomous branch. Under favorable conditions, they thought it better to have the men and women work together in every phase of the socialist movement. But they felt the masses of women were still backward, at least as any line of social progress was concerned and especially in the matter of socialism, and that it have proved difficult to induce them in any appreciable numbers to attend the sexually mixed locals, much less to join them. These women conceived of their separate organizations as a kind of preparatory school for women to learn about themselves, their history, and the traditions of their

---

[8] Spargo, *op.cit.*

sex. They believed that unless the men in the locals were particularly aggressive in their sympathies with the "woman question," they would be most unresponsive to the majority of women who were seeking the first steps in a socialist education. As for the locals where the men were openly hostile to any type of woman's organization, the women felt they had no choice but to go their own way. To them, it seemed a meaningless request to work in a Socialist Party — an ideal, perhaps, but not something actually feasible under the existing circumstances. Even in such places as New York City, where women's organizations had a relatively long history and were far advanced beyond an early educational stage, the New York Women's Conference in the spring of 1908 provoked only ridicule from the majority of male comrades.[9]

Even among those few women who were active in the Socialist Party, the proposal of a special Woman's Committee did not meet a consensus. But the strongest sentiment was conveyed in terms of hard realism; such women viewed the whole question of the Party's attitude toward the woman's movement as purely academic. As one able spokeswoman wrote: "It makes very little difference whether we approve of a separate organization of Socialist women or not. We have one — a real, live revolutionary movement, writing its own literature, managing its own newspapers, planning its own campaign." Since these organizations were composed largely of women who were not *members* of the Socialist Party, the Party could have no jurisdiction if the clubs did not wish to affiliate. The women who had dual memberships in women's clubs and in the Party saw the only logical solution as the creation of a special National Committee composed of women to do the needed propaganda work; they opposed the Party's *creating* a separate organization which would only conflict with the functions of those groups already in existence. They held that such a move would divide the ranks, whereas the main goal should be the attraction of women to the goals of socialism, and only secondarily into the Socialist Party.[10]

Since Spargo's proposal had been made into a formal resolution, the National Convention of May, 1908, attracted many women to Chicago. But the majority of women seemed determined to settle their own problems. Responding to a call from the Chicago women's groups, they gathered for discussion during the week prior to the convention. The first joint meeting

---

[9] Josephine C. Kaneko, "Separate Organizations," *Socialist Woman*, I (April 1908), 5; Theresa Malkiel, "Woman and the Socialist Party," *ibid.*, II (July 1908), 7.
[10] Jessie Molle, "The National Convention and the Woman's Movement," *International Socialist Review* VIII (May 1908, 688-90; Luella R. Krehbiel, "Woman and Socialism, *Socialist Woman*, II (July 1908), 7.

of the woman's Branch and the Socialist Woman's League, both Chicago organizations, was held on May 12 for the purpose of effecting a national organization of socialist women. The women agreed that it was expedient to follow the California example of 1904 and to attempt some sort of co-ordination among the numerous women's clubs. The following day eighty-five women assembled to discuss the proposition for a national organization. The first question on the agenda dealt with the role of the Socialist Party toward women. They decided to place a demand before the men at the National Convention to adopt a resolution favoring special agitation for woman's suffrage. Unless the Party officially came out in favor of woman's rights, any cooperation with it would be beyond discussion. The central question of this meeting was coordinating their activities. Mrs. Whilshire of *Appeal to Reason* said that many women had written her requesting some plan of action. After some deliberation on how to approach the study of socialism, she aided in the organization of the National Progressive League, which had then thirty-two branches and over three hundred paid members in different parts of the country. It was, Mrs. Wilshire claimed, the only national organization of women in the United States and she urged the women of the other clubs to join with her. A few of the women were willing to join the W.N.P.L., but the rest were divided over the choice of joining a new separate organization or allying with the regular-socialist locals. Arriving at no conclusion, the women voted to form a committee to study the matter more thoroughly and to report back to them later in the week. The substance of the committee's report favored a new federation of socialist women's clubs, recommending that each club already in existence appoint a member as correspondent to a committee set up in Chicago for that purpose.[11]

During the next week, the National Convention of the Socialist Party at last came to grips with the woman question. Even those male members who were absolutely opposed to women's organizations followed the lead of the Stuttgart Congress and endorsed the equal suffrage plank, making it clear at the same time that their decision was based on their loyalty to the International rather than on the strength of the feminists in their ranks. The women delegates, who numbered nineteen at this convention, debated the issue of the National Woman's Committee resolution. The Socialist Party majority report provided for a special committee of five, devoted to work or organization among women and supported with sufficient funds to

---

[11] See the May 1908 issue of *Socialist Woman* for several articles reporting the various meetings held in Chicago.

maintain a woman organizer in the field, to be supervised by the national party. But even among these women delegates, a minority report asked that "great care . . . be taken not to discriminate between men and women or take any steps which would result in a waste of energy and perhaps a separate woman's movement." After a brief debate, the majority report was adopted by the convention and the first Woman's Committee was elected with May Wood Simons as chairman.[12]

For many socialist women this historical event had no practical effect. The tensions between the women's clubs and the male-dominated locals continued to reinforce their basic assumption that under then-current conditions women's interests were not, and could not, be identified with those of men. During the summer months of 1908, the women's branches were still searching for a central organization, a special federation to furnish information, arrange national conventions, and increase socialist propaganda among working women and housewives. They felt that women all over the country wanted to learn organization, learn socialism, and learn economics; they wanted to be part of the movement, and they didn't want "to be bossed and put into the background by a lot of men still moved by instinctive capitalistic impulses of domination."[13] The growing wave of suffrage agitation increased their vigor to spread the propaganda of socialism among those women who were just awakening to a new political consciousness. As the National Woman's Committee became a functioning entity, the women in the various organizations were provided with the pamphlets, leaflets, reading lists — the tools they wanted for education — that a funded organization could afford. The Federation of Socialist Women Clubs, that finally adopted a constitution and by-laws in September, 1908, promised this service. But in effect, this Chicago-based organization, although corresponding with local women's clubs across the nation, was a paper organization. Without the Socialist Party behind it, the Federation was incapable of even raising money. On the other hand, the National Woman's Committee, although provided with only enough money from the Party treasury to staff a field organizer, was able to work through Party channels to raise enough money to keep the rest of the committee functioning. It organized benefits through the locals and tapped the wealthy members for special contributions. The New York local for example was fortunate to receive a gift from Louise Kneeland of $1000, earmarked for the women's fund.

By early 1909, even those women who once feared official ties with the

---

[12] *Proceedings* of the National Convention of the Socialist Party, May 1908, 301-06.
[13] Ida Crouch-Hazlett, "Women's Organizations," *Socialist Woman*, II (September 1908), 11.

Party were urging their sisters to join. One enthusiastic organizer wrote from Indiana, "The woman no longer sits alone at the meetings. . . . Now it is a matter of comment if there be no women at the Socialist propaganda meeting; and the men agitators print on their bills: 'Women Especially Invited!'" From across the country, women were reporting substantial increases of women members attending the local meetings. It was estimated that in Chicago and Kansas the numbers of women in the Party increased ten times within the year; "Everywhere that special attention has been give the matter, like results can be shown," a member reported.[14]

As women became an increasingly important sector of the Socialist Party organization, the ordinarily minor question of finances exemplified the internal tension. Traditionally, the women members, assumed to be wives of socialists, were allowed to pay one-third of the regular amount of dues. Apparently the male members, somewhat resentful of women's strong stance on equality, found the provision in the National Constitution somewhat inconsistent with the women's ideological goal. Proposing an amendment to the dues provision, the men urged the raising of women's allotment but keeping it less than the men's share. The women, in turn, reacted to this amendment as a distinction that suggested patronage, an objectionable "half-rate for children." The resolution adopted by the Woman's National Committee condemned "its implied inferiority and subserviance which smacks of that old chivalry which has ever granted to women these petty privileges and withheld from them equal responsibility with men."[15] On the local level, however, the financial matters were not settled so ideally. An organizer from Seattle described her "bitter experience":

> After the election of the nation committee on woman's work, we hastened to go before our local and put ourselves right by asking the local to make all women members of a committee of the whole to further the woman's work. At this time only a very few women belonged to the local ,and a large proportion of these are women who became interested in Socialism by attending the club.
> Recently we opened headquarters, which we kept open in the afternoons, had a woman in attendance to sell literature and to discuss the social question with any who might drop in, and we were planning to

---

[15] Resolutions adopted by the Woman's National Committee, reported in the *Weekly Bulletin* of the Socialist Party, Chicago, May 8, 1909.
[14] Mary Strickland, "What the New Year Should Mean to Socialists," New York *Call*, January 11, 1909; Mila Tupper Maynard, "Women in the Locals," *ibid.*, March 15, 1909.

extend our literature work, when lo! and behold! the local woke up to the fact that the woman were really handling some money, a part of their own dues, and spending it as they thought best! This would never do of course, since in this respect even a Socialist man still has a capitalist mind, and still thinks the purse strings belong to the male sex. Consequently our 10 cents per month was cut off, and as an equivalent, we were offered our room rent free! Well, the Woman's Club has taken a vacation. . . .[16]

The Woman's National Committee defined its duties in this way: 'to make intelligent Socialists and Suffragists of women and to secure their active membership in the Socialist Party," and proceeded to use its most active organizers across the country in setting up various subcommittees within the women's locals. Accepting the general recommendations of the 1908 convention, they utilized their resources for special propaganda and education among women, planning detailed prescriptions for efficient organization. The most popular method for attracting women proved to be agitation for suffrage, with the Party's own "Votes for Women" campaign. Although other committees were planned for the locals, such as membership, literature, children's education, and music committees, the current appeal of suffrage became such a powerful issue that many members of the party as a whole, as especially male members, accused the women of favoring the sex struggle over the class struggle. But the women were out to prove the Socialist Party had risen to champion woman's cause, bringing the declaration for enfranchisement from the Party platform to real life. One of the most popular features of the Committee's diverse program was one that they succeeded in making into a national, coordinated affair. Through the Party presses across the country, the women announced the fourth Sunday of February as "Woman's Day." Socialists throughout the country held demonstrations in favor of woman suffrage on February 23, 1909, and the event was met with such enthusiasm that it continued as an annual "Anticipation Day" for economic and political freedom for women, celebrated in the United States and Europe.[17]

Within a year of its inception, the Woman's National Committee proved itself capable of functioning as a national coordinating service, providing the

---

[16] Mrs. Anna Burgess, "Propaganda Among Women: The Bitter Experience of the Socialist Women of Seattle," New York *Call*, July 16, 1911.

[17] Woman's National Committee report, *Weekly Bulletin*, Chicago, June 17, 1909; Hebe, "Woman's Day," New York *Call*, January 23, 1910; Lena Morrow Lewis, "Woman's Day," *ibid.*, February 27, 1910.

women in the distant locals with literature, propaganda, and definite programs for organizing. They managed to win the support of the more prominent men in the Party, even Eugene Debs with his characteristic sentimental
glorifications of woman and motherhood. Special sections of the Party's
press, its newspapers, international and internal bulletins, and magazines,
were devoted to the woman question. In 1910 the National Woman's Committee was incorporated into the Party constitution and made a permanent
part of the bureaucracy. But despite its ability to win respect from the Party,
the Committee's success would ultimately be measured not by its popular
appeal but by its practical results.

III. The Woman Question

The Socialist women were confident that no one in the Party could fail to
be impressed with the rise of their organizations as a distinct force within
the movement. At the 1910 convention, the Woman's Committee reported
that new women's branches had been set up in 156 locals across the country
and that five states had organized state-wide women's committees. Their
success was symbolized by the election of the first woman, Lena Morrow
Lewis, to the National Executive Board, and they "rejoiced" that her election
was due solely to her outstanding agitational ability. Thus themselves impressed, the women demanded more autonomy within the Party and were
given a Party-funded correspondent to assist the enlarged seven-member
executive staff of the National Woman's Committee. For the first time, the
women gained floor space in the national office in Chicago, and a special
Women's Department was created for their clerical necessities. The women
delegates to the National Convention also displayed more interest in the
debates on the floor: they were elected to serve on most of the important
committees, and they expressed themselves unhesitatingly on questions
ranging from the new farm platform to immigration.

The 1910 Convention *seemed* a turning point for the socialist women,
and offered them a precedent for future labors within the Party. In the
immediate period following, they showed a willingness to forget their former attacks upon the men's failure to live up to the old sex-equality platform; sometimes they even congratulated their male comrades for casting
aside traditional prejudices against "feminine politics."[19] One socialist woman wrote: "Let us hope that this example of a peaceful intelligent mingling

---

[18] Mary E. Marcy, "Efficiency and Text," *ibid.*, May 8, 1910.
[19] Theresa Malkiel, "Woman and the National Congress," *ibid.*, May 29, 1910.

of the sexes will serve as a guide for the future" of society. And they compared their work with the futile attempts of women in other political
parties. They praised by contrast the Socialist Party and urged women to take
advantage of its program of full economic, social, and political freedom.
Thus by 1910, the women had resolved the initial problems of organization.
But the development of a positive program, based no longer simply on the
prejudices against the "inferior sex" but rather defined by their unique position as *Socialist* women in practical, organizational terms, remained to be
accomplished.

The previous emphasis on suffrage agitation was challenged by women
who wished to extend propaganda along more general socialist educational
lines. They felt that the suffrage question was being handled adequately by
the women's reform organization. The Party, for them, had a greater responsibility to the working woman and her special needs. This question of priority was debated extensively, and although no explicit conception determined
all their actions, many women rejected cooperation with the suffragists for
broader social appeals. Particularly in those states where women already
had the ballot, the Party could point to the negligible effect that socialist
propaganda had on voting results. Although proclaiming itself the vanguard
of all progressive movements in the United States, the Party claimed it gained
no immediate political benefits from woman suffrage, and could therefore
stress the need for less transient issues to build a socialist woman's
movement.[20]

The limited advantages of suffrage agitation sharpened the contradictions
for those women who believed their tactics should flow from fundamental
socialist theory. Despite the class-conscious rhetoric of their agitation,
it seemed to appeal not to the women who most needed political expression
in American society but rather to the same class from which the reformist-
suffragist organizations drew their membership — the professional women
and middle-class housewives. Special efforts to reach working-class women
through suffrage propaganda did not achieve the hoped-for results, since
the majority of working class women could ill afford the time to join locals.
Propaganda was then redirected to appeals around a more general oppression
of females. The tactics came nominally from a general theory that had been
their inspiration through the early days of the struggle, what they called a
"Materialist Conception of the Woman's Struggle," which the Socialist
women now integrated into the emerging Feminism of the decade.

The classic writings that most influenced their thinking were *Women*

---

[20] The Party Convention of 1910 debated suffrage as a key Party question. For the
highlights of the debate, see *The Progressive Woman,* June, 1910.

Under Socialism, by August Bebel, and *The Origins of the Family,* by Friedrich Engels. Taken with the anthropological analyses popular at the time, these two texts, unimpeachable for at least most American Socialists, provided women with a view of history that denied a biologically determined role for their sex. Both Bebel and Engels depicted the dawn of man as an era of cooperative struggle for survival, based upon primitive matriarchical structures. The exodus from this secular paradise had at once created the system of private ownership and woman's bondage within it. Over the ages the burden had fallen hardest upon her, for while her mate's dominant attitude had been acquisition and personal control, she had desperately attempted to conserve the family as best she could. Capitalism, as in so many other ways, both rendered the burden unendurable and created the pre-conditions for its elimination by creating the productive mechanization which potentially would provide plenty for all. The future civilization, like that in the dim past, would offer general cooperation and the realization of woman's desire to be an equal and to conserve the race as she had through the ages conserved the family.

The special appeal to women as women brought the socialists into the main line of the burgeoning Feminist movement, and by 1913 they observed that younger women were being attracted to radicalism primarily for their complete sexual emancipation. The Socialist women tried to bridge the gap to the older agitation by urging that the Feminist program consisted "very largely in what Socialists have been demanding for women for years and years," and by pointing out that only socialists understood complete freedom to be unattainable short of the common ownership of the means of production. As one woman socialist wrote: "The Socialist who is not a Feminist lacks breadth. The Feminist who is not a Socialist is lacking in strategy." Hence they held that whether women possessed the ballot or not, they would need to unite with all oppressed groups for a better society, and that the Socialist movement would ultimately provide women the courage to be in the forefront of the final battle "fighting for the destruction of masculine despotism and for the right of womankind."[21]

But with the concurrent passing of the suffrage issue and the ebbing of the inertia in the women's socialist movement, Feminism proved *as an agitational issue* to be unacceptable to the bulk of the socialist movement. Although the militant women insisted that Feminism could not be limited to

[21] Anita C. Block, "New York Socialists Women's Conference," New York *Call,* April 5, 1914; Louise W. Kneeland, "Feminism and Socialism," *New Review,* II (August 1914), 442; Mary White Ovington, "Socialism and the Feminist Movement," *ibid.,* II (March 1914), 146-47.

any one reform, the men and more orthodox socialist women generally offered a blanket criticism of Feminism and all the implications of agitation "along sex lines." Feminism, they held, was middle-class, and socialist-feminists were warned that their activity could swamp the party with non-wage earning elements. While an occasional middle-class woman could bring along her vitality and intelligence, a large number of them, it was thought, were bound to bring their reformist taints. Thus even a mild variety of Feminism, which clearly disavowed free love and the destruction of the family, was feared as a divider of the movement along sex lines. With all the odds against them, the socialist-feminists failed to respond successfully to this plea for a return to traditional socialist agitation on all fronts, and a new wave of "Male egotism" was evoked which, according to some women, was even more objectionable than the male attitudes dominating the party before 1908.

IV. The Declining Years, From 1912

During this period there were growing tensions within the Socialist Party which had undercut the development of an autonomous socialist women's agitational struggle and now worked against its revival. By 1910, American Socialism had accomplished basic propaganda tasks and entered a maturity, raising and sharpening internal differences that had been previously tolerated by nearly all concerned. Many Socialists long in the movement publicly warned against the influx of middle-class elements into the Party and the danger of encouraging agitation which resulted in the enrollment of non-wage-earners. More important, an internal Party struggle culminating in 1912 with the proscription of the advocacy of sabotage in Party ranks had the effect of tightening Party discipline against all potentially dissident elements. Finally, the success of "Constructive Socialist" locals, particularly the Milwaukee Social Democracy, provided the "lesson" of heavily concentrated agitation and propagandization within a city involving all socialists in a single-minded task. Cumulatively, therefore, women's agitation could have been seen to be divisive, disruptive and destructive to socialist energies. And without a body of important defenders within the ruling circles of the Party, women's agitation could not expect special treatment or solicitation for its case.

In retrospect, the true high point of women's agitation within the Socialist Party was the period around 1910 to 1912. Suffrage agitation died, for socialist purposes, as achievement loomed closer and the major political parties subsumed within them the energies that had been previously tapped by socialist women. There was an Indian Summer for socialist women in 1912-1913, as the vigorous national campaign and the residual effects of suffrage agitation swelled the women's ranks from ten percent to fifteen percent of the Party membership. But by 1913 the erosive effects of the changing conditions could already be seen.

The lack of an issue with the strength and popularity of suffrage, along with the Party's internal betrayal of the woman question, made impossible a clear program of organizational activities and stripped the agitational program to Socialism alone rather than feminism or suffrage. Even by 1913, the inertia of the women's socialist movement had slowed. The National Committee was no longer effective as a woman's committee, and prominent female socialists became increasingly involved in ordinary Party work, above all action against the coming war. When in 1914 a proposal was made at the Party Convention to abolish the Woman's National Committee, its (female) Correspondent from the Party's Woman Department applauded the prospective amendment. Though remaining nominally in existence, the Committee ceased to function in any significant way.

The most ominous sign was the death of the *Progressive Woman*. Like other Party publications, the *Woman* had never been a solvent financial venture, and from 1912 onward the Party had subsidized its existence. But aid was at best partial, and at no point adequate to make up the deficit or provide a sound financial basis for the magazine's expansion to its own expected circulation of 500,000. The Woman's Committee in 1914 sought to abandon the sinking ship, and the magazine was salvaged only momentarily by its transformation into the *Coming Nation*, a name which its editor Josephine Conger-Kaneko derived from the enormously popular Socialist paper of the 1890's. By mid-1914, the socialist women had no publication of their own and more than ever were forced to rely upon the mechanisms of a Party decreasingly concerned for the welfare of an autonomous group of women.

During the declining years of women's activities in the Socialist Party, the remarkable example of Margaret Sanger's struggle served to typify the organizational obstacles in the path of prospective radical feminists. Her class position, the unusual interests and ability she brought to her work, and the nature of her estrangement from the socialist movement further indicated the limits of Party flexibility, especially on questions of sexuality in practical organizational terms.[22]

Margaret Sanger's entry into the Socialist movement, like that of many

---

[22] Margaret Sanger, *Autobiography*, (New York: 1938) and *My Fight for Birth Control* (New York: 1931).

other women, came through her husband's activity (in this case in the New York Socialist Party). Frequently mingling with the salon crowd she came to associate a socialist perspective with her own ethical and humanitarian concerns. Although her anarchistic sentiments fostered an intellectual attraction to "individualistic" tendencies, the practical applications in an industrial society necessitated for her an organizational framework which she sought in the Socialist Party. She regularly attended local meetings with her husband, but only inadvertently did she become one of the most important activists in the movement. She was asked to replace an ailing speaker at one of the local women's meetings. Although she had never given a public speech before, she accepted on the condition that her topic be of her own choice. She had little confidence about her understanding of Marxian theory and decided to speak about her own specialty, sex education and hygiene.

Margaret Sanger's appearance and her introduction of the topic into public discussion generated enormous enthusiasm among women in the local, who repeatedly expressed their urgent needs for such information. Soon she was offering a series of lectures, during which so many questions were asked that Anita Block, editor of the New York *Call's* woman's page, asked Sanger to provide a regular column for publication. In this, her first experience at public writing, Margaret Sanger planned a series under the general title, "What Every Mother Should Know," in an effort to break through parents' rigid attitudes toward sexual development. Several weeks after its appearance, the title of the sequel column, "What Every Girl Should Know," was followed by the black-typed notation "NOTHING! By the order of the post-office department." For the first time, Margaret Sanger's work had been publicly censored.

Her writing for the *Call* continued sporadically into wartime, and even the censored article eventually appeared. But as she engaged in practical activities among working class women in New York and in such projects as the care of the children of strikers in Lawrence and Paterson, her sympathies were drawn increasingly to the direct actionists and syndicalists. She continually tried to work through the Socialist Party to disseminate birth control information among families of workers but met with constant frustration from the lack of help and the frequent scorn she received from the reformist socialist leadership. Meanwhile the IWW's Big Bill Haywood, a close personal friend, offered her contact with industrial workers and their wives. Finally, the attitude of the Socialists, that birth control would come with the victory of Socialism and was thus of negligible concern before the Revolution, turned her toward her original political inclination, anarchism.

In the spring of 1914, Margaret Sanger marked both her political anarchism and her desire to test censorship laws by founding a newspaper expressly devoted to women's liberation, the *Woman Rebel*. Across the masthead was emblazoned "No Gods, No Masters," and inside a mixture of rudimentary sex education and anti-political articles, such as "The Importance of Assassination in History." During the Colorado mining strike, she asked socialist women to send the fiercely-repressed miners guns rather than sympathy, adding that: "when 40,000 [socialist] women cannot follow up a protest by action, then truly it would appear that they have something other than their 'chains to lose.'" The *Woman Rebel* never reached any significant circulation, and since all issues were banned from the mails, it was generally limited to a few Eastern cities. After the seventh issue, Margaret Sanger was placed under indictment for "lewdness." Rather than face trial she fled to Europe.

A year earlier, Margaret Sanger's columns in the *Call* had opened a controversy within the Socialist Party, carried on in letters to the paper, which revealed the deep differences on matters of sexuality and woman's place generally.[23] As Anita Block noted, the purpose of the column was to "turn the searchlight on all those rotten spots which those in power today find it in their interest to keep dark and . . . keep turning on the light in one way or another even stronger and more penetrating until there is no part of our social structure that will not be clean and healthy and beautiful." Readers appreciative of the column sent in a variety of intense and even touching responses. One woman wrote of the loss of her "so-called innocence" which caused her husband to suspect wrongfully her past and destroy their marriage. On reading the column, the maligned woman's husband finally came to understand the possibility of a "natural" loss of virginity, thus ending his thoughtless persecution. Another woman, sixty-six years old and mother of eight, wrote that she learned more from Margaret Sanger's articles than "from any books or even from my own life." A male machinist, perhaps more typical of a sympathetic socialist reader, wrote that such lessons were important, for active socialists could not be recruited from a population sick with venereal disease. Above all, readers stressed the fact that the knowledge which Margaret Sanger made available was simply not accessible elsewhere. Even those who doubted the logic of such material in the *Call* often expressed their gratitude for her serious and factual presentations.

Readers unfriendly to Margaret Sanger's views revealed quite another side of American socialism. The most usual arguments against her column

---

[23] For typical articles, see the Woman's Page of the New York *Call*, December 1912 through 1913.

came from those crude materialists who stressed economic determinism. Capitalism, according to this argument, was the cause of prostitution, and indeed all of the "evils of the sex question;" only when socialism arrived would a healthy society come into existence. A more serious objection was offered to the very publication of knowledge of venereal disease, reasoning that it "placed the demands of FEAR and DISTRUST in the minds of hundreds of prospective wives and mothers," with the effect upon impressionable female readers of a discouragement towards marriage. One writer charged that Margaret Sanger's column would "produce a panic which would cause women to lose all confidence in men and cause them to withdraw their capital (themselves) from the marriage market." Like other critical correspondents, the writer felt that Margaret Sanger scorned the mental and spiritual in favor of the "animal being." Some critics even openly argued for an "eternal" inferior status of women. One writer who wondered whether adequate contraception might eradicate "mother love and the exquisite loyalty of the eternal female," confessed his hesitation "before subscribing to a practice that would have the least tendency to destroy the spiritual qualities of women. Undoubtedly as an expedient for the individual, [birth control] is absolutely moral, but when, as a fixed social policy, it assumes an influence upon the social conscious, its morality is questionable."

In responding to Margaret Sanger's attackers, Anita Block made clear the fundamental objection of some socialists to "What Every Girl Should Know": Sanger had brought the issue out of the abstractions of idyllic life under Socialism and into the realities of women's immediate struggle for full equality. The editor of *Call's* women's page assumed that her readers, as socialists, were more intelligent than non-socialists and consequently would be logically more open to the notion of women's special oppression. But the obstacles placed in front of Margaret Sanger's Party activity, and the failure of any decisive sector of the socialist organization to move to her defense, revealed the contradictory character of the socialists' radical sympathies. As a group, the socialists would more than any other sector of the nation's population affirm the *ultimate* equality of women and the viciousness of their exploitation under capitalism. Indeed, any rank-and-file socialists could articulate and intelligently discuss the radical theories of Engels and Bebel. But even the advanced sectors, to say nothing of the Party as a whole, rejected any notion of a *special* struggle for women, as they rejected generally the special struggles of blacks and even of unskilled workers. In retrospect, the socialists' position was historically understandable, for they viewed the coming of a socialist society as inevitable, smooth and not too far distant. But the situation in which radical theory seemingly justified conservative practice must have been all the more maddening for men and women who, like Margaret Sanger, had come to expect the socialist movement to represent the full liberating possibilities of mankind.

*   *   *

Like the apparent initial acceptance by the mass of socialists of Margaret Sanger's activities, the solicitations of the Party for the Women's National Committee and for the *Progressive Woman* had been deceptive. For as Margaret Sanger was judged by the irritation and even immediate danger she posed to the movement's internal stability, the National Committee and the magazine were judged by their results in recruiting females for the Party rolls, and any figure less than the goal the women had set — for fifty percent of the membership — was bound to be ultimately disappointing. Of course, such a figure was at all odds incredible: the Socialist Party drew predominately from the ranks of skilled workers, while women in the population as a whole were, with scattered exceptions, unskilled workers, workers' wives, or middle and upper-class housewives. Thus women's oppression was not generally felt at the point of production, and their needs were different and special. But the Party forced to extremes by internal disputes and the approaching world conflict, felt the necessity for such pragmatic yardsticks, and by such measurement there could be but one result for Margaret Sanger and the women as a group.

Yet, despite its rapid eclipse, the women's role within the Socialist Party was not a negligible one. At its best, it deeply touched the lives of the new women workers in mass trades such as garments, it moved leading radical literary figures such as Floyd Dell and Max Eastman, and it concentrated the energies of such outstanding women reformers as Margaret Sanger and Florence Kelley. More important, it left an indelible impression on the American radical movement, offering an early lesson—better than in any American radical movement since — of what women could do to link their sex-oppression with the general oppression of the social system.

Poems and Prose
Alta

if i were going to divide people, i would convince them that some are
better than others. some would get away with believing they were superior.
some would get away with believing they were inferior.
i could base this on race or class or money.
i could base this on sex. "men are better than women."
i could base this on age. "grownups are better than children."
or species. "people are better than other living things. a step between
         angels and insects."
or power. hippies know that cops are too perverse to be people. "They're pigs!"
       cops know that hippies are too perverse to be people. "They're animals!"
or personal guilt. you alone are perverse.
         you *are*, aren't you?
         well, you're the ONLY ONE, MUTHERFUCKER!

                    penus envy, they call it.
                    think how handy to have a thing
                    that poked out; you could just shove
                    it in any body, whang whang & come,
                    wouldn't have to give a shit.
                    you *know* you'd come!
                    wouldn't have to love that person,
                    trust that person.
                    whang whang & come.
                    if you couldn't get relief for free,
                    pay a little $, whang, whang & come.
                    you wouldn't have to keep. or abort.
                    wouldn't have to care about the kid.
                    wouldn't fear sexual violation.
                    penus envy, they call it.
                    the man is sick in his heart.
                    that's what i call it.

Printed by permission of Alta.

how the hell
am i supposed to
read your poem to another woman
and come out calm
oh yes dear very nice poem
when was she?
then like an ass
i read one about me
got all tickled
smiled up at you

4 months later you tell me
that poem was a put down

now i'm so busy wondering what
your words mean
that poems are meaningless

this is a very bitter, personal poem.
watch me read it in public
and watch the poets
snap their fingers and giggle.

if they like it they'll ask
if i was high when i wrote it

maybe i'll give up
and go live with a painter

ever go to a party with a
roomful of stoned poets?
the men ignore even me.

it's not that poets are queer,
they just haven't discovered women.

"the only person i lie to is the cleaning lady." - berkeley activist in WL

hmm. so i have too much work to do, the house and the kids and cooking and writing and editing and publishing and printing and teaching and reading at meetings. obviously too much to do. john also cleans the house and cares for the kids and cooks half the meals and writes and edits and publishes and prints and teaches and reads. he has too much to do. what now? a cleaning lady? a wife? a cook? a nanny? how about someone to do my typing? or better yet, my writing? while i'm busy making love to john, someone would be whanging out poems on this here electric whap whap. say, i know what, what about someone to make love for me? i could read or write great poems for the masses while some hireling could grunt and roll a couple of hours each week. all the time i spend nursing kia: why, some nanny could free me a couple of hours each *day!* and with my mind and talents, think what might happen! i'm too good for dishwashing, but the woman down the street isn't, besides i pay minimum wage.

i'm a package deal. come with 2 kids. malcom x's mom had a lover but he split cause she had 8 kids. she went insane from loneliness. (what man would want to take on "some other guy's kids?")

john wouldn't take me to the hills to fuck because i was "surrounded by kids." that is, i had one daughter who spent 3 hours in school each weekday. i asked my first husband if i could leave kia home with him and lori and he said no. "she's not *my* kid!" even when i asked to go to the mountains with john, he wouldn't let me. "what about the kids? bye-bye." so for 6 years i've resented lori and taken great pains to align myself with the man of the moment. i got babysitters for her so i could be with danny, gary, mark, bob, ron, migha, jeremy, kit, john. to a babysitter in reno she explained, "mommy leaves me but she always comes back." lorelei is old faithful, right? doesn't matter if i don't have time for her monday, she'll be there tuesday. but i can't let john think lori and i are allies or i'll never see him. no, no, i'm not with her, *shut up, lorelei,* no i'm a separate person, see? *goddamn you shut up!* see? i don't approve of her, i don't want to hear her either. "Time for daddy and me now, dear."

what i have done to my daughters. what i have done to them for a lousy piece of ass. either i resent them or agree to the bondage: become a jewish mother frantically tied to the kids, excluding the father because he excludes me. those are the roles i played because they were the only ones i saw. my 2 little kids have paid the dues for men who didn't know i was one person. i want those men to go thru everything i have gone thru, everything my daughters have gone thru. no more, no less. let them be rejected as undesirable because they have baby girls. let them be left home. let them be sexually unfulfilled. let them get suicidal when they wake up. let them live for the next 6 years the lives my daughters & i lived for the past 6 years. no more, *no less.*

I have just realized that the stakes are myself
I have no other
ransom money, nothing to break or barter but my life
my spirit measured out, in bits, spread over
the roulette table, I recoup what I can
nothing else to shove under the nose of the maitre de jeu
nothing to thrust out the window, no white flag
this flesh all I have to offer, to make the play with
this immediate head, what it comes up with, my move
as we slither over this board, stepping always
(we hope) between the lines

Diane di Prima

SECTION II:

Origins of Oppression

Women: The Longest Revolution

Juliet Mitchell

Juliet Mitchell is 29 years old and a lecturer in English literature at the University of Reading, England. Currently working on a book on the position of women, she is also an active member of the English Women's Liberation Movement.

The situation of women is different from that of any other social group. This is because they are not one of a number of isolable units, but half a totality: the human species. Women are essential and irreplaceable; they cannot therefore be exploited in the same way as other social groups can. They are fundamental to the human condition, yet in their economic, social and political roles, they are marginal. It is precisely this combination—fundamental and marginal at one and the same time—that has been fatal to them. Within the world of men their position is comparable to that of an oppressed minority: but they also exist outside the world of men. The one state justifies the other and precludes protest. In advanced industrial society, women's work is only marginal to the total economy. Yet it is through work that man changes natural conditions and thereby produces society. Until there is a revolution in production, the labor situation will prescribe women's situation within the world of men. But women are offered a universe of their own: the family. Like woman herself, the family appears as a natural object, but it is actually a cultural creation. There is nothing inevitable about the form or role of the family any more than there is about the character or role of women. It is the function of ideology to present these given social types as aspects of Nature itself. Both can be exalted paradoxically, as ideals. The 'true' woman and the 'true' family are images of peace and plenty: in actuality they may both be sites of violence and despair. The apparently natural condition can be made to appear more attractive than the arduous advance of human beings towards culture. But what Marx wrote about the bourgeois myths of the Golden Ancient World describes precisely women's realm': . . . in one way the child-like world of ancients appears to be superior, and this is so, insofar as we seek for closed shape, form and established limitation. The ancients provide a narrow satisfaction, whereas the modern world leaves us unsatisfied or where it appears to be satisfied with itself, is vulgar and mean.'

Women in Socialist Theory

The problem of the subordination of women and the need for their liberation was recognized by all the great socialist thinkers in the 19th century. It is part of the classical heritage of the revolutionary movement. Yet today, in the West, the problem has become a subsidiary, if not an invisible element in the preoccupations of socialists. Perhaps no other major issue has been so forgotten. In England, the cultural heritage of Puritanism, always strong on the Left, contributed to a widespread discussion of essentially conservative beliefs among many who would otherwise count themselves as 'progressive.' A *locus classicus* of these attitudes is Peter Townsend's remarkable statement: 'Traditionally Socialists have ignored the family or they have openly tried to waken it—alleging nepotism and the restrictions placed upon individual fulfillment by family ties. Extreme attempts to create societies on a basis other than the family have failed dismally. It is significant that a Socialist usually addresses a colleague as "brother" and a Communist uses the term "comrade". The chief means of fulfillment in life is to be a member of, and reproduce a family. There is nothing to be gained by concealing this truth.'[1]

How has this counter-revolution come about? Why has the problem of woman's condition become an area of silence within contemporary socialism? August Bebel, whose book *Woman in the Past, Present and Future* was one of the standard texts of the German Social-Democratic Party in the early years of this century, wrote: "Every Socialist recognizes the dependence of the workman on the capitalist, and cannot understand that others, and especially the capitalists themselves, should fail to recognize it also; but the same Socialist often does not recognize the dependence of women on men because the question touches his own dear self more or less nearly.'[2] But this genre of explanation—psychologistic and moralistic—is clearly inadequate. Much deeper and more structural causes have clearly been at work. To consider these would require a major historical study, impossible here. But it can be said with some certainty that part of the explanation for the decline

---

[1] Peter Townsend: *A Society for People*, in *Conviction*, ed. Norman Mackenzie (1958), pp. 119-20.
[2] August Bebel: *Die Frau und der Sozialismus* (1883), trans. H. B. Adams Walther: *Woman in the Past, Present and Future* (1885) p. 113.

in socialist debate on the subject lies not only in the real historical processes, but in the original weaknesses in the traditional discussion of the subject in the classics. For while the great studies of the last century all stressed the importance of the problem, they did not *solve* it theoretically. The limitations of their approach have never been subsequently transcended.

Fourier was the most ardent and voluminous advocate of women's liber-ation and of sexual freedom among the early socialists. In a well-known passage he wrote: 'The change in a historical epoch can always be determined by the progress of women towards freedom, because in the relation of woman to man, of the weak to the strong, the victory of human nature over brutality is most evident. The degree of emancipation of women is the natural measure of general emancipation.'[3] Marx quoted this formulation with appro-val in *The Holy Family*. But characteristically in his early writings he gave it a more universal and philosophical meaning. The emancipation of women would not only be as Fourier, with his greater preoccupation with sexual liberation saw it, an index of humanization in the civic sense of the victory of humaneness over brutality, but in the more fundamental sense of the progress of the human over the animal, the cultural over the natural: 'The relation of man to woman is the *most natural* relation of human being to human being. It indicates, therefore, how far man's *natural* behavior has become human, and how far his *human* essence has become a *natural* essence for him, how far his *human nature* has become *nature* for him.'[4] This theme is typical of the early Marx.

Fourier's ideas remained at the level of utopian moral injunction. Marx used and transformed them, integrating them into a philosophical critique of human history. But he retained the abstraction of Fourier's conception of the position of women as an index of general social advance. This in effect makes it merely a symbol—it accords the problem a universal importance at the cost of depriving it of its specific substance. Symbols are allusions to or derivations of something else. In Marx's early writings woman becomes an anthropological entity, an ontological category, of a highly abstract kind. Contrarily, in his later work, where he is concerned with describing the family, Marx differentiates it as a phenomenon according to time and place: ' . . . marriage, property, the family remain unattacked, in theory, because they are the practical basis on which the bourgeoisie has erected its domi-nation, and because in their bourgeois form they are the conditions which

[3] Charles Fourier: *Théorie des Quatre Mouvements*, in *Oeuvres Complétes* (1841) I 195; cit. Karl Marx: *The Holy Family* (1845, trans. 1956) p. 259.
[4] Karl Marx: *Private Property and Communism* (1844) in *Early Writings*, trans. T. B. Bottomore (1963), p. 154.

make the bourgeois a bourgeois . . .This attitude of the bourgeois to the conditions of his existence acquires one of its universal forms in bourgeois morality. One cannot, in general, speak of the family *'as such.'* Historically, the bourgeois gives the family the character of the bourgeois family, in which boredom and money are the binding link, and which also includes the bourgeois dissolution of the family, which does not prevent the family itself from always continuing to exist. Its dirty existence has its counterpart in the holy concept of it in official phraseology and universal hypocrisy. . . . (Among the proletariat) the concept of the family does not exist at all . . . In the 18th century the concept of the family was abolished by the philosophers, because the actual family was already in process of dissolution at the highest pinnacles of civilization. The internal family bond was dissolved, the separate components constituting the concept of the family were dissolved, for example, obedience, piety, fidelity in marriage, etc; but the real body of the family, the property relation, the exclusive attitude in relation to other families, forced cohabitation—relations produced by the existence of children, the structure of modern towns, the formation of capital, etc—all these were preserved, although with numerous violations because the existence of the family has been made necessary by its connection with the mode of production that exists independently of the will of bourgeois society.'[5] Or, later still, in *Capital:* 'It is, of course, just as absurd to hold the Teutonic-Christian form of the family to be absolute and final as it would be to apply that character to the ancient Roman, the ancient Greek, or the Eastern forms which, moreover, taken together form a series in historic development.'[6] What is striking is that here the problem of women has been submerged in an analysis of the family. The difficulties of this approach can be seen in the somewhat apocalyptic note of Marx's comments on the fate of the bourgeois family here and elsewhere (for example, in the *Communist Manifesto*). There was little historical warrant for the idea that it was in effective dissolution, and indeed could no longer be seen in the working-class. Marx thus moves from general philosophical formulations about women in the early writings to specific historical comments on the family in the later texts. There is a serious disjunction between the two. The common framework of both, of course, was his analysis of the economy, and of the evolution of property.

Engels

It was left to Engels to systematize these theses in *The Origin of the Family,*

[5] Karl Marx: *The German Ideology* (1845-46, trans. 1965), pp. 192-93.
[6] Karl Marx: *Capital* 1867. ed. 1961 I 490.

Private Property and the State, after Marx's death. Engels declared that the inequality of the sexes was one of the first antagonisms within the human species. The first class antagonism 'coincides with the development of the antagonism between man and woman in the monogamous marriage, and the first class oppression with that of the female sex by the male.'[7] Basing much of his theory on Morgan's inaccurate anthropological investigations, Engels nevertheless had some valuable insights. Inheritance, which is the key to his economist account, was first matrilineal, but with the increase of wealth became patrilineal. This was woman's greatest single setback. The wife's fidelity becomes essential and monogamy is irrevocably established. The wife in the communistic, partriarchal family is a public servant, with monogamy she becomes a private one. Engels effectively reduces the problem of woman to her capacity to work. He therefore gave her physiological weakness as a primary cause of her oppression. He locates the moment of her exploitation at the point of the transition from communal to private property. If inability to work is the cause of her inferior status, ability to work will bring her liberation:' . . . the emancipation of women and their equality with men are impossible and must remain so as long as women are excluded from socially productive work and restricted to housework, which is private. The emancipation of women becomes possible only when women are enabled to take part in production on a large, social, scale, and when domestic duties require their attention only to a minor degree.'[8] Or: 'The first premise for the emancipation of women is the reintroduction of the entire female sex into public industry . . . this . . . demands that the quality possessed by the individual family of being the economic unit of society be abolished.'[9] Engels thus finds a solution schematically appropriate to his analysis of the origin of feminine oppression. The position of women, then, in the work of Marx and Engels remains dissociated from, or subsidiary to, a discussion of the family, which is in its turn subordinated as merely a precondition of private property. Their solutions retain this overly economist stress, or enter the realm of dislocated speculation.

Bebel, Engels' disciple, attempted to provide a programmatic account of woman's oppression as such, not simply as a by-product of the evolution of the family and of private property: 'From the beginning of time oppression was the common lot of woman and the laborer. . . . *Woman was the first human being that tasted bondage,* woman was a slave *before the slave ex-*

---

[7] Friedrich Engels: *The, Origin of the Family, Private Property and the State* (1884), in Marx-Engels: *Selected Works* (1962) II 225.
[8] Ibid. II 311.
[9] Ibid. II 233.

isted.'[10] He acknowledged, with Marx and Engels, the importance of physical inferiority in accounting for woman's subordination, but while stressing inheritance, added that a biological element—her maternal function—was one of the fundamental conditions that made her economically dependent on the man. But Bebel, too, was unable to do more than state that sexual equality was impossible without socialism. His vision of the future was a vague reverie, quite disconnected from his description of the past. The absence of a strategic concern forced him into voluntarist optimism divorced from reality. Lenin himself, although he made a number of specific suggestions, inherited a tradition of thought which simply pointed to the *a priori* equation of socialism with feminine liberation without showing concretely how it would transform woman's condition: 'Unless women are brought to take an independent part not only in political life generally, but also in daily and universal public service, it is no use talking about full and stable democracy, let alone socialism'.[11]

The liberation of women remains a normative ideal, an adjunct to socialist theory, not structurally integrated into it.

The Second Sex

The contrary is true of De Beauvoir's massive work *The Second Sex*—to this day the greatest single contribution on the subject. Here the focus is the status of women through the ages. But socialism as such emerges as a curiously contingent solution at the end of the work, in a muffled epilogue. De Beauvoir's main theoretical innovation was to fuse the 'economic' and 'reproductive' explanations of women's subordination by a psychological interpretation of both. Man asserts himself as subject and free being by opposing other consciousnesses. He is distinct from animals precisely in that he creates and invents (not in that he reproduces himself), but he tries to escape the burden of his freedom by giving himself a spurious 'immortality' in his children. He dominates woman both to imprison another consciousness which reflects his own and to provide him with children that are securely his (his fear of illegitimacy). The notions obviously have a considerable force. But they are very atemporal: it is not easy to see why socialism should modify the basic 'ontological' desire for a thing-like freedom which De Beauvoir sees

[10] August Bebel, *op. cit* p. 7.
[11] V. I. Lenin: *The Tasks of the Proletoriat in Our Revolution* (1917), in *Collected Works* XXIV 70.

as the motor behind the fixation with inheritance in the property system, or the enslavement of women which derived from it. In fact she has since criticized this aspect of her book for idealism: 'I should take a more materialist position today in the first volume. I should base the notion of woman as *other* and the Manichean argument it entails not on an idealistic and *a priori* struggle of consciences, but on the facts of supply and demand. This modification would not necessitate any changes in the subsequent development of my argument.'[12] Concurrent, however, with the idealist psychological explanation, De Beauvoir uses an orthodox economist approach. This leads to a definite evolutionism in her treatment in Volume I, which becomes a retrospective narrative of the different forms of the feminine condition in different societies through time—mainly in terms of the property system and its effects on women. To this she adds various suprahistorical themes—myths of the eternal feminine, types of women through the ages, literary treatments of women—which do not modify the fundamental structure of her argument. The prospect for women's liberation at the end is quite divorced from any historical development.

Thus, the classical literature on the problem of woman's condition is predominantly economist in emphasis, stressing her simple subordination to the institutions of private property. Her biological status underpins both her weakness as a producer, in work relations, and her importance as a possession, in reproductive relations. The fullest and most recent interpretation gives both factors a psychological cast. The framework of discusion is an evolutionist one which nevertheless fails noticeably to project a convincing image of the future, beyond asserting that socialism will involve the liberation of women as one of its constituent 'moments'.

What is the solution to this impasse? It must lie in differentiating woman's condition, much more radically than in the past, into its separate structures, which together form a complex—not a simple— unity. This will mean rejecting the idea that woman's condition can be deduced derivatively from the economy or equated symbolically with society. Rather, it must be seen as a *specific* structure, which is a unity of different elements. The variations of woman's condition throughout history will be the result of different combinations of these elements— much as Marx's analysis of the economy in *Precapitalist Economic Formations* is an account of the different combinations of the factors of production, not a linear narrative of economic development. Because the unity of woman's condition at any one time is the

---

[12] Simone de Beauvoir: *Force of Circumstance* (1965), p. 192.

product of several structures, it is always 'overdetermined'.[13] The key structures can be listed as follows: Production, Reproduction, Sex and Socialization of children. The concrete combination of these produces the 'complex unity' of her position; but each separate structure may have reached a different 'moment' at any given historical time. Each then must be examined separately in order to see what the present unity is and how it might be changed. The discussion that follows does not pretend to give a historical account of each sector. It is only concerned with some general reflections on the different roles of women and some of their interconnections.

Production

The biological differentiation of the sexes and the division of labor have, throughout history, seemed an interlocked necessity. Anatomically smaller and weaker, woman's physiology and her psychobiological metabolism appear to render her a less useful member of a work-force. It is always stressed how, particularly in the early stages of social development, man's physical superiority gave him the means of conquest over nature which was denied to women. Once woman was accorded the menial tasks involved in maintenance whilst man undertook conquest and creation, she became an aspect of the things preserved: private property and children. All socialist writers on the subject mentioned earlier—Marx, Engels, Bebel, De Beauvoir —link the confirmation and continuation of woman's oppression after the establishment of her physical inferiority for hard manual work with the advent of private property. But woman's physical weakness has never prevented her from performing work as such (quite apart from bringing up children)—only specific types of work, in specific societies. In Primitive, Ancient, Oriental, Medieval and Capitalist societies, the *volume* of work per-

---

[13] See Louis Althusser, *Contradiction et Surdétermination* in *Pour Marx* (1965). Althusser advances the notion of a complex totality in which each independent sector has its own autonomous reality but each of which is ultimately, but only ultimately, determined by the economic. This complex totality means that no contradiction in society is ever simple. As each sector can move at a different pace, the synthesis of the different time-scales in the total social structure means that sometimes contradictions cancel each other out and sometimes they reinforce one another. To describe this complexity, Althusser uses the Freudian term 'over-determination.' The phrase *'unité de dupture'* (mentioned below) refers to the moment when the contradictions so reinforced one another as to coalesce into the conditions for a revolutionary change.

formed by women has always been considerable (it has usually been much more than this). It is only its form that is in question. Domestic labor, even today, is enormous if quantified in terms of productive labor.[14] In any case women's physique has never permanently or even predominantly relegated them to menial domestic chores. In many peasant societies, women have worked in the fields as much as, or more than men.

Physique and Coercion

The assumption behind most classical discussion is that the crucial factor starting the whole development of feminine subordination was women's lesser capacity for demanding physical work. But, in fact, this is a major oversimplification. Even within these terms, in history it has been woman's lesser capacity for violence as well as for work that has determined her subordination. In most societies woman has not only been less able than man to perform arduous kinds of work, she has also been less able to fight. Man not only has the strength to assert himself against nature, but also against his fellows. *Social coercion* has interplayed with the straightforward division of labor, based on biological capacity, to a much greater extent than generally admitted. Of course, it may not be actualized as direct aggression. In primitive societies women's physical unsuitability for the hunt is evident. In agricultural societies where women's inferiority is socially instituted they are given the arduous task of tilling and cultivation. For this coercion is necessary. In developed civilizations and more complex societies woman's physical deficiencies again become relevant. Women are no use either for war or in the construction of cities. But with early industrialization coercion once more becomes important. As Marx wrote: 'Insofar as machinery dispenses with muscular power, it becomes a means of employing laborers of slight muscular strength, and those whose bodily development is incomplete, but whose limbs are all the more supple. The labor of women and

---

[14] Apologists who make out that housework, though time-consuming, is light and relatively enjoyable, are refusing to acknowledge the null and degrading routine it entails. Lenin commented crisply: 'You all know that even when women have full rights, they still remain factually down-trodden because all housework is left to them. In most cases housework is the most unproductive, the most barbarous and the most arduous work a woman can do. It is exceptionally petty and does not include anything that would in any way promote the development of the woman'. (Collected Works XXX. 43). Today it has been calculated in Sweden, that 2,340 million hours a year are spent by women in housework compared with 1,290 million hours in industry. The Chase Manhattan Bank estimated a woman's overall working hours as averaging 99.6 per week.

children was, therefore, the first thing sought for by capitalists who used machinery.'[15]

René Dumont points out that in many zones of tropical Africa today men are often idle, while women are forced to work all day.[16] This exploitation has no 'natural' source whatever. Women may perform their 'heavy' duties in contemporary African peasant societies not for fear of physical reprisal by their men, but because these duties are 'customary' and built into the role structures of the society. A further point is that coercion implies a different relationship from coercer to coerced than exploitation does. It is political rather than economic. In describing coercion, Marx said that the master treated the slave or serf as the 'inorganic and natural condition of its own reproduction.' That is to say, labor itself becomes like other natural things—cattle or soil: 'The original conditions of production appear as natural prerequisites, *natural conditions of the existence of the producer,* just as his living body, however reproduced and developed by him, is not originally established by himself, but appears as his *prerequisite.*'[17] This is preeminently woman's condition. For far from woman's physical weakness removing her from productive work, her social weakness has in these cases evidently made her the major slave of it.

This truth, elementary though it may seem, has nevertheless been constantly ignored by writers on the subject, with the result that an illegitimate optimism creeps into their predictions of the future. For if it is just the biological incapacity for the hardest physical work which has determined the subordination of women, then the prospect of an advanced machine technology, abolishing the need for strenuous physical exertion would seem to promise, therefore, the liberation of women. For a moment industrialization itself thus seems to herald women's liberation. Engels, for instance, wrote: 'The first premise for the emancipation of women is the reintroduction of the entire female sex into public industry . . . And this has become possible only as a result of modern large-scale industry, which not only permits of the participation of women in production in large numbers, but actually calls for it and, moreover strives to convert private domestic work also into a public industry.'[18] What Marx said of early industrialism is no less, but

---

[15] Karl Marx: *Capital* I 394.
[16] 'The African woman experiences a three-fold servitude: through forced marriage; through her dowry and polygamy, which increases the leisure time of men and simultaneously their social prestige; and finally through the very unequal division of labor' René Dumont: *L'Afrique Noire est Mal Partie* (1962), p. 210.
[17] Karl Marx: *Precapitalist Economic Formations* op. cit. p. 87.
[18] Friedrich Engels, *op. cit.* II 233 & 311.

also *no more* true of an automated society:' . . . it is obvious that the fact of the collective working group being composed of individuals of both sexes and all ages, must necessarily, *under suitable conditions*, become a source of human development; although in its spontaneously developed, brutal, capitalistic form, where the laborer exists for the process of production, and not the process of production for the laborer, that fact is a pestiferous source of corruption and slavery.'[19] Industrial labor and automated technology both promise the preconditions for woman's liberation alongside man's—but no more than the preconditions. It is only too obvious that the advent of industrialization has not so far freed women in this sense either in the West or in the East. In the West it is true that there was a great influx of women into jobs in the expanding industrial economy, but this soon levelled out, and there has been relatively little increase in recent decades. De Beauvoir hoped that automation would make a decisive, qualitative difference by abolishing altogether the physical differential between the sexes. But any reliance on this in itself accords an independent role to technique which history does not justify. Under capitalism, automation could possibly lead to an ever-growing structural unemployment which would expel women— the latest and least integrated recruits to the labor force and ideologically the most expendable for a bourgeois society—from production after only a brief interlude in it. Technology is mediated by the total social structure and it is this which will determine woman's future in work relations.

Physical deficiency is not now, any more than in the past, a sufficient explanation of woman's relegation to inferior status. Coercion has been ameliorated to an ideology shared by both sexes. Commenting on the results of her questionnaire of working women, Viola Klein notes: 'There is no trace of feminist egalitarianism—militant or otherwise—in any of the women's answers to our questionaire; nor is it even implicity assumed that women have a 'Right to Work'."[20] Denied, or refusing, a role in *production*, woman does not even create the *pre*-conditions of her liberation.

Reproduction

Women's absence from the critical sector of production historically, of course, has been caused not just by their physical weakness in a context of coercion—but also by their role in reproduction. Maternity necessitates periodic withdrawals from work, but this is not a decisive phenomenon. It is

[19] Karl Marx: *Capital* I. 394.
[20] Viola Klein: *Working Wives*, Institute of Personnel Management Occasional Papers, No. 15 (1960), p. 13.

rather women's role in reproduction which has become, in capitalist society at least, the spiritual 'complement' of men's role in production.[21] Bearing children, bringing them up, and maintaining the home—these form the core of woman's natural vocation, in this ideology. This belief has attained great force because of the seeming universality of the family as a human institution. There is little doubt that Marxist analyses have underplayed the fundamental problems posed here. The complete failure to give any operative content to the slogan of 'abolition' of the family is striking evidence of this (as well as of the vacuity of the notion). The void thus created has been quickly occupied by traditional beliefs such as Townsend's quoted above.

The biological function of maternity is a universal, atemporal fact, and as such has seemed to escape the categories of Marxist historical analysis. From it follows—apparently—the stability and omnipresence of the family, if in very different forms.[22] Once this is accepted, women's social subordination—however emphasized, as an honourable, but different role (cf. the equal but 'separate' ideologies of Southern racists)—can be seen to follow inevitably as an *insurmountable* bio-historical fact. The casual chain then goes: Maternity, Family, Absence from Production and Public Life, Sexual Inequality.

The lynch-pin in this line of argument is the idea of the family. The notion that 'family' and 'society' are virtually co-extensive terms, or that an advanced society not founded on the nuclear family is now inconceivable, is widespread. It can only be seriously discussed by asking just what the family is—or rather what women's role in the family is. Once this is done, the problem appears in quite a new light. For it is obvious that woman's role in the family—primitive, feudal or bourgeois—partakes of three quite different structures: reproduction, sexuality, and the socialization of children. These are historically, not intrinsically, related to each other in the present modern family. Biological parentage is not necessarily identical with social parentage (adoption). It is thus essential to discuss: not the family as an unanalysed entity, but the separate *structures* which today compose it, but which may

---

[21] Maternity is *the* distinctive feature on which both sexes base their hopes: for oppression or liberation. The notion of woman's potential superiority on account of her procreative function reaches the absurd in Margherita Repetto: *Maternitá e Famiglia, Condizioni per la Libertà della Donna, Rivista Trimestrale* 11-12 (1964) but it is found even in Evelyne Sullerot: *Demain les Femmes* (1965).

[22] Philippe Ariès in *Centuries of Childhood* (1962) shows that though the family may in some form always have existed it was often submerged under more forceful structures. In fact according to Ariès it has only acquired its present significance with the advent of industrialization.

tomorrow be decomposed into a new pattern.

Reproduction, it has been stressed, is a seemingly constant atemporal phenomenon—part of biology rather than history. In fact this is an illusion. What is true is that the 'mode of reproduction' does not vary with the 'mode of production'; it can remain effectively the same through a number of different modes of production. For it has been defined till now, by its uncontrollable natural character. To this extent, it has been an unmodified biological fact. As long as reproduction remained a natural phenomenon, of course, women were effectively doomed to social exploitation. In any sense, they were not masters of a large part of their lives. They had no choice as to whether or how often they gave birth to children (apart from repeated abortion), their existence was essentially subject to biological processes outside their control.

Contraception

Contraception, which was invented as a rational technique only in the 19th century, was thus an innovation of world-historic importance. It is only now just beginning to show what immense consequences it could have, in the form of the pill. For what it means is that at last the mode of reproduction could potentially be transformed. Once child-bearing becomes totally voluntary (how much so is it in the West, even today?) its significance is fundamentally different. It need no longer be the sole or ultimate vocation of woman; it becomes one option among others.

Marx sees history as the development of man's transformation of nature, and thereby of himself—of human nature—in different modes of production. Today there are the technical possibilities for the humanization of the most natural part of human culture. This is what a change in the mode of reproduction could mean.

We are far from this state of affairs as yet. In France and Italy the sale of any form of contraception remains illegal. The oral contraceptive is the privilege of a moneyed minority in a few Western countries. Even here the progress has been realized in a typically conservative and exploitative form. It is made only for women, who are thus 'guinea-pigs' in a venture which involves both sexes.

The fact of overwhelming importance is that easily available contraception threatens to dissociate sexual from reproductive experience—which all contemporary bourgeois ideology tries to make inseparable, as the *raison d' etre* of the family.

Reproduction and Production

At present, reproduction in our society is often a kind of sad mimicry of production. Work in a capitalist society is an alienation of labor in the making of a social product which is confiscated by capital. But it can still sometimes be a real act of creation, purposive and responsible, even in conditions of the worst exploitation. Maternity is often a caricature of this. The biological product—the child—is treated as if it were a solid product. Parenthood becomes a kind of substitute for work, an activity in which the child is seen as an object created by the mother, in the same way as a commodity is created by a worker. Naturally, the child does not literally escape, but the mother's alienation can be much worse than that of the worker whose product is appropriated by the boss. No human being can create another human being. A person's biological origin is an abstraction. The child as an autonomous person inevitably threatens the activity which claims to create it continually merely as a *possession* of the parent. Possessions are felt as extensions of the self. The child as a possession is supremely this. Anything the child does is therefore a threat to the mother herself who has renounced her autonomy through this misconception of her reproductive role. There are few more precarious ventures on which to base a life.

Furthermore even if the woman has emotional control over her child, legally and economically both she and it are subject to the father. The social cult of maternity is matched by the real socio-economic powerlessness of the mother. The psychological and practical benefits men receive from this are obvious. The converse of women's quest for creation in the child is men's retreat from his work into the family: 'When we come home, we lay aside our mask and drop our tools, and are no longer lawyers, sailors, soldiers, statesmen, clergymen, but only men. We fall again into our most human relations, which, after all, are the whole of what belongs to us as we are in ourselves.'[23]

Unlike her non-productive status, her capacity for maternity *is* a definition of woman. But it is only a physiological definition. So long as it is allowed to remain a substitute for action and creativity, and the home an area of relaxation for men, women will remain confined to the species, to her universal and natural condition.

Sexuality

Sexuality has traditionally been the most tabooed dimension of women's

---

[23] J. A. Froude: *Nemesis of Faith* (1849), p. 103.

situation. The meaning of sexual freedom and its connection with women's freedom is a particularly difficult subject which few socialist writers have cared to broach. Fourier alone identified the two totally, in lyrical strophes describing a sexual paradise of permutations—the famous phalansteries. 'Socialist morality' in the Soviet Union for a long time debarred serious discussion of the subject within the world communist movement. Marx himself—in this respect somewhat less liberal than Engels—early in his life expressed traditional views on the matter: '. . . the sanctification of the sexual instinct through exclusivity, the checking of instinct by laws, the moral beauty which makes nature's commandment ideal in the form of an emotional bond—(this is) the spiritual essence of marriage.'[24]

Yet it is obvious that throughout history women have been appropriated as sexual objects, as much as progenitors or producers. Indeed, the sexual relation can be assimilated to the statute of possession much more easily and completely than the productive or reproductive relationship. Contemporary sexual vocabulary bears eloquent witness to this—it is a comprehensive lexicon of reification. Later Marx was well aware of this, of course: 'Marriage . . . is incontestably a form of exclusive private property.'[25] But neither he nor his successors ever tried seriously to envisage the implications of this for socialism, or even for a structural analysis of women's condition. Communism, Marx stressed in the same passage, would not mean mere 'communalization' of women as common property. Beyond this, he never ventured.

Some historical considerations are in order here. For if socialists have said nothing, the gap has been filled by liberal ideologues. A recent book, *Eros Denied* by Wayland Young, argues that Western civilization has been uniquely repressive sexually and in a plea for greater sexual freedom today compares it at some length with Oriental and Ancient societies. It is striking, that this book makes no reference whatever to women's status in these different societies, or to the different forms of marriage-contract prevalent in them. This makes the whole argument a purely formal exercise—an obverse of socialist discussions of women's position which ignores the problem of sexual freedom and its meanings. For while it is true that certain oriental or ancient (and indeed primitive) cultures were much less puritan than Western societies, it is absurd to regard this as a kind of 'transposable value' which can be abstracted from its social structure. In effect, in many of these societies sexual openness was accompanied by a form of polygamous exploitation which made it in practice an expression simply of masculine domination.

[24] Karl Marx: *Chapitre de Marriage. Oeuvres Complètes* ed. Molitor *Oeuvres Philosophiques.* I p. 25.
[25] Karl Marx: *Private Property and Communism, op. cit.* p. 153.

Since art was the province of man, too, this freedom finds a natural and often powerful expression in art—which is often quoted as if it were evidence of the total quality of human relationships in the society. Nothing could be more misleading. What is necessary, rather than this naive, hortatory core of historical example, is some account of the co-variation between the degrees of sexual liberty and openness and the position and dignity of women in different societies. Some points are immediately obvious. The actual history is much more dialectical than any liberal account presents it. Unlimited juridical polygamy—whatever the sexualization of the culture which accompanies it—is clearly a total derogation of woman's autonomy, and constitutes an extreme form of oppression. Ancient China is a perfect illustration of this. Wittfogel describes the extraordinary despotism of the Chinese *paterfamilias* —'a liturgical (semi-official) policeman of his kin group.'[26] In the West, however, the advent of monogamy was in no sense an *absolute* improvement. It certainly did not create a one-to-one equality—far from it. Engels commented accurately: 'Monogamy does not by any means make its appearance in history as the reconciliation of man and woman, still less as the highest form of such a reconciliation. On the contrary, it appears as the subjugation of one sex by the other, as the proclamation of a conflict between the sexes entirely unknown hitherto in prehistoric times.'[27] But in the Christian era, monogamy took on a very specific form in the West. It was allied with an unprecedented régime of general sexual repression. In its Pauline version, this had a markedly anti-feminine bias, inherited from Judaism. With time this became diluted—feudal society, despite its subsequent reputation for asceticism, practised formal monogamy with considerable actual acceptance of polygamous behaviour, at least within the ruling class. But here again the extent of sexual freedom was only an index of masculine domination. In England, the truly major change occurred in the 16th century with the rise of militant puritanism and the increase of market relations in the economy. Lawrence Stone observes: 'In practice, if not in theory, the early 16th century nobility was a polygamous society, and some contrived to live with a succession of women despite the official prohibition on divorce . . . But impressed by Calvinist criticisms of the double standard, in the late 16th century public opinion began to object to the open maintenance of a mistress.'[28] Capitalism and the attendant demands of the newly emergent bourgeoisie accorded women a new status as wife and mother. Her legal rights improved; there was vigorous controversy over her social position; wife-beating was

[26] Karl Wittfogel: *Oriental Despotism* (1957) p. 116.
[27] Friedrich Engels, *op. cit.* II 224.
[28] Lawrence Stone: *The Crisis of the Aristocracy* (1965), pp. 663-64.

condemned. 'In a woman the bourgeois man is looking for a counterpart, not an equal.'[29] At the social periphery woman did occasionally achieve an equality which was more than her feminine function in a market society. In the extreme sects women often had completely equal rights: Fox argued that the Redemption restored Prelapsarian equality and Quaker women thereby gained a real autonomy. But once most of the sects were institutionalized, the need for family discipline was re-emphasized and woman's obedience with it. As Keith Thomas says, the Puritans 'had done something to raise women's status, but not really very much.'[30] The patriarchal system was retained and maintained by the economic mode of production. The transition to complete effective monogamy accompanied the transition to modern bourgeois society as we know it today. Like the market system itself, it represented a historic advance, at great historic cost. The formal, juridical equality of capitalist society and capitalist rationality now applied as much to the marital as to the labor contract. In both cases, nominal parity masks real exploitation and inequality. But in both cases the formal equality is itself a certain progress, which can help to make possible a further advance.

For the situation today is defined by a new contradiction. Once formal conjugal equality (monogamy) is established, sexual freedom as such—which under polygamous conditions was usually a form of exploitation—becomes, conversely, a possible force for liberation. It then means, simply, the freedom for both sexes to transcend the limits of present sexual institutions.

Historically, then, there has been a dialectical movement, in which sexual expression was 'sacrificed' in an epoch of more-or-less puritan repression, which nevertheless produced a greated parity of sexual roles, which in turn creates the precondition for a genuine sexual liberation, in the dual sense of equality *and* freedom—whose unity defines socialism.

This movement can be verified within the history of the 'sentiments'. The cult of *love* only emerges in the 12th century in opposition to legal marital forms and with a heightened valorization of women (courtly love). It thereafter gradually became diffused, and assimilated to marriage as such, which in its bourgeois form (romantic love) became a *free* choice for *life*. What is striking here is that monogamy as an institution in the West anticipated the idea of love by many centuries. The two have subsequently been officially

[29] Simone de Beauvoir: *La Marche Longue* (1957), trans. *The Long March* (1958), p. 141.
[30] Keith Thomas: *Women and the Civil War Sects, Past and Present* No. 13 (1958), p. 43.

harmonized, but the tension between them has never been abolished. There is a formal contradiction between the voluntary contractual character of 'marriage' and the spontaneous uncontrollable character of 'love'—the passion that is celebrated precisely for its involuntary force. The notion that it occurs only once in every life and can therefore be integrated into a voluntary contract becomes decreasingly plausible in the light of everyday experience—once sexual repression as a psycho-ideological system becomes at all relaxed.

Obviously, the main breach in the traditional value-pattern has so far been the increase in premarital sexual experience. This is now virtually legitimized in contemporary bourgeois society. But its implications are explosive for the ideological conception of marriage that dominates this society: that of an exclusive and permanent bond. A recent American anthology *The Family and the Sexual Revolution* reveals this very clearly: 'As far as extramarital relations are concerned, the anti-sexualists are still fighting a strong, if losing, battle. The very heart of the Judeo-Christian sex ethic is that men and women shall remain virginal until marriage and that they shall be completely faithful after marriage. In regard to premarital chastity, this ethic seems clearly on the way out, and in many segments of the populace is more and more becoming a dead letter.'[31]

The current wave of sexual liberalization, in the present context, could become conducive to the greater general freedom of women. Equally it could presage new forms of oppression. The puritan-bourgeois creation of woman as 'counterpart' has produced the *precondition* for emancipation. But it gave statutory legal equality to the sexes at the cost of greatly intensified repression. Subsequently— like private property itself—it has become a brake on the further development of a free sexuality. Capitalist market relations have historically been a precondition of socialism; bourgeois marital relations (contrary to the denunciation of the *Communist Manifesto*) may equally be a precondition of women's liberation.

Socialization

Woman's biological destiny as mother becomes a cultural vocation in her role as socializer of children. In bringing up children, woman achieves her main social definition. Her suitability for socialization springs from her physiological condition; her ability to lactate and occasionally relative inability

[31] Albert Ellis: *The Folklore of Sex*, in *The Family and the Sexual Revolution* ed. E. M. Schur (1964) p. 35.

to undertake strenuous work loads. It should be said at the outset that suitability is not inevitability. Lévi-Strauss writes: 'In every human group, women give birth to children and take care of them, and men rather have as their speciality hunting and warlike activities. Even there, though, we have ambiguous cases: of course, men never give birth to babies, but in many societies . . . they are made to act as if they did.'[32] Evans-Pritchard's description of the Nuer tribe depicts just such a situation. And another anthropologist, Margaret Mead, comments on the element of wish-fulfillment in the assumption of a *natural* correlation of femininity and nurturance: 'We have assumed that because it is convenient for a mother to wish to care for her child, this is a trait with which women have been more generously endowed by a careful teleogical process of evolution. We have assumed that because men have hunted, an activity requiring enterprise, bravery, and initiative, they have been endowed with these useful aptitudes as part of their sex-temperament.'[33] However, the cultural allocation of rules in bringing up children—and the limits of its variability—is not the essential problem for consideration. What is much more important is to analyse the nature of the socialization process itself and its requirements.

Parsons in his detailed analysis claims that it is essential for the child to have two 'parents', one who plays an 'expressive' role, and one who plays an 'instrumental' role.[34] The nuclear family revolves around the two axes of generational hierarchy and of these two roles. In typically Parsonian idiom, he claims that 'At least one fundamental feature of the external situation of social systems—here a feature of the physiological organism—is a crucial reference point for differentiation in the family. This lies in the division of organisms into lactating and nonlactating classes.' In all groups, he and his colleagues assert, even in those primitive tribe discussed by Pritchard and Mead, the male plays the instrumental role *in relation* to the

[32] Claude Lévi-Strauss: *The Family*, in *Man, Culture and Society*, ed. H. L. Shapiro (1956), p. 274.
[33] Margaret Mead: *Sex and Temperament*, in *The Family and The Sexual Revolution*, op. cit. pp. 207-8.
[34] Talcott Parsons and Robert F. Bales: *Family, Socialization and Interaction Process* (1956), p. 313. 'The instrumental-expressive distinction we interpret as essentially the differentiation of function, and hence of relative influence, in terms of 'external' vs. 'internal' functions of the system. The area of instrumental function concerns relations of the system to its situation outside the system, to meeting the adaptive conditions of its maintenance of equilibrium, and 'instrumentally' establishing the desired relations to *external* goal-objects. The expressive area concerns the 'internal' affairs of the system, the maintenance of integrative relations between the members, and regulation of the patterns and tension levels of its component units.' (Ibid., p. 47).

wife-mother. At one stage the mother plays an instrumental and expressive role *vis-à-vis* her infant: this is pre-oedipally when she is the source of approval and disapproval as well as of love and care. However, after this, the father, or male substitute (in matrilineal societies the mother's brother) takes over. In a modern industrial society two types of role are clearly important: the adult familial roles in the family of procreation, and the adult occupational role. The function of the family as such reflects the function of the women within it; it is primarily expressive. The person playing the integrated-adaptive-expressive role cannot be off all the time on instrumental-occupational errands—hence there is a built-in inhibition of the woman's work outside the home. Parson's analysis makes clear the exact role of the maternal socializer in contemporary American society.[35] It fails to go on to state that other aspects and modes of socialization are conceivable. What is valuable in Parson's work is simply his insistence on the central importance of socialization as a process which is constitutive of any society (no Marxist has so far provided a comparable analysis). His general conclusion is that: 'It seems to be without serious qualification the opinion of competent personality psychologists that, though personalities differ greatly in their degrees of rigidity, certain broad fundamental patterns of 'character' are laid down in childhood (so far as they are not genetically inherited) and are not radically changed by adult experience. The exact degree to which this is the case or the exact age levels at which plasticity becomes greatly diminished, are not at issue here. The important thing is the fact of childhood character formation and its relative stability after that.'[36]

Infancy

This seems indisputable. One of the great revolutions of modern psychology has been the discovery of the decisive specific weight of infancy in the course of an individual life—a psychic time disproportionately greater than the chronoligical time. Freud began the revolution with his work on infantile sexuality; Klein radicalized it with her work on the first year of the infant's life. The result is that today we know far more than ever before how delicate and precarious a process the passage from birth to childhood is for everyone. The fate of the adult personality can be largely decided in the initial months of life. The preconditions for the latter stability and inte-

[35] One of Parsons' main theoretical innovations is his contention that what the child strives to internalize will vary with the content of the reciprocal role relationships in which he is a participant. R. D. Laing, in *Family and Structure* (1966) contends that a child may internalize an entire system—i.e. 'the family.'
[36] Talcott Parsons: *The Social System* (1952), p. 227.

gration demand an extraordinary degree of care and intelligence on the part of the adult who is socializing the child, as well as a persistence through time of the same person.

These undoubted advances in the scientific understanding of childhood have been widely used as an argument to reassert women's quintessential maternal function, at a time when the traditional family has seemed increasingly eroded. Bowlby, studying evacuee children in the Second World War, declared: 'essential for mental health is that the infant and young child should experience a warm, intimate and continuous relationship with his mother,'[37] setting a trend which has become cumulative since. The emphasis of familial ideology has shifted away from a cult of the biological ordeal of maternity (the pain which makes the child precious, etc.) to a celebration of mother-care as a social act. This can reach ludicrous extremes: 'For the mother, breast-feeding becomes a complement to the act of creation. It gives her a heightened sense of fulfilment and allows her to participate in a relationship as close to perfection as any that a woman can hope to achieve ... The simple fact of giving birth, however, does not of itself fulfil this need and longing. . . . Motherliness is a way of life. It enables a woman to express her total self with the tender feelings, the protective attitudes, the encompassing love of the motherly woman.'[38] The tautologies, the mystifications (an *act* of creation, a *process* surely?) the sheer absurdities . . . 'as close to perfection as any woman can hope to achieve' . . . point to the gap between reality and ideology.

Familial Patterns

This ideology corresponds in dislocated form to a real change in the pattern of the family. As the family has become smaller, each child has become more important; the actual *act* of reproduction occupies less and less time and the socializing and nurturance process increase commensurately in significance. Bourgeois society is obsessed by the physical, moral and sexual problems of childhood and adolescence.[39] Ultimate responsibility for these is

[37] John Bowlby, cit. Bruno Bettelheim: *Does Communal Education work? The Case of the Kibbutz*, in *The Family and the Sexual Revolution, op. cit.* p. 295.
[38] Betty Ann Countrywoman, in *Redbook* (June, 1960), cit. Betty Friedan: *The Feminine Mystique* (1963), p. 58.
[39] David Riesman, while correctly observing this, makes a rather vain criticism of it: 'There has been a tendency in current social research influenced as it is by psychoanalysis, to over-emphasize and over-generalize the importance of very early childhood in character formation. . . It is increasingly recognized, however, that character may change greatly after this early period. . . Cultures differ widely not only in their timing of the various steps in character formation but also in the agents they rely on at each step.' *The Lonely Crowd* (1950), pp. 38-39.

placed on the mother. Thus the mother's 'maternal' role has retreated as her socializing role has increased. In the 1890's in England a mother spent 15 years in a state of pregnancy and lactation; in the 1960's she spends an average of four years. Compulsory schooling from the age of five, of course, reduces the maternal function very greatly after the initial vulnerable years.

The present situation is then one in which the qualitative importance of socialization during the early years of the child's life has acquired a much greater significance than in the past—while the quantitative amount of a mother's life spent either in gestation or child-rearing has greatly diminished. It follows that socialization cannot simply be elevated to the woman's new maternal vocation. Used as a mystique, it becomes an instrument of oppression. Moreover, there is no inherent reason why the biological and social mother should coincide. The process of socialization is, in the Kleinian sense, invariable—but the person of the socializer can vary.

Bruno Bettelheim observing Kibbutz methods notes that the child who is reared by a trained nurse (though normally maternally breast-fed) does not suffer the back-wash of typical parental anxieties and thus may positively gain by the system.[10] This possibility should not be fetishized in its turn (Jean Baby, speaking of the post-four-year-old child, goes so far as to say that 'complete separation appears indispensable to guarantee the liberty of the child as well as of the mother.'[11]) But what it does reveal is the viability of plural forms of socialization—neither necessarily tied to the nuclear family, nor to the biological parent.

Conclusion

The lesson of these reflections is that the liberation of women can only be achieved if *all four* structures in which they are integrated are transformed. A modification of any one of them can be offset by a reinforcement of another, so that mere permutation of the form of exploitation is achieved. The history of the last 60 years provides ample evidence of this. In the early 20th century, militant feminism in England or the USA surpassed the labor movement in the violence of its assault on bourgeois society, in pursuit of suffrage. This political right was eventually won. Nonetheless, though a simple completion of the formal legal equality of bourgeois society, it left the socio-economic situation of women virtually unchanged. The wider legacy of the suffrage was nil: the suffragettes proved quite unable

[10] Bruno Bettelheim: *Does Communal Education Work? The Case of the Kibbutz*, p. 303. From *The Family and Social Revolution op. cit.*
[11] Jean Baby: *Un Monde Meilleur* (1964), p. 99.

to move beyond their own initial demands, and many of their leading figures later became extreme reactionaries. The Russian Revolution produced a quite different experience. In the Soviet Union in the 1920's, advanced social legislation aimed at liberating women above all in the field of sexuality: divorce was made free and automatic for either partner, thus effectively liquidating marriage; illegitimacy was abolished, abortion was free, etc. The social and demographic effects of these laws in a backward, semi-literate society bent on rapid industrialization (needing, therefore, a high birth-rate) were—predictably—catastrophic. Stalinism soon produced a restoration of iron traditional norms. Inheritance was reinstated, divorce inaccessible, abortion illegal, etc. 'The State cannot exist without the family. Marriage is a positive value for the Socialist Soviet State only if the partners see in it a lifelong union. So-called free love is a bourgeois invention and has nothing in common with the principles of conduct of a Soviet citizen. Moreover, marriage receives its full value for the State only if there is progeny, and the consorts experience the highest happiness of parenthood,' wrote the official journal of the Commissariat of Justice in 1939.[12] Women still retained the right and obligation to work, but because these gains had not been integrated into the earlier attempts to abolish the family and free sexuality no general liberation has occurred. In China, still another experience is being played out today. At a comparable stage of the revolution, all the emphasis is being placed on liberating women in *production*. This has produced an impressive social promotion of women. But it has been accompanied by a tremendous repression of sexuality and a rigorous puritanism (currently rampant in civic life). This corresponds not only to the need to mobilize women massively in economic life, but to a deep cultural reaction against the corruption and prostitution prevalent in Imperial and Kuo Ming Tang China (a phenomenon unlike anything in Czarist Russia). Because the exploitation of women was so great in the *ancien régime,* women's participation at village level in the Chinese Revolution was uniquely high. As for reproduction, the Russian cult of maternity in the 1930's and 1940's has not been repeated for demographic reasons: indeed, China may be one of the first countries in the world to provide free State authorized contraception on a universal scale to the population. Again, however, given the low level of industrialization and fear produced by imperialist encirclement, no all-round advance should be expected.

It is only in the highly developed societies of the West that an authentic

---

[12] *Sotsialisticheskaya Zakonnost* (1939. No. 2, cit. N. Timasheff: *The Attempt to Abolish the Family in Russia,* in *The Family,* ed. N. W. Bell and E. F. Vogel (1960), p. 59.

liberation of women can be envisaged today. But for this to occur, there must be a transformation of all the structures into which they are integrated, and an *'unité le rupture'*.[13] A revolutionary movement must base its analysis on the uneven development of each, and attack the weakest link in the combination. This may then become the point of departure for a general transformation. What is the situation of the different structures today?

1. Production: The long-term development of the forces of production must command any socialist perspective. The hopes which the advent of machine technology raised as early as the 19th century have already been discussed. They proved illusory. Today, automation promises the *technical* possibility of abolishing completely the physical differential between man and woman in production, but under capitalist relations of production, the *social* possibility of this abolition is permanently threatened, and can easily be turned into its opposite, the actual diminution of woman's role in production as the labor force contracts.

This concerns the future, for the present the main fact to register is that woman's role in production is virtually stationary, and has been so for a long time now. In England in 1911 30 per cent of the work-force were women; in the 1960's 34 per cent. The composition of these jobs has not changed decisively either. The jobs are very rarely 'careers'. When they are not in the lowest positions on the factory-floor they are normally white-collar auxiliary positions (such as secretaries)—supportive to masculine roles. They are often jobs with a high 'expressive' content, such as 'service' tasks. Parsons says bluntly: 'Within the occupational organization they are analogous to the wife-mother role in the family.'[11] The educational system underpins this role-structure. Seventy-five per cent of 18-year-old girls in England are receiving neither training nor education today. The pattern of 'instrumental' father and 'expressive' mother is not substantially changed when the woman is gainfully employed, as her job tends to be inferior to that of the man's to which the family then adapts.

Thus, in all essentials, work as such—of the amount and type effectively available today—has not proved a salvation for women.

2. Reproduction: Scientific advance in contraception could, as we have seen, make involuntary reproduction—which accounts for the vast majority of births in the world today, and for a major proportion even in the West—a

---

[43] See Louis Althusser: *op.cit.* See note 13.
[44] Parsons and Bales, *op. cit* p. 15n.

phenomenon of the past. But oral contraception—which has so far been developed in a form which exactly repeats the sexual inequality of Western society—is only at its beginnings. It is inadequately distributed across classes and countries and awaits further technical improvements. Its main initial impact is, in the advanced countries, likely to be psychological—it will certainly free women's sexual experience from many of the anxieties and inhibitions which have always afflicted it.[15] It will definitely divorce sexuality from procreation, as necessary complements.

The demographic pattern of reproduction in the West may or may not be widely affected by oral contraception. One of the most striking phenomena of very recent years in the United States has been the sudden increase in the birth-rate. In the last decade it has been higher than that of under-developed countries such as India, Pakistan and Burma. In fact, this reflects simply the lesser economic burden of a large family in conditions of economic boom in the richest country in the world. But it also reflects the magnification of familial ideology as a social force. This leads to the next structure.

3. Socialization: The changes in the composition of the work-force, the size of the family, the structure of education, etc.—however limited from an ideal standpoint—have undoubtedly diminished the societal function and importance of the family. As an organization it is not a significant unit in the political power system, it plays little part in economic production and it is rarely the sole agency of integration into the larger society; thus at the macroscopic level it serves very little purpose.

The result has been a major displacement of emphasis on to the family's psycho-social function, for the infant and for the couple.[16] Parsons writes: 'The trend of the evidence points to the beginning of the relative stabilization of a *new* type of family structure in a new relation to a general social structure, one in which the family is more specialized than before, but not in any general sense less important, because the society is dependent *more* exclusively on it for the performance of *certain* of its vital functions.'[17] The vital nucleus of truth in the emphasis on socialization of the child has been discussed. It is essential that socialists should acknowledge it and integrate it

---

[15] Jean Baby records the results of an enquiry carried out into attitudes to marriage, contraception and abortion of 3,191 women in Czechoslovakia in 1959: 80 per cent of the women had limited sexual satisfaction because of fear of conception. *Op. cit.* p. 82n.

[16] See Berger and Kellner: *Marriage and the Construction of Reality, Diogenes* (Summer 1964) for analyses of marriage and parenthood 'nomic-building' structure.

entirely into any programme for the liberation of women. It is noticeable that recent 'vanguard' work by French Marxists—Baby, Sullerot, Texier—accords the problem its real importance. However, there is no doubt that the need for permanent, intelligent care of children in the initial three or four years of their lives can (and has been) exploited ideologically to perpetuate the family as a total unit, when its other functions have been visibly declining. Indeed, the attempt to focus women's existence exclusively on bringing up children, is manifestly harmful to children. Socialization as an exceptionally delicate process requires a serene and mature socializer—a type which the frustrations of a *purely* familial role are not liable to produce. Exclusive maternity is often in this sense 'counter-productive'. The mother discharges her own frustrations and anxieties in a fixation on the child. An increased awareness of the critical importance of socialization, far from leading to a restitution of classical maternal roles, should lead to a reconsideration of them—of what makes a good socializing agent, who can genuinely provide security and stability for the child.

The same arguments apply, *a fortiori*, to the psycho-social role of the family for the couple. The beliefs that the family provides an impregnable enclave of intimacy and security in an atomized and chaotic cosmos assumes the absurd—that the family can be isolated from the community, and that its internal relationships will not reproduce in their own terms the external relationships which dominate the society. The family as refuge in a bourgeois society inevitably becomes a reflection of it.

4. Sexuality: It is difficult not to conclude that the major structure which at present is in rapid evolution is sexuality. Production, reproduction, and socialization are all more or less stationary in the West today, in the sense that they have not changed for three or more decades. There is, moreover, no widespread *demand* for changes in them on the part of women themselves—the governing ideology has effectively prevented critical consciousness. By contrast, the dominant sexual ideology is proving less and less successful in regulating spontaneous behaviour. Marriage in its classical form is increasingly threatened by the liberalization of relationships before and after it which affects all classes today. In this sense, it is evidently the weak link in the chain—the particular structure that is the site of the most contradictions. The progressive potential of these contradictions has already been emphasized. In a context of juridical equality, the liberation of sexual experience

---

[47] Parsons and Bales, *op. cit.* pp. 9-10.

from relations which are extraneous to it—whether procreation or property
—could lead to true inter-sexual freedom. But it could also lead simply to
new forms of neocapitalist ideology and practice. For one of the forces behind the current acceleration of sexual freedom has undoubtedly been the
conversion of contemporary capitalism from a production-and-work ethos
to a consumption-and-fun ethos. Riesman commented on this development
early in the 1950's: ' . . . there is not only a growth of leisure, but work itself
becomes both less interesting and less demanding for many . . . more than
before, as job-mindedness declines, sex permeates the daytime as well as the
playtime consciousness. It is viewed as a consumption good not only by the
old leisure classes, but by the modern leisure masses.'[18] The gist of Riesman's
argument is that in a society bored by work, sex is the only activity, the only
reminder of one's energies, the only competitive act; the last defence against
vis inertiae. This same insight can be found, with greater theoretical depth,
in Marcuse's notion of 'repressive de-sublimation'—the freeing of sexuality
for its own frustration in the service of a totally co-ordinated and drugged
social machine.[19] Bourgeois society at present can well afford a play area of
premarital *non*-procreative sexuality. Even marriage can save itself by increasing divorce and remarriage rates, signifying the importance of the institution itself. These considerations make it clear that sexuality, while it
presently may contain the greatest potential for liberation—can equally well
be organized against any increase of its human possibilities. New forms of

---

[18] Riesman, *op. cit.* p. 154.

[19] Marcuse offers the prospect of a leisure society produced by automation and the
consequent shift from a Promethean to an Orphic ethos (eroticism over work-
effort); and sees in this the true liberation of sexual energy for its own aesthetic
end. Though he illustrates the difference (*Eros and Civilization* (1955), pp. 144-56),
this notion is too close to images of primitive societies dominated by the aura of
maternal relaxation: ' . . . satisfaction . . . would be *without toil*—that is, without
the rule of alienated labor over the human existence. Under primitive conditions,
alienation has *not yet* arisen because of the primitive character of the needs
themselves, the rudimentary (personal or sexual) character of the division of
labor, and the absence of an institutionalized hierarchial specialization of
functions. Under the "ideal" conditions of mature industrial civilization, alienation
would be completed by general automatization of labor, reduction of labor time
to a minimum, and exchangeability of functions, . . . the reduction of the working
day to a point where the mere quantum of labor time no longer arrests human
development is the first prerequisite for freedom.' (*Ibid.*, p. 138). Against the consumer use of sex illustrated by Riesman Marcuse poses the necessity for equal
distribution of leisure, and hence the 'regression to a lower standard of life'; a
new set of values ('gratification of the basic human needs, the freedom from
guilt and fear . . .') against an automated-TV culture. This is premature.

reification are emerging which may void sexual freedom of any meaning. This is a reminder that while one structure may be the *weak link* in a unity like that of woman's condition, there can never be a solution through it alone. The utopianism of Fourier or Reich was precisely to think that sexuality could inaugurate such a general solution. Lenin's remark to Clara Zetkin is a salutary, if over-stated, corrective: 'However wild and revolutionary (sexual freedom) may be, it is still really quite bourgeois. It is, mainly, a hobby of the intellectuals and of the sections nearest them. There is no place for it in the Party, in the class conscious, fighting, proletariat.'[50] For a general solution can only be found in a strategy which affects *all* the structures of women's exploitation. This means a rejection of two beliefs prevalent on the left:

Reformism: This now takes the form of limited ameliorative demands: equal pay for women, more nursery-schools, better retraining facilities, etc. In its contemporary version it is wholly divorced from any fundamental critique of women's condition or any vision of their real liberation (it was not always so). Insofar as it represents a tepid embellishment of the *status quo*, it has very little progessive content left.

Voluntarism: This takes the form of maximalist demands—the abolition of of the family, abrogation of all sexual restrictions, forceful separation of parents from children—which have no chance of winning any wide support at present, and which merely serve as a substitute for the job of theoretical analysis or practical persuasion. By pitching the whole subject in totally intransigent terms, voluntarism objectively helps to maintain it outside the framework of normal political discussion.

What, then, is the responsible revolutionary attitude? It must include both immediate and fundamental demands, in a single critique of the *whole* of women's situation, that does not fetishize any dimension of it. Modern industrial development, as has been seen, tends towards the separating out of the originally unified function of the family—procreation, socialization, sexuality, economic subsistence, etc—even if this 'structural differentiation' (to use a term of Parsons') has been checked and disguised by the maintenance of a powerful family ideology. This differentiation provides the real historical basis for the ideal demands which should be posed: structural differentiation is precisely what distinguishes an advanced from a primitive society

---

[50] Clara Zetkin: *Reminiscences of Lenin* (1925, trans. 1929), pp. 52-53.

(in which all social functions are fused *en bloc*).[51]

In practical terms this means a coherent system of demands. The four elements of women's condition cannot merely be considered each in isolation; they form a structure of specific interrelations. The contemporary bourgeois family can be seen as a triptych of sexual, reproductive and socializatory functions (the woman's world) embraced by production (the man's world)— precisely a structure which in the final instance is determined by the economy. The exclusion of women from production—social human activity—and their confinement to a monolithic condensation of functions in a unity—the family—which is precisely unified in the *natural part* of each function, is the root cause of the contemporary *social* definition of women as *natural* beings. Hence the main thrust of any emancipation movement must still concentrate on the economic element—the entry of women fully into public industry. The error of the old socialists was to see the other elements as reducible to the economic; hence the call for the entry of women into production was accompanied by the purely abstract slogan of the abolition of the family. Economic demands are still primary, but must be accompanied by coherent policies for the other three elements, policies which at particular junctures may take over the primary role in immediate action.

Economically, the most elementary demand is not the right to work or receive equal pay for work—the two traditional reformist demands— but *the right to equal work itself*. At present, women perform unskilled, uncreative, service jobs that can be regarded as 'extensions' of their expressive familial role. They are overwhelmingly waitresses, office-cleaners, hair-dressers, clerks, typists. In the working-class occupational mobility is thus sometimes easier for girls than boys—they can enter the white-collar sector at a lower level. But only two in a hundred women are in administrative or managerial jobs, and less than five in a thousand are in the professions. Women are poorly unionized (25 per cent) and receive less money than men for the

---

[51] (See Ben Brewster: *Introduction to Lukács on Bukharin, New Left Review* No. 39, p. 25). The capitalist mode of production separates the family from its earlier immediate association with the economy, and this marginality is unaffected directly by the transformation of the relations of production from private to public ownership in the transition to a socialist society. As the essence of woman's contemporary problem derives from this marginality, for this problem, *but for this problem only*, the distinction between industrial and preindustrial societies is the significant one. Categories meaningful for one element of the social totality may well be irrelevant or even pernicious if extended to the whole of historical development. Similar arguments, but principally lack of space in a short article must excuse the total neglect of problems arising from class distinctions in the functions and status of women.

manual work they do perform: in 1961 the average industrial wage for women was less than half that for men, which, even setting off part-time work, represents a massive increment of exploitation for the employer.

Education

The whole pyramid of discrimination rests on a solid extra-economic foundation—education. The demand for equal work, in Britain, should above all take the form of a demand for an *equal educational system*, since this is at present the main single filter selecting women for inferior work-roles. At present, there is something like equal education for both sexes up to 15. Thereafter three times as many boys continue their education as girls. Only one in three 'A'-level entrants, one in four university students is a girl. There is no evidence whatever of progress. The proportion of girl university students is the same as it was in the 1920's. Until these injustices are ended, there is no chance of equal work for women. It goes without saying that the content of the educational system, which actually instils limitation of aspiration in girls needs to be changed as much as methods of selection. Education is probably the key area for immediate economic advance at present.

Only if it is founded on equality can production be truly differentiated from reproduction and the family. But this in turn requires a whole set of non-economic demands as a complement. Reproduction, sexuality, and socialization also need to be free from coercive forms of unification. Traditionally, the socialist movement has called for the 'abolition of the bourgeois family'. This slogan must be rejected as incorrect today. It is maximalist in the bad sense, posing a demand which is merely a negation without any coherent construction subsequent to it. Its weakness can be seen by comparing it to the call for the abolition of the private ownership of the means of production, whose solution—social ownership—is contained in the negation itself. Marx himself allied the two, and pointed out the equal futility of the two demands:' . . . this tendency to oppose general private property to private property is expressed in animal form; *marriage* . . . is contrasted with the communty of women, in which women become communal and common property.'[52] The reasons for the historic weakness of the notion is that the family was never analysed structurally—in terms of its different functions. It was a hypostasized entity; the abstraction of its abolition corresponds to the abstraction of its conception. The strategic concern for socialists should be for the equality of the sexes, not the abolition of the family. The conse-

[52] Karl Marx: *Private Property and Communism, op. cit.* p. 153.

quences of this demand are no less radical, but they are concrete and positive, and can be integrated into the real course of history. The family as it exists at present is, in fact, incompatible with the equality of the sexes. But this equality will not come from its administrative abolition, but from the historical differentiation of its functions. The revolutionary demand should be for the liberation of these functions from a monolithic fusion which oppresses each. The dissociation of reproduction from sexuality frees sexuality from alienation in unwanted reproduction (and fear of it), and reproduction from subjugation to chance and uncontrollable casuality. It is thus an elementary demand to press for free State provision of oral contraception. The legalization of homosexuality—which is one of the forms of non-reproductive sexuality—should be supported for just the same reason, and regressive campaigns against it in Cuba or elsewhere should be unhesitatingly criticized. The straightforward abolition of illegitimacy as a legal notion as in Sweden and Russia has a similar implication; it would separate marriage civically from parenthood.

From Nature to Culture

The problem of socialization poses more difficult questions, as has been seen. But the need for intensive maternal care in the early years of a child's life does not mean that the present single sanctioned form of socialization—marriage and family—is inevitable. Far from it. The fundamental characteristic of the present system of marriage and family is in our society its *monolithism*: there is only one institutionalized form of inter-sexual or inter-generational relationship possible. It is that or nothing. This is why it is essentially a denial of life. For all human experience shows that intersexual and intergenerational relationships are infinitely various—indeed, much of our creative literature is a celebration of the fact—while the institutionalized expression of them in our capitalist society is utterly simple and rigid. It is the poverty and simplicity of the institutions in this area of life which are such an oppression. Any society will require some institutionalized and social recognition of personal relationships. But there is absolutely no reason why there should be only one legitimized form—and a multitude of unlegitimized experience. Socialism should properly mean not the abolition of the family, but the diversification of the socially acknowledged relationships which are today forcibly and rigidly compressed into it. This would mean a plural range of institutions—where the family is only one, and its abolition implies none. Couples living together or not living together, long-term unions with children, single parents bringing up children, children socialized by conventional rather than biological parents, extended kin groups, etc,—all these could be encompassed in a range of institutions which matched the free invention and variety of men and women.

It would be illusory to try and specify these institutions. Circumstantial accounts of the future are idealist and worse, static. Socialism will be a process of change, of becoming. A fixed image of the future is in the worst sense ahistorical; the form that socialism takes will depend on the prior type of capitalism and the nature of its collapse. As Marx wrote: 'What (is progress) if not the absolute elaboration of (man's) creative dispositions, without any preconditions other than antecedent historical evolution which makes the totality of this evolution—i.e., the evolution of all human powers as such, unmeasured by any *previously established* yardstick— an end in itself? What is this, if not a situation where man does not reproduce himself in any determined form, but produces his totality? Where he does not seek to remain something formed by the past, but is the absolute movement of becoming?'[53] The liberation of women under socialism will not be 'rational' but a human achievement, in the long passage from Nature to Culture which is the definition of history and society.

---

[53] Karl Marx. *Precapitalist Economic Formations, Op. cit.* p. 85.

A Historical and Critical Essay for Black Women

Patricia Haden, Donna Middleton
and Patricia Robinson

This article was written by three women from different social stratas in the black society and three different age groups. Donna Middleton is sixteen from a petit-bourgeois family. Pat Haden is twenty-two and on welfare, and Pat Robinson is forty-three and has had ten years of experience in psychiatric social work in mental health clinics and family agencies in Boston, Los Angeles and New York City. For five years she has had a private practice and been psychiatric consultant to Planned Parenthood of Lower Westchester.

It is time for the black woman to take a look at herself, not just individually and collectively but historically, if she is to avoid sabotaging and delaying the black revolution. Taking a look at yourself is not simply good tactics; it is absolutely necessary at this time in the black movement when even black radical males are still so insecure about their identity and so full of revolutionary phantasies, that they can not reach out to the black woman in revolutionary love—to urge us to begin to liberate ourselves, to tell the truth, "Black women, you are the most pressed down of us all. Rise up or we as Black men can never be free!"

No black man can or should ever think he can liberate us. Black men do not have our economic, social, biologic and historic outlook. We are placed by those, who have historically formed and manipulated the values in this society, white males, at the very bottom of all these perspectives. There is so much scorn and fear of WOMEN, ANIMAL AND BLACK in this western culture and since we are all three, we are simply kept out of

Printed by permission of the authors.

history. Except for certain "house women," history is made only by males. The word *animal* is used by most males to mean a hated and despicable condition, and anything that is hated is simultaneously feared. Black women get "put down" as "bitch dogs" and "pussies" by western white and black men, especially those who so smugly overestimate their brain power flying from campus to campus "rapping" about reason and SOUL. Their heads "blow out" this "intellectual" and "educated" *spiel* on white and black power. They back it up, like males have always done down through written history, with Gods in their own image. What a "come down" it is to these males, that they so often have to slip away from Harlem and Wall Street— to "take a crap." And how they struggle against the fact that, like so many animals, they are born of the female and from the moment of their leaving our dark wombs, they, like all animals, begin to die! Yet we black women in our deepest humanity love and need black men so, we hesitate to revolt against them and go for ourselves.

If we black women "get" a few of the "goodies," and we have bought all that jive put down on us by our field nigger families who all our lifetime pushed and hustled to be just simple house niggers, our anger and frustration go underground. We don't dare to endanger what we have been conditioned to accept as "making it"—a little glass house full of "T.V. crap." We become nervous-nagging-narrow-minded murderers of ourselves and our children. We turn our madness and frustrations into other channels—against other black women and against our oppressed white sisters. We even trip out on "smokes." We psyche out on sex with some cat that is as "hung-up" as we are. Then we got the nerve to break into the "bag" of cleanliness, godliness, and "I'm better than you are, baby!"

If we are poor black women, one night in the streets we explode. That small razor cupped in our fingers slashes his hated black face, that face that reflects our own. We look at him and see ourselves for what we really are — traitors to ourselves as poor black women and traitors to him, our street-brother, because we let him get to where he's at now—not a man just a "jive-time turkey." We did not confront him long ago because our minds were not "wrapped." But now we can hear, see, feel our mistakes through his actions against us, towards his children and his mother. Now he's going to try to prove himself a man — "walk that walk, talk that talk." He's still hanging on to his "jive thing." He "bops" on the corner and "raps" that he's straight. "I'm coming to my people!" He's still out there "fucking" with his drugs and talking "shit." We lunge and sink our knife deep into his chest to blot out this awful truth. His blood oozes and stops while ours gushes from between our legs. Nothing gets born. We just end up murderers of the future of our people.

If we feel ourselves to be college-educated and politically aware, we end up nothing but common opportunists, playing the role of some dreamed-up African Queen, like we "gonna" rule some black country somewhere with some "dashiki cat" acting haughty and ending up a "tripped out" black king. It does not matter to us that it is a historical fact that our own feudal period in Africa was cruelly oppressive to black women and peasants; that in Africa this warring and exploitive period was only interrupted by the landing of the European colonialist and slave trader. The African chiefs and their cliques were selling troublesome relatives and rival tribesmen to Europeans then, just as *now* three-fourths of the so-called African states-men are wheeling and dealing to sell the riches of their land and the labor of their people under neo-colonialism.

We want desperately to feel black but we also need to feel superior to whitey. We want to take his place. We really want to take over his system and rule over and exploit *everyone*. We want to be black masters and missies and have white maids and big white houses. We go to college to get good jobs and bring our learning back to the people in the streets. We're "jiving"—we're going to college to be social workers, NAACP'ers, teachers, doctors, lawyers to keep the minds of the poor messed up and confused. We're going to college to be a part of the system.

All of us caught in this white male-jive, that was meant to keep us hooked, exploited and oppressed, groove on this big white world of male supremacy, this way-out white capitalism. We hold tight to that little capi-tal, clothes, furniture and bank account, because if we lose it we'd have to go back to that old feeling of "I ain't nothing, I ain't nowhere!" We are scared to death of that "big dick," the military-industrial complex. But how we give all praise to its power and tell all our friends how you can't beat the man and his system.

PART II

Myths unite people and steer their culture. They are the dreams and hopes; they are the fears and confusions of a people. They are found in their folk tales, customs, in their religious and economic systems. Myths are not about real people but they do express the movement of opposites, which is con-tradiction. The deep thoughts and everyday attitudes of human beings are full of contradictions. Like electrical energy these thoughts that may oppose each other at times, and may join together at other times, move whole peoples into action. They also keep a society steadily moving in one direction or keep it in general peace with itself and its neighbors.

The American Dream is a myth. If you trace it symbolically and historically, it is a long route away from the ANIMAL BODY, and from the LAND, away from the WOMAN and away from BLACK to condensed wealth (which is capital and in the American Dream is money, machines and property), to the CITIES, to MAN and to WHITE.

It is now the historical time to examine this myth that has made dead things and their creators sacred and over-valued by us.

Black women in the U.S. are so systematically left out of this society that we do not have an important part in producing the products bought and sold in this economy. We are civil servants, domestic servants and servants to our families. We have no Gods in our own image, even though South American women through Catholicism have the Black Madonna. We are separated from black men in the same way that white women have been separated from white men. But we are even less valued by white and black males because we are not white. The American Dream is white and male when examined symbolically. We are the exact opposite — black and female and therefore carry the stigma, almost religious in nature, of the scorned and feared outcaste.

The western world was built on much more than colonialism and imperialism. It was also built on a split in the minds of men that thoroughly separated male from female as well as the body from the mind. This mind-blowing phenomenon caused all things having to do with the animal body to be repressed unconsciously. It is a fact of the psyche that repressed feelings, like oppressed peoples, do not stay repressed. Repressed feelings, like living energy, struggle against the force of repression to rise to consciousness. Repression of feelings that we have learned, through the conditioning of myths, are unacceptable is a constant struggle.

Oppression of unacceptable people—unacceptable to those who rule and reenforced by myths from their imagination—is also a constant struggle between those who oppress and those who are oppressed. The oppressed, like repressed feelings, struggle to rise into the open and be free. This is an example of the movement of opposites and contradiction.

Men who controlled the making of myths and culture after the overthrow of women managed to banish women and what they had always symbolized to a psychic underworld, a chaotic hell of folktales and fables. *Animals, women* and *black* became the underground witches and demons in men's minds. Men denied themselves their own feminine nature, inherent in their bisexuality. This mental split enabled the male to deny the fact that he was an animal, to struggle against the darkness and towards the light and to do away with the fact of his dependence on women for his vital nourishment before and after birth. He could now ripple his large muscles and dream of soaring one day to the heavens where he could be in charge and therefore worshipped as the God of Light and the Heavens—an Apollo. The woman's body which receives, hosts and gives forth the future of the species is inherently powerful. Her body and power had to be overthrown and suppressed when the male felt overwhelmed by this power and responded with the desperate need to take power from the woman. His desperate need became a living force in his use of external power over others and in the repression of his own femininity.

Some thousands of years ago, the female was considered the Goddess of the Universe from which heaven and earth sprang. Certainly this myth conforms to basic reality—out of one comes two. The female bears both the male and the female. The Adam and Eve myth that has for so long been an important part of black women's education through our part time father—the negro minister—and our devoutly religious black mothers turns this basic reality on its head and into its opposite. The male gives birth through the magical intervention of an all-powerful male God. The rib of Adam is plucked out and made into woman by this powerful medicine man who resembles in action the African and Asian tribal priest. Indeed this is a powerful myth for it does grant the role of man in human creation but at the same time it utterly denies women's role. Deep down we black women still believe this clever religious tale that puts us out of creation. The fact that we do exposes our terrible dependence on outside authority and our fear of thinking for and trusting ourselves.

Anthropologists have been able to trace the animal family to the first human family, and they observe that the male's only role early in human history was insemination. Then he drifted off, leaving the female to take care of herself during pregnancy, birth and the nursing of the young. When man and women began to live together what can be called culture began. But women controlled the first fruit or surplus, the child, by reason of its long need for protection before it can take care of itself.

This was concrete power over the child and the male in those places with a warm climate with food and water readily available. In this Garden of Eden, there was no real need for a male food gatherer, a hunter. When the male came to live with the female more often, parents and an extended family in a culture began. The children were molded and conditioned by all manner of rituals and folk stories. Their education kept them under control and made them ready to follow the customs and rules set up by parents—first the female, then the male.

Today in the time of the cities, cybernetics, nuclear power and space exploration, white men have developed a man-made body, the self-regulating machine. It can operate a whole series of machines and adjust itself much as our human brain is able to readjust to the needs of our body and to operate the human body. It can also do the mental and physical work of men's bodies. At last man has done away with the practical need for his own human form. Now he must turn his attention to the danger the woman's body has always posed to his rule. He struggles to perfect artificial insemination and a machine host for the human foetus. He concerns himself with the biological control of reproduction of the species. Those white males who rule the free (capitalist) world understand that if they are to keep their rule over women and so-called lesser men, they must stop being dependent on their bodies and must perfect machines which they can control absolutely.

PART III

When any group must be controlled and used, their Gods, their religion, their land and their tools of survival must be taken away from them. These are all reflections of themselves and their inner being as well as practical means to living. This must be done by force at first.

In the days when all the forest was evergreen, before the parakeet painted the autumn leaves red with the color from his breast, before the giants wandered through the woods with their heads above the tree-tops; in the days when the sun and moon walked the earth as man and wife, and many of the great sleeping mountains were human beings; in those far off days witchcraft was known only to the women of Onaland (Tierra del Fuego, South America). They kept their own particular lodge, which no man dared approach. The girls, as they neared womanhood, were instructed in the magic arts, learning how to bring sickness and even death to all those who displeased them.

The men lived in abject fear and subjugation. Certainly they had bows and arrows with which to supply the camp with meat, yet, they asked what use were such weapons against the witchcraft and sickness? This tyranny of the women grew from bad to worse until it occurred to the men that a dead witch was less dangerous than a live one. They conspired together to kill off all the women; and there ensued a great massacre, from which not one woman in human form escaped.

The legend goes on to describe how the men waited for the little girls to grow up so they could have wives. Meanwhile, they plotted how they would have their own lodge or secret society from which all women would forever be excluded. The lowly servant tasks would be performed only by women. They would be frightened into submission by means of demons drawn from men's minds.

This is only one of thousands of such legends taken from all parts of the world that indicate some great crisis did occur where leadership of society was taken away from the women by force. We blacks have a splendid oral tradition and respect for the history that comes to us through our older women. Much of their practical advice has kept our spirits up—advice on how to doctor our children, make delicious dinners out of scraps the white world throws away, get meaning from our dreams—and tales about how they felt about the time of slavery and how they overcame the master. For those of us who want to break out of the subtle oppression of all black women, stories from the past have been used extensively in our research. We have begun to feel sure that before written history men had great fear of women and a sense of being oppressed by their inner and reproductive powers. The "Great Earth Mother" could bring forth life and inexplicably take it away. This was one kind of power—internal power. In all the folktales it could only be overcome through external power—force. It is possible that long ago there was a time when women were murdered in some massive genocide, her ancient God-like reflection destroyed along with her temples. Archeologists have found such temples in Asia and northern Africa along with statues of some female Goddess. But it is better for women to make the historical connections about these remains since black and white males still need to rule over us and cannot be depended upon to be free of male prejudice against women. It is enough for now that we note that men were determined at one time in the past to have external power over women, and her symbolic representative nature.

For men to keep themselves in power over women, they had to make up new myths and tales that would frighten and subdue women. As in all situations where one class oppresses another, both groups begin to believe the new myths and the oppressed begin to repress themselves. Religions have been one of the major means by which all oppressed people have been seduced into helping in their own oppression while giving some small rewards that do not endanger the ruling class's position at the top. It usually gives to the people one or two rulers or Gods and Goddesses at the top with none of the contradictions of common parents. These are very special and all-powerful parents. Below them are various classes or groups arranged in a descending order—a hierarchy. Members from those groups at the bottom may be chosen by the higher class for forceful control of the lower classes. Historically, armies and the police force have come from these lower classes, and employment in such forces gave these members of a "lower order" feelings of prestige and status. African religions have the Great Earth Mother still in the symbol of the moon Goddess whose monthly phases match the woman's menstrual cycle. Poor black women of today still plant their city gardens according to the phases of the moon. They are the descendants of the very early African women who produced the first food that was not simply collected. The first farmers in Africa were women, and both women and the land were valued and worshiped. The African women who tilled the land came to own it and what it produced. She controlled the human product, the child, for only she knew whose child it was. African males were almost superfluous except for their sexual mating role. The African woman had sacred and religious power through her reflection as the Great Earth Mother and the moon goddess. She had social and economic power through ownership of the land which was shared and divided among all women of the village. All products that were surplus were stored and shared communally. And only the African women knew the origins of the future of the tribe, the children.

African males who did not need to hunt often because food was readily available formed secret councils in reaction to this female dominance. Unlike the more aggressive African hunting and herding societies, the males from these agricultural communities were elected to such lodges.

Men from other tribes were encouraged to join so that a secret council might spread through many tribes over a large area. The sacred divinities were still often female. The moon, symbol of the Great Mother, remained part of their life. These secret societies did not absolutely exclude women. She was kept symbolically among the group's Gods.

These secret societies gradually developed into councils of chiefs and elders. The communal village that had formerly been dominated by the African female was eventually ruled by a male, tribal aristocracy. These males were administrators and did not take part in agriculture. They controlled and decided on all the economic and social relations within the tribe and between tribes. They had great prestige and absolute authority. This period began somewhere around 1250 B.C. when Iron and other metals were discovered in Africa. More complex labor production beyond agriculture was possible. Males were able to mine the earth and women began to lose control of the land. Men worked the metal and women made pottery and did the basket weaving. In the fields men still cleared the brush but women were now chained to the land. Along with her children, she became the "slave labor force" for the village, planting and caring for the crops.

African villages became more complex and frequently were overrun by herding and hunting tribes. These were restless men with domesticated animals that could be traded and made into wealth and capital. With their fierce competitiveness and need for individual accomplishment, female worship and female shrines were smashed and replaced with male monuments and objects of worship. Women, like the animals, were made into property and traded for other objects of wealth and prestige. African women had been overwhelmed by force over a long period and by the time of the Moslem religion around 700 A.D., polygamy has absolutely subjugated the African female. A male aristocracy ruled over the village class structure. It was on this feudal development in African society that European feudal states were able to build a cooperative venture with African chiefs for the beginning of the slave trade.

Many black male theorists prefer to call the African village, before the coming of white colonialism, a commune where land was owned by the tribe. The male aristocracy was not always hereditary and changed hands many times. They insist that the gifts the peasants and women and children had to give to the elders was part of their communal tradition. The division of labor between males and females also existed between the young, the married and the elders. Women were not cruelly exploited because there were many brave queens. There was no true class system as described by Marx from his European point of reference. African males and chiefs did not cooperate with the European slave trader.

PART IV

James Boggs, in an unpublished manuscript, writes:

> "Black men from the time they were captured back in Africa with the help of the tribal chiefs lost their domination over the black woman. For a long period in black slave society in the United States there was no domination of the female by the male. Both were entirely dominated by the whites. African male domination continued in the African bush; where hardly touched by the white settlers, African elders could continue their male supremacist customs and control of the land."

Essentially the white master controlled the black slave family and slave groupings by superior force of arms. The main responsibility of the field female slave was to produce male babies—the labor commodity needed for the master's fields. Male field slaves were used as studs. The stories that come down to us by word of mouth from our slave great-grandmothers tell of stag pens throughout Virginia and South Carolina where "black bucks" were made to mate with white indentured females from England.

This agreement was a good basis for establishing faithful house slaves that looked to the physical comfort and entertainment of the master and his family. There was a type of Southern plantation owner who dreamed that he was an aristocrat and engaged in rituals practiced by the feudal barons of Europe. These light-skinned blacks played the role of parlor entertainers. They dressed in European clothes and were educated to speak several languages. Before the civil war it was this high-yellow caste of negroes who were given the privilege of a college education.

This enabled many of them to step into state senatorships and into Congress during Reconstruction. The majority who received such privileges were men. Very few women, unless talented like the poetess Phyllis Wheatley, ever received special education and none were allowed, of course, to be State Senators or Congresswomen. Women, white and black, were not allowed to vote. The black male received the vote not the black female.

The first form of solidified relations between black male and female were generally decided by the master who thought that a certain black was so good, so talented as a mechanic, shoemaker or a carpenter, that he ought to settle down with the cook or the dressmaker for the mistress. This was a "taming" process and such slaves naturally identified with the master and the mistress, imitated them and had great social prestige among the other slaves. This arrangement was carried on among a few field slaves particularly if they had some talent that could be exploited. Such men could be trusted to be field foreman, slave quarter guards and bounty hunters who returned escaped slaves to the plantation for money. Many black male slaves were able to buy their freedom in the South. Carter G. Woodson, a careful historian, points out that by 1860 there were about 250,000 Southern free blacks. (For a study of the free blacks before the Civil War see Carter G. Woodson, *The Negro In our History*.) Northern black males were often fugitive slaves or had bought their freedom or been given their freedom for service in the Revolutionary War. By 1800 there were almost 25,000 free slaves in the North. Black females escaped and worked as domestic servants in order to buy their children's freedom. The mother of David Walker was able to give him an education and by 1830 he had written his famous appeal to the slaves to rise up against their masters. From Boston he had it distributed through negro sailors to Southern slaves.

Free Southern blacks were able to become wealthy through their skilled labor, even without their civil rights. The Northern free black was kept out of the infant industries and had to work at very menial tasks or be a house servant. In "Free Negro Owners of Slaves in the United States in 1830" by Carter G. Woodson, 3,777 black "heads of families" were reported in the U.S. Bureau of Census as slave owners.

They were black males who bought and sold slaves and imitated European landlords on the property they held. They were few in number but they became the basis of the small Southern black middle-class. This class of black males with their wives began that Negro aristocratic class that is so praised in our black history courses today. The white master had developed a successful slave hierarchy that supported his rule at the top and decreased the need for constant force against the slave population.

The middle-class black female was not the head of such free black slave-owning families. The majority of her sisters who were house servants were sexual objects for the master even as they were allowed a house-slave husband. Even if she had been taught to read and write, she was not considered by the master to have the skills needed to be an artisan or a worker in the plantation repair shops. She was kept in women's "place", sewing, cooking, laundry work. Her white mistress was that object that showed the wealth of the master. The black female in the plantation house did the mistress' work and imitated her. The petty privileges she received in clothing and "white" food gave her some comfort but no strong reflection of human worth, for the white woman was a female and *every* female was subjected to male rule.

Among the field slaves the master could not control the male-female relationship to the extent he could control the house slave's relationships. Among field slaves, man-woman ties were very unstable. The male could be sold, beaten, killed for reasons bearing on the productivity of his labor, e.g., his age, his speed and usefulness in the fields, number of children from his matings, the degree of submissiveness to the slave role. His brutal oppression and distance from privilege and social status his "house nigger" brothers enjoyed, planted the seeds of hatred and revolt. The master could be paternalistic to the house slaves but was forced by the fear of retaliation to be hostile and sadistic to the field slaves.

The field woman was a laborer beside her man, a begetter of children, who was let out to other plantations for breeding. She was responsible for cooking, feeding and caring for the slave children and field men. She was a mid-wife and if she rose in social status through her "doctoring," then she became a mammy to the white children.

Unlike her "house" sister, she was not as valued as a sex object by her white master nor was she easily accessible, being all day in the fields and all evening in the slave quarters. Older slave woman had some status among the slaves just through age. They were advisers and negotiators between the slaves themselves and occasionally when they negotiated with the master they held the honorary title of "Auntie." These women were active in slave marriages, providing the famous broom over which the slave couple jumped to seal their union.

Generally the black male field slave's position in the slave economy was similar to the position of the male during the early agricultural stages of history when women owned the land and controlled the agricultural surplus and the children. He had no responsibility for an extended family unit beyond the sexual act and conception—which he of times had to steal if he was not assigned. The family unit was, as in earlier history, the mother and the children, but usually only for a limited time. Extended family units were not helpful to increased production and the economic use of labor.

The black woman who worked in the "big house" acted not as a dominator over the black male but as his protector and savior. Her primary strategy was to allow herself to be sexually used, often to save the life of the black male. She could speak out to the master and to the white foreman, if she pleased him with good sex and good earthy care of his children, roles which the master's "woman" was seldom allowed to pursue. As a vocal link between the white man and the black man, the black woman often forced opinions and bargained successfully for whatever pitiful reforms were possible under slavery.

The black woman under slavery was close to the land, to the human body, wise and saintly in her service to human beings. Kept out of small plantation crafts and limited to biological production and "cropping," she remained more like her African sisters who still are African peasants and exploited by African males and European landlords. She cared for white and black and in this very act, discovered a basic similar humanity that transcended the color of skin and class. Though she was cruelly exploited, and, like all women in a male-supremacist's culture, not as valued, she went inward and downward. If women have inner power because of their subjugation and reproductive role then the black slave women had it in abundance.

The white patriarchy, where the middle-class merchant and landowner still "aped" his European feudal lord, was reenforced and reflected in the Christian religion. The majority of Southern masters were Protestants and with this religion's one all-powerful male God, it exactly imitated the white-power-hierarchy. Catholicism had the lesser deity, Mary, and in European Catholic countries there had existed the Black Madonna, the goddess of fertility. But the Black Madonna disappears from North American Catholicism, except for in Mexico. She has been traced back to the Egyptian goddess, Isis, and very possibly she is the submerged and underground, prehistoric Great Earth Mother. These European immigrants, now stately Lords and Masters, were not descendants of kings. They were refugees from their own middle-class in Europe who had taken power from the kings in the 1700's. They were socially and economically unsure of themselves, not ever having ruled by "divine right." Racism and sexism are necessary defenses of white and black males who feel economically and socially insecure. The Black Madonna could not appear in the United States where white males felt so weak inside themselves and so tentative in their power over the Red Man and the black slave population. The black woman would be denied this reflection of herself as the black man was denied his black God.

The black field male was ruled out of the life of the black woman by order of the "acting king" and slave master. She was left only with her children and with her paternal master who, through slavery, gave her some refuge. He provided a male Jesus in his image and later appointed "His Messenger," the circuit-rider, a tested and faithful "house nigger" to spread the "word of God," which is always the word of the Master and the ruling class. The lower-class whites were similarly seduced with their "blood and thunder" travelling preachers. The black woman succumbed as had all lower-classes before her to the rule of the great white father. And even in the nights with her black man, she cried out for Jesus in exultation and delight. The Negro minister was the gentle, black father, magical in his ministrations to his flock. When external power overwhelmed the black woman she could reach out for the magic and spirit of deliverance through the all-powerful male, black and white.

PART V

Among freed slave society there was a loose family relationship, particularly among field slaves, who were still tied to the land they could not own. They were free in name but enslaved in fact. Northern industrialization speeded up when the Southern landlords and Northern capitalists made their peace pact during Reconstruction. If the Southern rulers cooperated in this new stage of capitalism, providing raw materials and open markets for the northern factory finished products, they would be allowed to rule over their own affairs again. Negroes would be the South's cheap labor force while the mass of poor European immigrants would be the cheap labor force for the northern industry. So the black man hired himself out as a hired hand and as the lowest of factory employees. The black woman remained the farm worker and common laborer anchored to the land and the children.

Whites receded from direct domination of the black family to indirect domination. Black males still had to accede to a white boss on whom he depended for a job. The black woman could achieve a slightly higher status by being a domestic. It paid less than the male jobs but more than farm labor. It was only during World War II that the black woman, like the black male, was allowed into factories in great numbers. Both had to do the lowest, most menial jobs and the black woman got paid much less. A minority of black women, usually from the Northern middle-class, succeeded in becoming professionals—professional "house women" who turned away from the mass of poor black women.

The black male looked up to his white boss and his material possessions. The master's property was the white woman, humiliated and oppressed herself; his land was taken from the Indians by force; his factories had been built on the exploitation of poor whites; his education was full of myths of white and male supremacy; his culture was European and full of monstrous class-struggle. This was the American Dream; this was capitalism; and for all this the black man lusted. Any black man who wanted "in" to this system and a higher status, felt he needed a high-yellow woman or better a white woman to show that he had made it. In the North, a few black men could get a white woman, descended from indentured slavery and usually economically and socially oppressed herself.

After emancipation the black man got his black woman but his range of domination was only in the home, not in the public arena. The white man could still counter the black man's orders to "his woman" by removing him from a job, from a home or from the land. Only in the small area of the black family could the black man hit back during slavery, after emancipation and practically up to the present time. The use of the black woman as a whipping post reflected the stigma the black man carried within himself from the white ruling class. He was not a man because he had "no loot," "no bread," no status, but he did bear one saving symbol of the American Dream. He was male. Since this was a male supremacist culture, he could pit himself against his male antagonist. Capitalism favored individualism and competition, so if the black man struggled hard and long enough he could overthrow the white male and get to the "goodies" of capitalism. He was not about to stop and care about all the world's people whom capitalism used and "took from." Don't talk to him about Communism and Marxist-Leninism and the rule of society by the poor. He wanted his "piece."

When this tortured black animal could not beat the master, he beat his black woman. She retaliated by any means necessary. The middle-class Negro woman was just as caught up in the American Dream. She became a pitful caricature of the white female, bleaching her skin, straightening her hair, following the fashions, speaking good English. After World War II she began to find herself less favored by black males who did not feel shy toward white women after their experience outside of the country with European and Japanese females. What did the black male need with a poor imitation of the white woman when he could get the real thing. The black and white woman were unaware that both of them were objects, symbols only of the rising social and economic status of the white and black male. White women were part of the "goodies" of the American Dream, like a white-on-white-in-white Cadillac. The middle-class Negro women had to strive to be more like the white woman if she was to compete. It could not occur to her, because of her narrow view of life, that she was not the symbol the black man with capitalist ambitions needed in the American Dream. There was one small exception; if she was light-skinned with "white folks" hair, then she might be chosen.

The black woman fought back against her man. She struggled to get the "simple goodies." Just a little comfortable furniture, some pretty clothes for herself and education for the children. As she grew older and learned to hustle perhaps she could even get a house that she could rent out to poorer women on welfare. If she really made it she could have a fancy car. The house and the furnishings were the top of the American Dream for her. But her man usually could not share it. He always had a bigger dream, male dreams of power over others, and he destroyed himself in chasing that dream power.

In the U.S. black men and women of all classes have grown to love the white man's money, property, military power. This is for them the only goal. They tremble in envy as they dream of taking the master's place. But the bitter joke is that money, property, machines, all capital, are only symbols of power. They have been made through the efforts of common working people, who had no choice but to allow these products of their labor to be appropriated by a ruling class of desperate males — frightened males who felt impelled to prove to themselves and all other "lesser" men, women and children that they were not only men but super-men. These symbols were the adornments and possessions of kings and queens. Later these images of wealth and prestige were taken over by rich merchants who had overthrown the kings. This ridiculous middle-class was not content to have power over the masses of poor people, but they also imitated the feudal kings they had overthrown.

No force of arms can control whole masses of people forever. The oppressed must be deceived into believing that the ruling class is next to God.

They must believe that this ruling class is magically, awesomely powerful. Then they will offer themselves up to it and imitate it. But first, they must have learned to despise and hate themselves. This is achieved by the ruling class who removes from them by force all those habits, customs, tools, dwelling places and their Gods—all of which reflect the fact that they exist and that they ARE people of dignity. These must be replaced by foreign, humiliating symbols that show the oppressed daily that they belong in an inferior position. Finally, when these lower-class people have only the labor of their bodies, not the products of their labor, they must even sell that. They sell their bodies for pitiful wages which are supposed to reflect a "fact" that they are not "worth" more. They must literally sell themselves, their very bodies, to those in the middle-class who own the land and the factories, the areas of production upon which all our lives depend. Then they are truly alienated and the plunder of the people is complete. Now they will cooperate in their own oppression.

This aggressive white male rule is actually based not on force, but on long-term seduction. It is an illusion that males and whites are superior and more powerful. But we black and white women believe it. Their power over us exists because we permit it. We permit it because we have been thoroughly seduced, robbed of our gods, the fruit of our wombs, our land and what we produced on it and made wards of males, if we are middle-class, and wards of the state, if we are poor black women. We have lost the ability to think for ourselves which is the first step in owning ourselves.

Marxism is a structure that has faithfully patterned the movement of history. It charts the struggle of the repressed dreams of oppressed people to rise and return to their proper equilibrium—where the oppressed can own themselves, the products of their labor and the fruits of their land in which their valiant ancestors are buried; where they are no longer assessed by an aristocracy, in the image of sacred gods, for gifts that can only be added to ruling class's profits and stored wealth; where the oppressed recognize that their ruling classes are robbers and criminals and that their greed only reveals their terrible weakness. The ruling class does not know whether it exists unless it rules and has power to own other people. They really are paper tigers, after all.

The American Dream is a bold, heady, ruthless dream away from the black woman, the very image of the Great Earth Mother — the black mother whose body flows with the phases of the moon and who exists even today, symbolically, in the form of the Black Madonna. For us black women, "MOTHERFUCKER," is a definitive, historical term symbolizing the first murder, the murder of the Great Earth Mother, repeated endlessly to this day.

From our historical viewpoint the murder was begun by black men and later taken up by white men. Then we black women took it up ourselves. The murder has now become the murder of ourselves. This defends us from the fearsome but inevitable, historical duty to overthrow this massive and oppressive, white, male, supremacists culture which can endure only through capitalism, imperialism and neo-colonialism.

Social unrest, wars and insurrections, the weakening of the ruling classes as these thieves fall out with one another—all these loosen the inner bonds of the oppressed and manipulated individuals and the outer bonds of exploited human beings. Political education plus our experience of greater and more hysterical force on the part of the declining ruling class frees our minds of the effects of years of seduction.

It is said that all true revolutions begin from the bottom-up and from the inside-out and that such revolutions are irreversible. Black women have the capacity to know the truth and be free of this pervading manipulation. Many poor black women radiate this internal power. Outside of this society, they dedicate themselves to their children, stubbornly they resist and sabotage the system. They are "rude," "lazy," "always late," "always having babies out-of-wedlock." Most important, they are more aware of class oppression than racial oppression and in the future this kind of awareness will stand them in good stead for it is written, "And the meek shall inherit the earth."

Historical and political understanding of ourselves and our actual place in the American Dream is more important at this time than the gun. We black women look at our backwardness, our colossal ignorance and political confusion and want to give up. We do not like ourselves or each other. Our contradictory feeling about our black brothers, who seem simultaneously to move forward and backward, are increased by their continual cautioning that we must not move on our own or we will divide the movement. About all that we will mess-up will be their black study, black power, cultural nationalism hustle. Forget black capitalism, because when the master offers you "his thing," you know it's over! There have been other movements in history when revolutionary males have appeared conservative, opportunistic or just "stopped at the pass," and revolutionary women have always forged ahead of the males at this time to take the revolution to a deeper stage.

Black revolutionary women are going to be able to smash the last myths and illusions on which all the "jive-male oppressive power" depends. We are not alone anymore. This country no longer holds one well-armed united majority against an unarmed minority . . . There is a whole bunch of brown, and yellow poor folks out there in the world that the ruling, middle-class of this country have used and abused, stolen from to sell our shoddy goods at way-out prices. They are fighting back now, taking over those U.S. companies that sucked their people and their land. They are putting out the

United States Army and capitalist investors as they did in China and Cuba.

But a new stage of history really began when the poor Vietnamese men, women and children beat up and killed a whole lot of white and black "cats," who had decided it was easier to fight little, brown, poverty-stricken people than fight the "Man." One-half of these courageous South Vietnamese NFL fighters are women and children and they have proved that no U.S. male, black or white, got what it takes to destroy a people who have decided in their guts to own themselves and their land. That is power U.S. males have forgotten, but not black women, especially those of us who are poor.

White males are only in the image of God and supernaturally powerful with unbeatable instruments of death, in our own "messed-over" minds— not in the revolutionary world beyond the borders of the United States. All that "Big Daddy" and "head of family" shit is possible because we "play the game"—"ego-tripping" black men and ourselves. If our minds are together, we can work, think and decide everything for ourselves. It is only a cruel, capitalist system that "digs" money, property and "white broads" more than people, that forces us to be the "dependents" of men and wards of the state. We recognize that black males are frail human beings, born of women who love them, not for their "dick power" or their "bread" but for their gentle, enduring and powerful humanity.

It is important for black women to remind themselves occasionally that no black man gets born unless we permit it—even after we open our legs. That is the first, simple step to understanding the power that we have. The second is that all children belong to the women because only we know who the mother is. As to who is the father—well, we can decide that, too—any man we choose to say it is. And that neither the child nor MAN was made by God.

Third, we are going to have to put ourselves back to school, do our own research and analysis. We are going to have to argue with and teach one another, grow to respect and love one another. There are a lot of black chicks, field niggers wanting to be house niggers, who will fight very hard to keep this decaying system because of the few, petty privileges it gives them over poor, black women. Finally, we are going to have to give the brothers a helping hand here and there because they will be "uptight" not only with "the enemy" but with us. But at the same time we've got to do our own thing and get our own minds together.

All revolutionaries, regardless of sex, are the smashers of myths and the destroyers of illusion. They have always died and lived again to build new myths. They dare to dream of a Utopia, a new kind of synthesis and equilibrium.

Psychology Constructs the Female, or the Fantasy Life of the Male Psychologist

Naomi Weisstein

Imagine Naomi Weisstein's wonder when, after completing her postdoctoral fellowship in mathematical biology at the University of Chicago (after obtaining her Ph.D. in psychology from Harvard in 2½ years) she was told by the 12 institutions to which she had been recommended for jobs that they couldn't hire her because she lacked the qualifications. It was enough to make one join Women's Liberation, which she did, in 1966; at present she is active in the Chicago Women's Liberation Union, and plays piano in a Women's Liberation rock group. She is Associate Professor of psychology at Loyola University in Chicago, where her major research is in visual perception and neural models of visual process.

It is an implicit assumption that the area of psychology which concerns itself with personality has the onerous but necessary task of describing the limits of human possibility. Thus when we are about to consider the liberation of women, we naturally look to psychology to tell us what 'true' liberation would mean: what would give women the freedom to fulfill their own intrinsic natures.

Psychologists have set about describing the true natures of women with a certainty and a sense of their own infallibility rarely found in the secular world. Bruno Bettelheim, of the University of Chicago, tells us (1965) that "we must start with the realization that, as much as women want to be good scientists or engineers, they want first and foremost to be womanly companions of men and to be mothers."

Erik Erikson of Harvard University (1964), upon noting that young women

A revised and expanded version of "Kinder, Küche, Kirche as Scientific Law: Psychology Constructs the Female", *motive* nos. 6 and 7, March/April, 1969, pp. 78-85, by permission of the author. (Biographical sketch of author taken from the *motive* issue)

often ask whether they can "have an identity before they know whom they will marry, and for whom they will make a home," explains somewhat elegiacally that: "Much of a young woman's identity is already defined in her kind of attractiveness and in the selectivity of her search for the man (or men) by whom she wishes to be sought. . . . "Mature womanly fulfillment, for Erikson, rests on the fact that a woman's ". . . somatic design harbors an 'inner space' destined to bear the offspring of chosen men, and with it, a biological, psychological, and ethical commitment to take care of human infancy."

Some psychiatrists even see the acceptance of woman's role by women as a solution to societal problems. "Woman is nurturance . . ." writes Joseph Rheingold (1964), a psychiatrist at Harvard Medical School, ". . . anatomy decrees the life of a woman . . . when women grow up without dread of their biological functions and without subversion by feminist doctrine, and therefore enter upon motherhood with a sense of fulfillment and altruistic sentiment, we shall attain the goal of a good life and a secure world in which to live it." (p. 714)

These views from men who are assumed to be experts reflect, in a surprisingly transparent way, the cultural consensus. They not only assert that a woman is defined by her ability to attract men, they see no alternative definitions. They think that the definition of a women in terms of a man is the way it should be; and they back it up with psychosexual incantation and biological ritual curses. A woman has an identity if she is attractive enough to obtain a man, and thus, a home; for this will allow her to set about her life's task of "joyful altruism and nurturance."

Business Certainly Does Not Disagree

If views such as Bettelheim's and Erikson's do indeed have something to do with real liberation for women, then seldom in human history has so much money and effort been spent on helping a group of people realize their true potential. Clothing, cosmetics, home furnishings, are multi-million dollar businesses: if you don't like investing in firms that make weaponry and flaming gasoline, then there's a lot of cash in "inner space." Sheet and pillowcase manufacturers are concerned to fill this inner space:

"Mother, for a while this morning, I thought I wasn't cut out for married life. Hank was late for work and forget his apricot juice and walked out without kissing me, and when I was all alone I started crying. But then the postman came with the sheets and towels you sent, that look like big bandana handkerchiefs, and you know what I thought? That those big red and blue handkerchiefs are for girls like me to dry their tears on so they can get busy and do what a housewife has to do. Throw open the windows and start getting the house ready, and the dinner, maybe clean the silver and put new geraniums in the box. *Everything to be ready for him when he walks through that door."* (Fieldcrest 1966; emphasis added.)

Of course, it is not only the sheet and pillowcase manufacturers, the cosmetics industry, the home furnishings salesmen who profit from and make use of the cultural definitions of man and woman. The example above is blatantly and overtly pitched to a particular kind of sexist stereotype: the child nymph. But almost all aspects of the media are normative, that is, they have to do with the ways in which beautiful people, or just folks, or ordinary Americans, or extraordinary Americans should live their lives. They define the possible; and the possibilities are usually in terms of what is male and what is female. Men and women alike are waiting for Hank, the Silva Thins man, to walk back through that door .

It is an interesting but limited exercise to show that psychologists and psychiatrists embrace these sexists norms of our culture, that they do not see beyond the most superficial and stultifying media conceptions of female nature, and that their ideas of female nature serve industry and commerce so well. Just because it's good for business doesn't mean it's wrong. What I will show is that it *is wrong*; that there isn't the tiniest shred of evidence that these fantasies of servitude and childish dependence have anything to do with women's true potential; that the idea of the nature of human possibility which rests on the accidents of individual development of genitalia, on what is possible today because of what happened yesterday, on the fundamentalist myth of sex organ causality, has strangled and deflected psychology so that it is relatively useless in describing, explaining or predicting humans and their behavior. It then goes without saying that present psychology is less than worthless in contributing to a vision which could truly liberate — men as well as women. The central argument of my paper, then, is this. Psychology has nothing to say about what women are really like, what they need and what they want, essentially because psychology does not know. I want to stress that this failure is not limited to women; rather, the kind of psychology which has addressed itself to how people act and who they are has failed to understand, in the first place, why people act the way they do, and certainly failed to understand what might make them act differently.

The kind of psychology which has addressed itself to these questions divides into two professional areas: academic personality research, and clinical psychology and psychiatry. The basic reason for failure is the same in both these areas: the central assumption for most psychologists of human personality has been that human behavior rests on an individual and inner dynamic, perhaps fixed in infancy, perhaps fixed by genitalia, perhaps simply arranged in a rather immovable cognitive network. But this assumption is rapidly losing ground as personality psychologists fail again and again to get consistency in the assumed personalities of their subjects (Block, 1968). Meanwhile the evidence is collecting that what a person does and who he believes himself to be, will in general be a function of what people around him expect him to be, and what the overall situation in which he is acting implies that he is. Compared to the influence of the social context within which a person lives, his or her history and "traits," as well as biological makeup, may simply be random variations, "noise" superimposed on the true signal which can predict behavior.

Some academic personality psychologists are at least looking at the counter evidence and questioning their theories; no such corrective is occurring in clinical psychology and psychiatry. Freudians and neo-Freudians, Adlerians and neo-Adlerians, classicists and swingers, clinicians and psychiatrists, simply refuse to look at the evidence against their theory and practice. And they support their theory and their practice with stuff so tranparently biased as to have absolutely no standing as empirical evidence.

To summarize: the first reason for psychology's failure to understand what people are and how they act is that psychology has looked for inner traits when it should have been looking for social context; the second reason for psychology's failure is that the theoreticians of personality have generally been clinicians and psychiatrists, and they have never considered it necessary to have evidence in support of their theories.

Theory Without Evidence

Let us turn to this latter cause of failure first: the acceptance by psychiatrists and clinical psychologists of theory without evidence. If we inspect the literature of personality, it is immediately obvious that the bulk of it is written by clinicians and psychiatrists, and that the major support for their theories is "years of intensive clinical experience." This is a tradition started by Freud. His "insights" occurred during the course of his work with his patients. Now there is nothing wrong with such an approach to theory *formulation*; a person is free to make up theories with any inspiration which works: divine revelation, intensive clinical practice, a random numbers table. But he is not free to claim any validity for his theory until it has been tested and confirmed. But theories are treated in no such tentative way in ordinary clinical practice. Consider Freud. What he thought constituted evidence violated the most minimal conditions of scientific rigor. In *The Sexual Enlightenment of Children* (1963), the classic document which is supposed to demonstrate empirically the existence of a castration complex and its connection to a phobia, Freud based his analysis on the reports of the father of the little boy, himself in therapy, and a devotee of Freudian theory. I really don't have to comment further on the contamination in this kind of evidence. It is remarkable that only recently has Freud's classic theory on the sexuality of women - the notion of the double orgasm - been actually tested physiologically and found just plain wrong. Now these who claim that fifty years of psychoanalytic experience constitute evidence enough of the essential truths of Freud's theory should ponder the robust health of the double orgasm. Did women, until Masters and Johnson (1966), believe they were having two different kinds of orgasm? Did their psychiatrists cow them into reporting something that was not true? If so, were there other things they reported that were also not true? Did psychiatrists ever learn anything different than what their theories had led them to believe? If clinical experience means anything at all, surely we should have been done with the double orgasm myth long before the Masters and Johnson studies.

But certainly, you may object, "years of intensive clinical experience" is the only reliable measure in a discipline which rests for its its findings on insight, sensitivity, and intuition. The problem with insight, sensitivity, and intuition, is that they can confirm for all time the biases that one started out with. People used to be absolutely convinced of their ability to tell which of their number were engaging in witchcraft. All it required was some sensitivity to the workings of the devil.

Years of intensive clinical experience is not the same thing as empirical evidence. The first thing an experimenter learns in any kind of experiment which involves humans is the concept of the "double blind." The term is taken from medical experiments, where one group is given a drug which is presumably supposed to change behavior in a certain way, and a control group is given a placebo. If the observers or the subjects know which group took which drug, the result invariably comes out on the positive side for the new drug. Only when it is not known which subject took which pill, is validity remotely approximated. In addition, with judgments of human behavior, it is so difficult to precisely tie down just what behavior is going on, let alone what behavior should be expected, that one must test again and again the reliability of judgments. How many judges, blind, will agree in their observations? Can they replicate their own judgments at some later time? When, in actual practice, these judgment criteria are tested for clinical judgments, then we find that the judges cannot judge reliably, nor can they judge consistently; they do no better than chance in identifying which of a certain set of stories were written by men and which by women; which of a whole battery of clinical test results are the products of homosexuals and which are the products of heterosexuals (Hooker, 1957), and which, of a battery of clinical test results *and* interviews (where questions are asked such as "Do you have delusions?," (Little & Schneidman, 1959) are products of psychotics, neurotics, psychosomatics, or normals. Lest this summary escape your notice, let me stress the implications of these findings. The ability of judges, chosen for their clinical expertise, to distinguish male heterosexuals from male homosexuals on the basis of three widely used clinical projective tests - The Rorschach, the TAT, and the MAP - was *no better than chance.* The reason this is such devastating news, of course, is that sexuality is supposed to be of fundamental importance in the deep dynamic of personality; if what is considered gross sexual deviance cannot be caught, then what are psychologists talking about when they, for example, claim that at the basis of paranoid psychosis is "latent homosexual panic?" They can't even identify what homosexual anything is, let alone "latent homosexual panic."[1] More frightening, expert clinicians cannot be consistent on what diagnostic category to assign to a person, again on the basis of both tests and interviews; a number of normals in the Little & Schneidman study were described as psychotic, in such categories as "schizophrenic with homosexual tendencies" or "schizoid character with depressive trends." But most disheartening, when the judges were asked to rejudge the test protocols some weeks later, their diagnoses of the same subjects on the basis of the same protocols differed markedly from their initial judgments. It is obvious that even simple descriptive conventions in clinical psychology cannot be consistently applied; that these descriptive conventions have any explanatory significance is therefore, of course, out of the question.

As a graduate student at Harvard some years ago, I was a member of a seminar which was asked to identify which of two piles of a clinical test, the TAT, had been written by males and which by females. Only four students out of twenty identified the piles correctly, and this was after one

---

[1] It should be noted that psychologists have been as quick to assert absolute truths about the nature of homosexuality as they have about the nature of women. The arguments presented in this paper apply equally to the nature of homosexuality; psychologists know nothing about it; there is no more evidence for the "naturalness" of homosexuality. Psychology has functioned as a pseudo-scientific buttress for a patriarchal ideology and patriarchal social organization: women's liberation and gay liberation fights against a common victimization.

and a half months of intensively studying the differences between men and women. Since this result is below chance—that is, this result would occur by chance about four out of a thousand times—we may conclude that there *is* finally a consistency here; students are judging knowledgeably within the context of psychological teaching about the differences between men and women; the teachings themselves are simply erroneous.

You may argue that the theory may be scientifically 'unsound' but at least it cures people. There is no evidence that it does. In 1952, Eysenck reported the results of what is called an 'outcome of therapy' study of neurotics which showed that, of the patients who received psychoanalysis the improvement rate was 44%; of the patients who received psychotherapy· the improvement rate was 64%; and of the patients who received no treatment at all the improvement rate was 72%. These findings have never been refuted; subsequently, later studies have confirmed the negative results of the Eysenck study. (Barron & Leary, 1955; Bergin, 1963; Cartwright and Vogel, 1960; Truax, 1963; Powers and Witmer, 1951) How can clinicians and psychiatrists, then, in all good conscience, continue to practice? Largely by ignoring these results and being careful not to do outcome-of-therapy studies. The attitude is nicely summarized by Rotter (1960) (quoted in Astin, 1961): "Research studies in psychotherapy tend to be concerned with psychotherapeutic procedure and less with outcome . . . to some extent, it reflects an interest in the psychotherapy situation as a kind of personality laboratory". Some laboratory.

The Social Context

Thus, since clinical experience and tools can be shown to be worse than useless when tested for consistency, efficacy, agreement, and reliability, we can safely conclude that theories of a clinical nature advanced about women are also worse than useless. I want to turn now to the second major point in my paper, which is that, even when psychological theory is constructed so that it may be tested, and rigorous standards of evidence are used, it has become increasingly clear that in order to understand why people do what they do, and certainly in order to change what people do, psychologists must turn away from the theory of the causal nature of the inner dynamic and look to the social context within which individuals live.

Before examining the relevance of this approach for the question of women, let me first sketch the groundwork for this assertion.

In the first place, it is clear (Block, 1968) that personality tests never yield consistent predictions; a rigid authoritarian on one measure will be an unauthoritarian on the next. But the reason for this inconsistency is only now becoming clear, and it seems overwhelmingly to have much more to do with the social situation in which the subject finds himself than with the subject himself.

In a series of brilliant experiments, Rosenthal and his co-workers (Rosenthal and Jacobson, 1968; Rosenthal, 1966) have shown that if one group of experimenters has one hypothesis about what they expect to find, and another group of experimenters has the opposite hypothesis, both groups will obtain results in accord with their hypotheses. The results obtained are not due to mishandling of data by biased experimenters; rather, somehow, the bias of the experimenter creates a changed environment in which subjects actually act differently. For instance, in one experiment, subjects were to assign numbers to pictures of men's faces, with high numbers representing the subject's judgment that the man in the picture was a successful person, and low numbers representing the subject's judgment that the man in the picture was an unsuccessful person. The experimenters read the same set of instructions to two groups of subjects, and were required to say nothing else than what was in the instructions. One group of experimenters was told that the subjects tended to rate the faces high; another group of experimenters was told that the subjects tended to rate the faces low. Each group of experimenters was instructed to follow precisely the same procedure: they were required to read to subjects a set of instructions, and *to say nothing else*. For the 375 subjects run, the results showed clearly that those subjects who performed the task with experimenters who expected high ratings gave high ratings, and those subjects who performed the task with experimenters who expected low ratings gave low ratings. How did this happen? The experimenters all used the same words; it was something in their conduct which made one group of subjects do one thing, and another group of subjects do another thing.

The concreteness of the changed conditions produced by expectation is a fact, a reality: even with animal subjects, in two separate studies (Rosenthal & Fode, 1960; Rosenthal & Lawson, 1961), those experimenters who were told that rats learning mazes had been especialy bred for brightness obtained better learning from their rats than did experimenters believing their rats to have been bred for dullness. In a very recent study, Rosenthal & Jacobson (1968) extended their analysis to the natural classroom situation. Here, they tested a group of students and reported to the teachers that some among the students tested "showed great promise." Actually, the students so named had been selected on a random basis. Some time later, the experimenters retested the group of students: those students whose teachers had been told that they were "promising" showed real and dramatic increments in their IQ's as compared to the rest of the students. Something in the conduct of the teachers towards whom the teachers believed to be the "bright" students, made those students brighter.

Thus, even in carefully controlled experiments, and with no outward or conscious difference in behavior, the hypotheses we start with will influence enormously the behavior of another organism. These studies are extremely important when assessing the validity of psychological studies of women. Since it is beyond doubt that most of us start with notions as to the nature of men and women, the validity of a number of observations of sex differences is questionable, even when these observations have been made under carefully controlled conditions. Second, and more important, the Rosenthal experiments point quite clearly to the influence of social expectation. In some extremely important ways, people are what you expect them to be, or at least they behave as you expect them to behave. Thus, if women, according to Bettelheim, want first and foremost to be good wives and mothers, it is extremely likely that this is what Bruno Bettelheim, and the rest of society, want them to be.

There is another series of brilliant social psychological experiments which point to the overwhelming effect of social context. These are the obedience experiments of Stanley Milgram (1965) in which subjects are asked to obey the orders of unknown experimenters, orders which carry with them the distinct possibility that the subject is killing somebody.

In Milgram's experiments, a subject is told that he is administering a learning experiment, and that he is to deal out shocks each time the other "subject" (in reality, a confederate of the experimenter) answers incorrectly. The equipment appears to provide graduated shocks ranging upwards from 15 volts through 450 volts; for each of four consecutive voltages there are verbal descriptions such as "mild shock," "danger, severe shock," and, finally, for the 435 and 450 volt switches, a red XXX marked over the switches. Each time the stooge answers incorrectly the subject is supposed to increase the voltage. As the voltage increases, the stooge begins to cry in pain; he demands that the experiment stop; finally, he refuses to answer at all. When he stops responding, the experimenter instructs the subject to continue increasing the voltage; for each shock administered the stooge shrieks in agony. Under these conditions, about 62.5% of the subjects administered shock that they believed to be possibly lethal.

No tested individual differences between subjects predicted how many would continue to obey, and which would break off the experiment. When forty psychiatrists predicted how many of a group of 100 subjects would go on to give the lethal shock, their predictions were orders of magnitude below the actual percentages; most expected only one-tenth of one per cent of the subjects to obey to the end.

But even though *psychiatrists* have no idea how people will behave in this situation, and even though individual differences do not predict which subjects will obey and which will not, it is easy to predict when subjects will be obedient and when they will be defiant. All the experimenter has to do is change the social situation. In a variant of Milgram's experiment, two stooges were present in addition to the "victim;" these worked along with the subject in administering electric shocks. When these two stooges refused to go on with the experiment, only ten per cent of the subjects continued to the maximum voltage. This is critical for personality theory. It says that behavior is predicted from the social situation, not from the individual history.

Finally, an ingenious experiment by Schachter and Singer (1962) showed that subjects injected with adrenalin, which produces a state of physiological arousal in all but minor respects identical to that which occurs when subjects are extremely afraid, became euphoric when they were in a room with a stooge who was acting euphoric, and became extremely angry when they were placed in a room with a stooge who was acting extremely angry.

To summarize: If subjects under quite innocuous and non-coercive social conditions can be made to kill other subjects and under other types of social conditions will positively refuse to do so; if subjects can react to a state of physiological fear by becoming euphoric because there is somebody else around who is euphoric or angry because there is somebody else around who is angry; if students become intelligent because teachers expect them to be intelligent, and rats run mazes better because experimenters are told the rats are bright, then it is obvious that a study of human behavior requires, first and foremost, a study of the social contexts within which people move, the expectations as to how they will behave, and the authority which tells them who they are and what they are supposed to do.

Biologically Based Theories

Two theories of the nature of women, which come not from psychiatric and clinical tradition, but from biology, can be disposed of now with little difficulty.

The first biological theory of sex differences argues that since females and males differ in their sex hormones, and sex hormones enter the brain (Hamburg & Lunde in Maccoby, 1966), there must be innate differences in "nature." But the only thing this argument tells us is that there are differences in physiological state. The problem is whether these differences are at all relevant to behavior. Recall that Schachter and Singer (1962) have shown that a particular physiological state can itself lead to a multiplicity of felt emotional states, and outward behavior, depending on the social situation.

The second theory is a form of biological reductionism: sex role behavior in some primate species is described, and it is concluded that this is the "natural" behavior for humans. Putting aside the not insignificant problem of observer bias (for instance, Harlow, 1962, of the University of Wisconsin, after observing differences between male and female rhesus monkeys, quotes Lawrence Sterne to the effect that women are silly and trivial, and concludes that "men and women have differed in the past and they will differ in the future"), there are a number of problems with this approach.

The most general and serious problem is that there are no grounds to assume that anything primates do is necessary, natural, or desirable in humans, for the simple reason that humans are not non-humans. For instance, it is found that male chimpanzees placed alone with infants will not "mother" them. Jumping from hard data to ideological speculation researchers conclude from this information that *human* females are necessary for the safe growth of human infants. It would be as reasonable to conclude, following this logic, that it is quite useless to teach human infants to speak, since it has been tried with chimpanzees and it does not work.

One strategy that has been used is to extrapolate from primate behavior to "innate" human preference by noticing certain trends in primate behavior as one moves phylogenetically closer to humans. But there are great difficulties with this approach. When behaviors from lower primates are directly opposite to those of higher primates, or to those one expects of humans, they can be dismissed on evolutionary grounds — higher primates and/or humans grew out of that kid stuff. On the other hand, if the behavior of higher primates is counter to the behavior considered natural for humans, while the behavior of some lower primate is considered the natural one for humans, the higher primate behavior can be dismissed also, on the grounds that it has diverged from an older, prototypical pattern. So either way, one can select those behaviors one wants to prove as innate for humans. In addition, one does not know whether the sex-role behavior exhibited is dependent on the phylogenetic rank, or on the environmental conditions (both physical and social) under which different species live.

Is there then any value at all in primate observations as they relate to human females and males? There is a value but it is limited: its function can be no more than to show some extant examples of diverse sex-role behavior.

It must be stressed, however, that this is an extremely limited function. The extant behavior does not begin to suggest all the possibilities, either for non-human primates or for humans. Bearing these caveats in mind, it is nonetheless interesting that if one inspects the limited set of existing non-human primate sex-role behaviors, one finds, in fact, a much larger range of sex-role behavior than is commonly believed to exist. "Biology" appears to limit very little; the fact that a female gives birth does not mean, even in non-humans, that she necessarily cares for the infant (in marmosets, for instance, the male carries the infant at all times except when the infant is feeding (Mitchell, 1969)); "natural" female and male behavior varies all the way from females who are much more aggressive and competitive than males (e.g., Tamarins, see Mitchell, 1969) and male "mothers" (e.g., Titi monkeys, night monkeys, and marmosets, see Mitchell, 1969)[2] to submissive and passive females and male antagonists (e.g., rhesus monkeys).

But even for the limited function that primate arguments serve, the evidence has been misused. Invariably, only those primates have been cited which exhibit exactly the kind of behavior that the proponents of the biological basis of human female behavior wish were true for humans. Thus, baboons and rhesus monkeys are generally cited: males in these groups exhibit some of the most irritable and aggressive behavior found in primates, and if one wishes to argue that females are naturally passive and submissive, these groups provide vivid examples. There are abundant counter examples, such as those mentioned above (Mitchell, 1969); in fact, in general, a counter example can be found for every sex-role behavior cited, including, as mentioned in the case of marmosets, male "mothers."

But the presence of counter examples has not stopped florid and overarching theories of the natural or biological basis of male privilege from proliferating. For instance, there have been a number of theories dealing with the innate incapacity in human males for monogamy. Here, as in most of this type of theorizing, baboons are a favorite example, probably because of their fantasy value: the family unit of the hamadryas baboon, for instance, consists of a highly constant pattern of one male and a number of females and their young. And again, the counter examples, such as the invariably monogamous gibbon, are ignored.

An extreme example of this maiming and selective truncation of the evidence in the service of a plea for the maintenance of male privilege is a

---

[2] All these are lower-order primates, which makes their behavior with reference to humans unnatural, or more natural; take your choice.

[3] Schwarz-Belkin (1914) claims that the name was originally *Mouse*, but this may be a reference to an earlier L. Tiger (putative).

recent book, *Men in Groups (1969)* by a man who calls himself Tiger.[3] The central claim of this book is that females are incapable of honorable collective action because they are incapable of "bonding" as in "male bonding." What is "male bonding"? Its surface definition is simple: " . . . a particular relationship between two or more males such that they react differently to members of their bonding units as compared to individuals outside of it" (pp. 19-20). If one deletes the word male, the definition, on its face, would seem to include all organisms that have any kind of social organization. But this is not what Tiger means. For instance, Tiger asserts that females are incapable of bonding; and this alleged incapacity indicates to Tiger that females should be restricted from public life. Why is bonding an exclusively male behavior? Because, says Tiger, it is seen in male primates. All male primates? No, very few male primates. Tiger cites two examples where male bonding is seen: rhesus monkeys and baboons. Surprise, surprise. But not even all baboons: as mentioned above, the hamadryas social organization consists of one-male units; so does that of the Gelada baboon. (Mitchell, 1969). And the great apes do not go in for male bonding much either. The "male bond" is hardly a serious contribution to scholarship; one reviewer for *Science* has observed that the book " . . . shows basically more resemblance to a partisan political tract than to a work of objective social science," with male bonding being " . . . some kind of behavioral phlogiston" (Fried, 1969, p. 884).

In short, primate arguments have generally misused the evidence; primate studies themselves have, in any case, only the very limited function of describing some possible sex-role behavior; and at present, primate observations have been sufficiently limited so that even the range of possible sex-role behavior for non-human primates is not known. This range is not known since there is only minimal observation of what happens to behavior if the physical or social environment is changed. In one study (Itani, 1963), different troops of Japanese macaques were observed. Here, there appeared to be cultural differences: males in 3 out of the 18 troops observed differed in their amount of aggressiveness and infant-caring behavior. There could be no possibility of differential evolution here; the differences seemed largely transmitted by infant socialization. Thus, the very limited evidence points to some plasticity in the sex-role behavior of non-human primates; if we can figure out experiments which massively change the social organization of primate groups, it is possible that we might observe great changes in behavior. At present, however, we must conclude that, since non-human primates are too stupid to change their social conditions by themselves, the "innateness" and fixedness of their behavior are simply not known. Thus, even if there were some way, which there isn't, to settle on the behavior of a particular primate species as being the "natural" way for humans, we would not know whether or not this were simply some function of the present social organization of that species. And finally, once again it must be stressed that even if non-human primate behavior turned out to be relatively fixed, this would say little about our behavior. More immediate and relevant evidence, i.e., the evidence from social psychology, points to the enormous plasticity in human behavior, not only from one culture to the next, but from one experimental group to the next. One of the most salient features of human social organization is its variety; there are a number of cultures where there is at least a rough equality between men and women (Mead, 1949). In summary, primate arguments can tell us very little about our "innate" sex-role behavior; if they tell us anything at all, they tell us that there is no one biologically "natural" female or male behavior, and that sex-role behavior in non-human primates is much more varied than has previously been thought.

In brief, the uselessness of present psychology with regard to women is simply a special case of the general conclusion: one must understand social expectations about women if one is going to characterize the behavior of women.

How are women characterized in our culture, and in psychology? They are inconsistent, emotionally unstable, lacking in a strong conscience or super-ego, weaker, "nuturant" rather than productive, "intuitive" rather than intelligent, and, if they are at all "normal," suited to the home and the family. In short, the list adds up to a typical minority group stereotype of inferiority (Hacker, 1951): if they know their place, which is in the home, they are really quite lovable, happy, childlike, loving creatures. In a review of the intellectual differences between little boys and little girls, Eleanor Maccoby (1966) has shown that there are no intellectual differences until about high school, or, if there are, girls are slightly ahead of boys. At high school, girls begin to do worse on a few intellectual tasks, such as arithmetic reasoning, and beyond high school, the achievement of women now measured in terms of productivity and accomplishment drops off even more rapidly. There are a number of other, non-intellectual tests which show sex differences: I choose the intellectual differences since it is seen clearly that women start becoming inferior. It is no use to talk about women being different but equal; all of the tests I can think of have a "good" outcome and a "bad" outcome. Women usually end up at the "bad" outcome. In light of social expectations about women, what is surprising is not that women end up where society expects they will; what is surprising is that little girls don't get the message that they are supposed to be stupid until high school; and what is even more remarkable is that some women resist this message even after high school, college, and graduate school.

My paper began with remarks on the task of the discovery of the limits of human potential. Psychologists must realize that it is they who are limiting discovery of human potential. They refuse to accept evidence, if they are clinical psychologists, or, if they are rigorous, they assume that people move in a context-free ether, with only their innate dispositions and their individual traits determining what they will do. Until psychologists begin to respect evidence and until they begin looking at the social contexts within which people move, psychology will have nothing of substance to offer in this task of discovery. I do not know what immutable differences exist between men and women apart from differences in their genitals; perhaps there are some other unchangeable differences; probably there are a number of irrelevant differences. But it is clear that until social expectation for men and women are equal, until we provide equal respect for both men and women, our answers to this question will simply reflect our prejudices.

REFERENCES

Astin, A. W., "The functional autonomy of psychotherapy." *American Psychologist*, 1961, *16*, 75-8.

Barron, F. & Leary, T., "Changes in psychoneurotic patients with and without psychotherapy." *Consulting Psychology*, 1955, *19*, 239-245.

Bregin, A. E., "The effects of psychotherapy: negative results revisited." *Journal of Consulting Psychology*, 1963, *10*, 244-250.

Bettelheim, B., "The commitment required of a woman entering a scientific profession in present day American society." *Woman and the Scientific Professions*, The MIT symposium on American Women in Science and Engineering, 1965.

Bleck, J., "Some reasons for the apparent inconsistency of personality." *Psychological Bulletin*, 1968, *70*, 210-212.

Cartwright, R. D. & Vogel, J. L., "A comparison of changes in psychoneurotic patients during matched periods of therapy and no-therapy." *Journal of Consulting Psychology*, 1960, *24*, 121-7.

Erikson, E., "Inner and outer space: reflections on womanhood." *Daedalus*, 1964, *93*, 582-606.

Eysenck, H.J., "The effects of psychotherapy: an evaluation." *Journal of Consulting Psychology*, 1952, *16*, 319-324.

Fieldcrest — Advertisement in the *New Yorker*, 1965.

Fried, M.H., "Mankind excluding woman," review of Tiger's *Men in Groups*. *Science*, 1969, *165*, pp. 883-4.

Freud, S., *The Sexual Enlightenment of Children*, Collier Books Edition, 1963.

Goldstein, A.P. & Dean, S.J., *The investigation of Psychotherapy: Commentaries and Readings*. John Wiley & Sons, New York: 1966.

Hamburg, D.A. & Lunde, D.T., "Sex hormones in the development of sex differences in human behavior." In Maccoby, ed., *The Development of Sex Differences*, Stanford University Press, 1966, pp. 1-24.

Hacker, H.M., "Women as a minority group." *Social Forces*, 1951, *30*, 60-69.

Harlow, H.F., "The heterosexual affectional system in monkeys." *The American Psychologist*, 1962, *17*, 1-9.

Hooker, E., "Male Homosexuality in the Rorschach." *Journal of Projective Techniques*, 1957, *21*, 18-31.

Itani, J., "Paternal care in the wild Japanese monkeys, *Macaca fuscata*." In C.H. Southwick, ed., *Primate Social Behavior*. Princeton: Van Nostrand, 1963.

Little, K.B. & Schneidman, E.S., "Congruences among interpretations of psychological and anamestic data." *Psychological Monographs*, 1959, *73*, 1-42.

Maccoby, Eleanor E., "Sex differences in intellectual functioning," in Maccoby, ed., *The development of sex differences*, Stanford University Press, 1966, pp. 25-55.

Masters, W.H. & Johnson, V.E., *Human Sexual Response*, Little Brown: Boston, 1966.

Mead, M., *Male and Female: A Study of the sexes in a changing world*, William Morrow, New York, 1949.

Milgram, S., "Some Conditions of Obedience and Disobedience to Authority." *Human Relations*, 1965a, *18*, 57-76.

Milgram, S., "Liberating effects of group pressure." *Journal of Personality and Social Psychology*, 1965b, *1*, 127-134.

Mitchell, G.D., "Paternalistic behavior in primates." *Psychological Bulletin* 1969, *71*, pp. 399-417.

Powers, E. & Witmer, H., *An experiment in the prevention of deliquency*, New York: Columbia University Press, 1951.

Rheingold, J., *The fear of being a woman*. Grune & Stratton, New York, 1964.

Rosenthal, R., "On the social psychology of the psychological experiment: The experimenter's hypothesis as unintended determinant of experimental results." *American Scientist*, 1963, *51*, 268-283.

Rosenthal, R., *Experimenter effects in Behavioral Research*. New York: Appleton-Century Crofts, 1966.

Rosenthal, R. & Jacobson, L., *Pygmalion in the classroom: teacher expectation and pupil's intellectual development.* New York: Holt Rinehart & Winston, 1968.

Rosenthal, R. & Lawson, R., "A longitudinal study of the effects of experimenter bias on the operant learning of laboratory rats." Unpublished manuscript, Harvard University, 1961.

Rosenthal, R. & Fode, K.L., "The effect of experimenter bias on the performance of the albino rat." Unpublished manuscript, Harvard University, 1960.

Rotter, J.B., "Psychotherapy." *Annual Review of Psychology,* 1960, *11,* 381-414.

Schachter, S. & Singer, J.E., "Cognitive, social and physiological determinants of emotional state." *Psychological Review,* 1962, *69,* 379-399.

Schwartz-Belkin, M., "Les Fleurs de Mal," in *Festschrift for Gordon Piltdown,* Ponzi Press, New York, 1914.

Tiger, L., *Men in Groups,* Random House, New York, 1969.

Truax, C.B., "Effective ingredients in psychotherapy: an approach to unraveling the patient-therapist interaction." *Journal of Counseling Psychology,* 1963, 10, 256-263.

after the second miscarriage
i'm tired
grieving for dead children
empty belly again
breasts small, not full
what kind of woman
after awhile
it
gets so
all
your tears are
private

Alta

SECTION III:

Work and the Family

The American Family: Decay and Rebirth

Selma James

*Selma James was born in Brooklyn in 1930,
She is now active in England in Women's
Liberation and in the struggle against
racism. During the 1950's she spent five
years in the West Indies working for Federation and national independence.*

PREFACE

The following essay, written in 1956, was to be a chapter of a book on American civilization. The book, to be written by members of a small Marxist organization, was never completed and the essay remains in draft. The founder of that organization, C.L.R. James, wrote the introduction, which appears here in excerpted form.

It was impossible to bring the essay up to date without des-troying its original merit. So I have added a postscript to give some indication of present thinking. It is in parts abstract. But my ex-perience in Women's Liberation here in England impelled me at least to attempt that aspect of the redefinition of socialism which Women's Liberation, of all liberation movements, most acutely poses.

Selma James
London, June 1970

Introduction

The family is the whole civilization in embryo. There the social practices, aims and ideals of the civilization are not merely taught but practiced under those conditions and between individuals where human affections are inseparably intertwined with the social disci-plines of the society. In the family are laid the foundations of atti-tudes to the world, the form and content of relations to the sexes

An expanded version of an article printed in *Radical America*, vol. IV, no. 2, Feb-ruary, 1970. Printed by permission of the author.

and to one's fellow human beings. There is not, and can never be, any substitute for it. It is a fundamental form of human existence and for that very reason it changes, must change, according to fundamental changes in the forms and conditions of society itself. The Hindu patriarchal family, a community in itself; the family of the medieval peasant and artisan, an economic unit, where the father ruled despotically because he was responsible for the economic life of the family; the family of the frontier where the woman handled the rifle as easily as the cradle and gained status in consequence; the middle-class family of Victorian times, built on order and authority in a social climate where prosperity was threatened by obvious dangers — all these are examples of the family which corresponded to the needs of a particular society and various classes in that particular society. But different as were all of these, they had this in common, that they were founded on an authority which inculcated the authoritarian character of society as a whole, and that authority found its immediate and most obvious expression in the authority of the man over the woman. It is that authority which, as we have seen in economic relations, is being challenged from one end of modern society to the other. And the American woman, brought up in the democratic and social freedoms of the United States, has challenged it as it has been challenged in no modern country. The battle she is waging, with all its victories and defeats, is a part of the general struggle for complete democracy, in the plant as well as in the home.

C.L.R. James

The American Women and the Family

We intended to give, first, as close a picture as possible of the women of the American middle-class, for society does *not* consist exclusively or mainly of workers. No fundamental change in society can take place at all unless large sections of the middle-class actively support it, or at any rate are in sympathy with it. And they will do this only because they feel that it opens a way for them to rid themselves of burdens which are crushing them as members of the middle-classes. More important, an examination of the situation of these women, free of oppressive laws, with enough money to rid them of economic cares, shows very precisely the stupidity of "the higher standard of living" philosophy and its uselessness as a means of understanding the crisis in society.

The young woman of the middle-class has fought for and achieved in the United States the reputation and the actual status of great social, legal and political equality. Not only has she had the vote for years, but divorce in many states takes six weeks on the grounds of mental cruelty or ony other superficial grounds. Birth control is commonly accepted and easy to obtain. Some states award not only the children, but half the property to a divorced woman. Eighteen is the legal age of consent but it is not strictly enforced and in fact is not enforceable except in case of scandal. She is born into a milieu and tradition which apparently ensures her personal freedom and constant and uninhibited association with men. She goes to the university, often co-educational, to study what she is interested in. She is, as soon as she reaches maturity, her own mistress, traveling where and when she wants to travel and making her own way in the world. She decides who will be her boy friends and practices her own code of morals, which for her most often means sexual freedom.

Her wealth of experiences in social life and education lead her to believe that the future belongs to her. Aspirations of marriage and a family are for her new worlds and situations to conquer, to manage, and to control successfully. Nothing can conquer, manage or control her, for her restraints are either self-imposed or do not exist at all. All new relations are, for her, relations to be modernized, tailor-made, to suit herself. She, with the co-operation of some modern young man, is going to create a modern relationship based on equality of the sexes and no compromise of that principle will ever be tolerated.

This has been the spirit of the young women on the campuses in American universities for many years, whose free walk and blue jeans were the symbols of their belligerent struggle for woman's equality.

It is these same women who, once having married, are shocked by the realities of life and the inability of personal resolution, no matter how strong and how correctly motivated, to except them from the real human relations of their country.

In marriage, the middle-class woman had to face for the first time the fact that, although she and her husband had came from the same backgrounds, had gone to the same kind of university, had worn the same blue jeans, had stayed out until the same late hours of the night and had had almost the same number of sleeping partners before marriage, the feeling of the necessity for her personal development which came so natural to her, was not at all natural to him. As a matter of fact, what came naturally and most easily to him was for her to assume the traditional role of home, children and subordination to his needs and whims.

In marriage she came face to face with the fact that whatever ideas, liberal and tending towards a fully human relationship with his wife, he may have, her husband, as all men, had been conditioned and condemned by the dominance of men in past civilizations and the influence that this exercises in every sphere of human life today.

The average man born into the world, from the very beginning is imbued with one attitude to the male sex and another attitude to the female sex. His early years are spent almost entirely with women so that he is conditioned to look to women for certain of the essential, primary needs of his nature. The child is then brought up in kindergarten where once more he is subjected to the influence of women. In his early schooldays, he is again placed under the influence of women. He leaves this feminine influence to become the pupil of men and to mix with men just at the moment when he is able to control himself and to feel his useful growing strength. Consequently, there is created in his whole personality a distinction between activity, independence, work and masculinity; and relaxation, emotional needs and women.

Until this division which creates a man of a certain type, formed for dominance in society and in personal relations, until these educational practices are abolished, women will find that all the formal and legal and abstract equality which they may win, will never do away with this particular type of masculine personality which is the product of past societies and is at odds with modern social conditions.

But though it is a relic of the past, it is re-enforced by some of the most powerful forces in modern life. To take only one: the advertising industry in the United States, within comparatively recent times, has launched upon the American people and the world a conception of "voluptuous woman" as the indispensable encouragement to buying everything from toilet paper to cheap editions of the classics. Morning, noon and night, from every newspaper, every hoarding, there is hammered into the masculine head, juvenile, adult and child, the message that life consists of first work, and afterwards woman, woman, woman, presented in as many varieties of physical charms as the ingenuity of the layout man can devise. It is at the same time cause and effect of the diseased relationship of the sexes in modern life. Its particular and pervading viciousness is that it is in direct opposition to the struggle of women to establish in the minds of men a concept of themselves as fundamentally human beings seeking to establish social relations of freedom and equal shared responsibility, and not as houris in some harem of the Arabian Nights.

It is clear that we are dealing with fundamental problems, which are not to be solved by slogans, by Congress, or under the leadership of Communist or Socialist parties. What we point out is that these are the problems which make or break a social order and that vast millions of people are involved in it to the point of desperation, in their most intimate personal lives. And in this case, the American middle-class, there is no question of a low standard of living. We concentrate here on the women, but it is obvious that if women are degraded then the possibilities of a profound and satisfying relationship between the sexes are destroyed.

The Unending Need to Decide

Not only men, but women themselves are caught between the two different conceptions in the development of their personalities. Though the middle-class woman is brought up in a society where women are relatively free, at every moment, in spite of personal and physical freedom, she herself is affected by the constant example of traditional feminine behavior, the product of past relations of society. She is still educated in the art of catching a man, and in the art of keeping him, using feminine wiles and tricks centuries old. This at the same time that her ideas and personality are turned to revolt against any attempt to inhibit or curb her equality or to force her into a feminine mold. It is therefore not only between herself and her man that there is a clash. The clash is inside herself, a reflection of the two societies into which she is born.

From this flows a perpetual disruption of woman's personality creating a permanent problem which her mother, and most certainly her grandmother, never knew. The least demand that her husband makes upon her sets up within her the necessity of decision. If she subordinates herself to his demands and thereby gives up an ounce of her hard-won freedom, she is acting against her principles. If she refuses to subordinate herself to his demands and demonstrates to him and to herself that she can't be pushed around, she is splitting her personality deep inside of her, digging into and tearing against those aspects of her personality which are fundamental to her because they are not ideas, but absorbed assumptions and patterns of behavior from all the life around her.

The very presence of the need to decide, decide, decide, on every issue, big or small, creates not only a social crisis but an internal personal crisis. She is confronted with what the whole of society has trained her for and held up before her as ideal femininity, on the one hand, and, on the other hand, what she as a modern individual needs and what society has told her she must have, especially as a middle-class American.

No matter what she decides, the very fact that any demand or request, legitimate or not, calls for a principled decision, a decision for or against the cause of women's equality, has destroyed her chances for a fruitful and harmonious relationship. To find it necessary to weigh and measure, to be cut off from spontaneous pleasure in doing for other members of the family, to feel no innate assurance that they are willing to help and are feeling mutual concern, for every issue to be a principled issue, is to say that the individual woman finds in the family itself the worst characteristics of the chaotic world just outside the door, its tensions, antagonisms and inhumanity. This dis-spirited, disunited, unsheltered haven lies just under the surface and accurately describes millions of American homes.

People need to live in harmony with the society of which they are members. What they need as individuals and what society demands of them cannot be in conflict. They cannot constantly be forced to make intellectual decisions between different social systems as they do now, because of the transitional and antagonistic character of the life they live.

These antagonisms have been growing for decades. But here (as in labor relations) they have reached a climax. Society has got to find new foundations in which people can live instinctively and naturally without having a dozen times a day to work out problems of ethics, philosophy, and moral and social behaviour.

Men did not make this sex war. But their role in it is of necessity a defense of the old manner of life. As soon as women demanded human freedoms for themselves, the family began to crumble, because the modern family is incompatible with the freedom of woman. Any challenge on the part of women of their subordination has the immediate effect of breaking up the family. It is impossible for a woman to look upon herself as an independent human being with independent needs and at the same time subordinate herself to her family and to the needs of her husband's occupation, as the modern family demands that she do. Conversely, it is impossible for her to maintain the struggle without destroying the family, as we now know it. Yet she must maintain the struggle.

Who Knows the Biological Nature of Woman?

Meanwhile, however, there are certain prejudices and illusions, buttressed often by high scientific authority, which are deeply rooted in the society and which will finally be torn up only when the soil on which they have grown is reploughed and resettled. But it is enough to point them out, in relation to our philosophy of society, to see how superficial they really are.

For many generations it has been claimed that woman is biologically constructed for what we shall call, for want of a better word, femininity. Scientists and non-scientists state with a great show of evidence that women are, as far as their metabolism is concerned, unstable. Their whole structure is shaped for the bearing of children and their emotionalism, physical and psychological instability all point to a biological basis for their feminine role.

People who today in good faith repeat these things are swimming in deeper waters than they know. Just the same type of argument was used for centuries to maintain the privileges of aristocrats over serfs, of white men over Blacks, of imperialists over the Asian peoples. All those mighty scientific structures are now in ruins.

If woman is biologically fit only for femininity, then the whole trend of modern democratic rights and freedom for women is wrong, and tens upon tens of millions of women, ever-increasing, who see freedom and equality as imperative steps to their own sense of well being have to be told that they are wrong. Hitler did that, in the course of his ruining Germany. Only a totalitarian state can dare to do this and its punishment will be swift, in the chaos that will result from the violent reversal of the movement towards freedom and the absolute impossibility of restoring the old relations. We do not know what the biological nature of woman is, and we all probably shall never know. All that we know is that under certain social conditions of the past, woman has been *forced* to play the role of femininity, the definition of which varies enormously from society to society.

As the industrial revolution has developed and to some degree has begun to free woman from economic dependence, the limitations due to her supposed biological weakness have grown less and less. If there is any remote possibility of finding out what her biological limitations are, and what men's are, it can only come when she is perfectly free to shape her own destiny as a social being, to have all the privileges and all the responsibilities of freedom in a free society. But even this is in all probability a purely abstract idea. All human beings today are social beings, their biological strengths and weaknesses subordinated to the powerful, dominating, irresistible shaping of human life by the vast industrial and social complexity of modern society. It seems to us impossible at any future time to abstract from this society some purely physical characteristics and call these "the biological nature" of women. Of the same superficial character is the supposed masculinity inherent in men. There is not the slightest biological reason why from the very beginning men and women do not share equally in the care of the infant and children, and this would strike a mortal blow at the educational processes which today condition men (and women) to a shape of personality totally unfitted for the modern world. We must have the vision of a free society and only that will make sense of the remorseless struggle that goes on today in countless homes and the increasing spectre of a society where the old family relationships are disintegrating day by day and there are no new ones to take their place.

As in all such titanic struggles, where millions of people are involved in relationships, many of which are intangible, victories and defeats go side by side, even though the general trend is forward.

The absence of this vision of the possibility of a different and new society, once the middle-class woman had achieved all the formal and legal rights that there were to achieve, have caused her, in recent years, to suffer a defeat. After the war, the American press and women's magazines opened up a powerful campaign to change the situation, the overwhelming antagonisms of which had become intolerable for men and frustrating for women. What could they offer to these women who had fought a ferocious battle but who had achieved only formal equality and little change in actual personal relations? Their only answer was back to the kitchen, back to being baby machines, back to the old fashioned ways. It was clear that the battle had reached its limits on the basis that is was being fought. Formal equality had appeared to have been achieved. It had brought only frustration. But one great gain had been achieved. With all formal barriers dissolved, American women, believing, as all Americans, that everything can be fixed by proper management of a situation, were for the first time faced with the actual relation between what American society promises and what it actually gives. The barriers being removed, the question had come to the surface.

Many of these women, seeing for the first time the breadth of the crisis, have said that it does not pay to fight, and have capitulated once more, at least partially, to the domination of their husbands and their homes. A whole generation of middle-class women have switched their courses in universities from the arts to the art of homemaking, from the sciences to child-care, and from the struggle for equality to the struggle to subordinate personality, desires and intellect to the will of their husbands. Their slogans are: Cater to your husband, and enjoy motherhood. Vain retreat. The family has not appreciably changed in any basic way as a result. But these women at least are no longer externally compelled to wage a never-ending war. But this defeat is only temporary. The new generation is fighting the battle all over again, and the failure of the parents is constantly brought home to them by the failures of the children.

A glance at two specific types of women of the middle class will complete this picture of the class and show how hopeless is their position unless seen in the context of a total change in society.

The Exceptional Woman

From the middle-class has arisen a section of women, who, faced with the choice of modern home life or no home life, have chosen no home life. They have chosen instead, a career. Though some of them are married and may even have a child, the marriage is quite business-like and the child is very often a concession to the husband. The center of the lives of these women uniquely is outside the home.

These are ordinarily women of good looks, exceptional intellect, energy or force, or exceptional opportunity. It is because of this that they find middle-class life for a woman so intolerable. It is also because of this that they can make their way out of it, into the professions. Their trade mark is the man-tailored suit, envy of men and hatred of women. They waver from excessive femininity to excessive masculine aggressiveness, from maudlin sentimentalism to crudeness, brutality and all the excesses which are commonly associated with men. They are ordinarily restless and what bothers all women seems to fester in them, each masculine wrong against them felt by their very flesh.

Their banner is sexual freedom, because sexual subordination appears to them the last stronghold of their repudiation of being women, a condition they despise. They repudiate family relations in order to outdo men in what they presume to be a masculine attitude and thus break the only human outlet which women are allowed in this society. But they are not fighting for a new society, with new and expansive human outlets. They are fighting for themselves, for position, for power and for domination. In the desire for all of these, they outdo men. In order to achieve what they want, they go to any lengths of cruelty and intrigue and when they do not achieve what they believe is rightfully theirs, power and domination over men and other women, they wail that discrimination has been shown against them because they are women and they never had a chance.

It is quite in keeping with the hypocrisy on the question of the crisis of American sex relations that these women executives, these top dress designers, these female politicians are the only examples that official society can find of the equality the American woman enjoys and the roads which they claim are constantly opening up to her, the success of the career woman being proof.

While one section of them becomes the efficient and energetic servants of large firms, the other section joins the Communist Party or other radical groups which claim to practice women's equality and which promise these women state power "when the party wins."

For these women, to dominate is the only alternative to being dominated. Their struggle, therefore, is not to be equal but to dominate, and it extends from the kitchen to the office and back to the bedroom. At their best their individual successes offer not even a palliative for social questions. At their worst, they are the proof, too monstrous to be a lie, that either women find themselves in the stream of history which is moving them and all of society to a new world, or their struggle can only degenerate into a selfish, atomized fight, destroying relations with men, family and other human beings, and in the process destroying themselves.

At the opposite scale, we have seen in recent years those who have not the financial ease of the middle-class but aspire to it. Most typical are those women who huddle with their husbands and families in the project houses thrown up. around campuses for ex-soldiers studying under the G.I. Bill. There the retreat from the struggle for equality is at its most pitiful. In tiny apartments with paper-thin walls sit many young women with one, two or three children, children who are breast-fed not from any innate desire, but in order, as the new books tell them, to prove they are women at all. They do not accompany their husbands on the campus, but sit at home with their children, comfort their men for the exams, typing their final papers, and racing to keep up with what their husbands are doing, so that at night they can carry on (rational) conversations, and not just talk about the neighbors and the kids. For, though they have retreated, they are unable to go back completely to the lives of their mothers. These young women work hard at their modern families, help their struggling men, swallow their fierce modern prides and follow in the wake of their husbands, trying desperately not to be left behind.

When their men have their degrees and begin the business of making money, it will fall on the shoulders of these young women to submit their children to a ceaseless round of piano lessons, dancing lessons, elocution lessons, so that not only the wife, car, house and furniture, but the children as well will most accurately express the income level of their fathers.

They may, if their husbands are successful, be relieved of the burden of child care and housekeeping by servants or black day workers. For those women it will be worse. They can read their future by looking at the middle-aged women around them. The leisure time that servants will allow them is the one disease in their predestined course for which there is no cure. For these women, so accurately described by many, many observers, have nothing to do. They may become some of the women who nag their husbands ceaselessly for things which they do not want in the hopes that their men will take as much interest in them as all their leisure insists that they take in themselves. They may become some of the women who live from cocktail party to cocktail party, in the hopes of a slight or more serious flirtation to take the edge off the bordom and give their lives some excitement and spice. They may eventually be some of the women who end up in Las Vegas or Reno two or three times, each time with wounded prides, bitter resentments and large alimony suits, willing at the drop of a hat to tell anyone who will listen the sad story of what that man did to them after they had done so much for him. Or perhaps they will not like the scandal and, when their children marry, they, with all the human involvement and maternal domination removed from their grasp, will become the characteristic fortyish mother-in-law whose lives feed solely upon their unwelcomed interference in the lives of the new generation. If they are, they will begin to understand and take seriously *The Ladies Home Journal* which has been telling them for years to prepare for this empty period in their lives by developing a hobby. A section of them will fill a good deal of this empty period in beauty parlors and doctors' offices, the former to keep them looking young in a country which respects only young women, and the later for dieting and prescriptions for nervous ailments. These women are the best known and most pitiable women in American society.

Whatever happens to them, they will never be filled with the satisfaction that what they are doing is necessary to the world, or necessary even to themselves. They will not have known either the equality which they believed at one time was their rightful heritage, nor will they know the guiltlessness and peace of mind of the old fashioned woman who did what she was told, and lived a narrow and restricted life. But, since she knew no other, she felt that when she had done what she was told and done it well, she had fulfilled her life and therefore could be at peace with the world.

For, when these women turned back, they could not turn back all the way. The women before them had destroyed the past, with its evils and with its compensations. The old fashioned woman who subordinated herself to her man did so because she knew nothing else to do. But every compromise these modern women make they must do consciously, and this cannot avoid engendering deep bitterness which, from time to time, explodes against both their men and their children. In reality it is a bitterness against society for placing them in the position of having to compromise. Society degrades these women by demanding nothing of them; it must be prepared for the fury this inevitably unleashes. The difficulty of these women is that they share the assumptions of the society which oppresses them, and it is devastating to fight a whole network of relations which, though they are tearing you apart, you accept unquestioningly. This is the great liberation of modern middle class women. (See Postscript)

But the battle itself, when seen in the totality of the American people struggling to emancipate themselves, is an indication of the inescapable trends of the future. Though it appears to have suffered defeat, it is one of the great social experiences of contemporary America, pregnant with consequences and the conclusions that can be legitimately drawn from it.

The Historical Perspective

Americans are looked upon as a materialistic people. De Tocqueville did not think so. And of Americans today it is totally untrue. The leaders and rulers of American society, incapable of offering to the people any serious social, cultural or spiritual values, help to create this false picture of American life by their perpetual harping on goods and gadgets, and the "ever higher standard of living." In reality, the American people, in its large majority, fall back on material goods in default of what they lack eternally and cannot find, some system of values to correspond to the energy and sense of power given to them by the magnificent territory, their special historical past, and their mastery of material things. They seek in vain. They will have to create one for themselves. More than that. It *is* being created. That is what we are writing about.

This gross materialism of the American ruling class is doomed to total defeat and one signal proof is this very experience of the well-to-do middle class woman. She has had a "high standard of living." Official society has turned all its forces upon her. One small part of American technology is in her kitchen and her garage. Her life, her home, her family, her income have been held up as the official American ideal in movies, on the radio, on television, and above all, in the press and in advertisements. And yet what is the result? *She has rejected it.* Rich as the bribe has been, she has not been bribed into acceptance of the role cut out for her. She has fought for personal freedom and personal equality in the finest American tradition and if she has for the time being temporarily retreated, it is only because for the time being she sees no way out. Let the vulgarians who rule American society, set its tone (and paint the false pictures that exist of us outside the United States), let them note and tremble how widely spread is the opposition in the United States to their "higher standard of living" philosophy and how knit into the very structure of the American personality is the desire for a free and equal society.

And here we want to make the first vital connection between the position of women and labor relations.

Far removed as they are, from each other, yet the masses of workers in American industry, plants and offices, and the women of the middle-class have this in common, that in the two most important spheres of social life, production relations and family relations, they are embattled and unappeasable enemies of the principles and values of the existing social order. Both seek essentially the same thing, freedom and equality, the one in the co-operative character of the labor process, the other in family life. Both know they must have it, or life is not worth living. History begins to move when widely separated sections of society recognize that they have a common enemy and common aims.

This is *our* philosophy of history.

Everyone knows that before the Civil War there was a crisis in the production relations of slavery. (If the escape of thousands of slaves every year from production was not a crisis in the production relations of slavery, then what is a crisis?) It shook the whole nation, and among those shaken were middle-class women who joined the Abolition Movement and *raised the banner of legal equality for women.* So close was the relation between the two that the first meeting for women's rights had Frederick Douglass, the great Black Abolitionist, orator and statesman, as its chairman.

Today the social forces, needs and values have shifted. But all sections have moved. In production relations the crisis is in industry itself against bureaucratic domination which ruins the very purpose of industry. In family relations it is against personal domination in the family which ruins the very purpose of the family. These are the types of forces that alter the channels in which history has run for centuries. We do not say that all middle-class women will rush to embrace a labor movement that has shown its determination to clean out the Augean stables of American capitalism. They will come in stages, the bolder ones at first, then more, usually younger ones. Some who do not come will be sympathetic, some of those who retreat will be demoralized. The children and the youth will come in droves, for Americans, even well-to-do ones, have little of that class consciousness and hostility to working people as such which so divides European peoples. Wealth as such does not mean so much to them because the confidence that wealth can easily be created is still very strong in the consciousness of the country as a whole. When the nation, in its vital forces, does move, the preachers on the text of the higher standard of living will preach to empty benches. As it is, few listen to them today.

A great deal of what we have said here is not new. The middle-class woman has not lacked acute observers who have analyzed her situation today with ability and penetration. The difference between them and us is that they can come to no conclusion and the best of them, after going a certain distance, stop short, and even sometimes destroy the validity of the conclusions at which they have arrived because they will not, in fact they cannot, recognize that the only solutions to the problems which they analyze is the total reorganization of society on new foundations. For the problems created by a society which has come into existence during the last 50 years, they insist on seeking solutions within the old foundations and the old framework, which are now utterly outmoded in every sphere, economic, social and political. And because of this, few of them seem to be aware that the same battle is being fought by millions of working class women, and from their very position in society, these have gone a long way, not in solving this great problem (nothing but a total reorganization of society will solve that), but towards showing the way in which it must and *will* ultimately be solved.

The Working Class Woman

The movement of history towards a new social order is not simple. Listening to the ideas, aspirations and complaints of middle-class women, a woman of the working class has mixed reactions. She may feel sympathy and even identify with them because she too is a woman and because the working class woman is also faced with her husband's disinterest in her, that is, in the daily problems that she faces. In the course of the conversation, that sympathy and identity are often expressed, but in the company of her "own kind," she is apt to be more articulate and more accurate, and expresses what she instinctively feels are class divisions, at the same time that she holds to the original alliance with her sisters of whatever class. For, sympathetic or not, the working class woman has her own problems, her own aspirations, her own distinct methods of coping with her situation and, even more fundamental, her own instincts and attitudes. Though she is born into the same world and at the same time as her middle-class counterpart, it is not merely income level which divides them. The instincts and attitudes arise from the different traditions of their backgrounds and their actual situations. The power of working class women in this struggle is due to the fact that they recognize, are compelled to recognize that the woman question, for them, is rooted in the relations of production.

The working class woman is at the disposal of her household and her household is at the disposal of the needs of her husband's job. What her husband earns, that is what the family lives on. How many clothes she buys or whether she has to make clothes, whether she has a washing machine or washes clothes by hand, whether the family lives in a crowded apartment or in a house with enough room for the family, all of these things are decided by the kind of job her husband has. The shift that he works determines her schedule. How hard he works determines how much peacemaking she will have to do, and how much help, if any, she can expect from him. Where her husband works determines what part of town they live in, and if there are no jobs in that town, then all the family and social ties have to be forgotten and she and her children go where he can find work.

The housewife, though she is not herself dominated by any direct boss or time clock knows that she is dominated by what has to be done in relation to her husband's job. Her responsibility is to see that he is at the disposal of industry. This is the type of profound knowledge of social realities which no academic education can give and which is often the task of academic education to hide. She is learning that there is no solution to her problems as a woman unless there is a total change in the conditions under which her husband works. This knowledge makes her the leader of her well-to-do sister in the struggle for the emancipation of women in distinction from the struggle for legal equality which in its time was led by middle-class women.

Let us get some idea of her life, the things that matter, whether she has voted Democratic or Republican. Popular magazines and able journalists do not spend much time on her, except to tell her how to do better what she resents doing at all.

Since being a housewife allows no creative expression outside the home, women often try to put all that they have as human beings into the management and decoration of their homes. And for most working class women, it does take all that they have to make some of the places they live in liveable, let alone attractive, on one insufficient paycheck. It is a witness to the narrow lives they lead that women spend so much time, thought and energy on their homes, for they have had in the past no other direction for their creative social instincts, except their homes and families.

What is denied a working class woman as a productive individual she tries to compensate for, as much as she can afford, in consumption.†

Yet one of the fundamental standards of the working class community is

---

†To make consumption the enemy, however, is to deny the problem, not expose it; she is starved of expression of her individual creative powers and reduced to the performer of a particular function—being a housewife.

the importance of the unity of the family, not only wife and husband, but sisters and brothers, aunts, uncles and cousins. Though the family unit has broken up and physically separated, this tradition still remains. It is this standard which emerges in all that a working class woman does for her home. She is not only doing for the expression of her own personality. She is doing for "my family."

For the working class, and the woman as a part of it, it is foreign to make intellectual decisions on personal matters. Their lives are spent making the best of a bad situation, trying to squeeze out all the personal happiness that they can from an inhuman setup, which is constantly threatening to subordinate and drain them completely in the work that they do. In that world, people tend to do what is easiest, not tying themselves up in the knot of rigid principles, but attempting to lead spontaneous lives to the degree that this is possible. Her aim is to pool resources where the family is concerned, each adult giving freely for the good of the whole, and children trained to do the same. The contribution of the man is the paycheck. In that world, it is not only foreign, but a destructive imposition for a woman to figure how much she is owed and how much is owed to her, to constantly measure her share in the distribution of income or responsibility. The problems are too urgent.

This has been so for a long time. What is new is that with this background, women of the working class are waging a fierce battle to break down the traditional spheres of man's work and women's. She wages bitter war for help in the house from her husband and her children. This battle is not a struggle to be arithmetically equal. It is first of all to lighten her burden, something which she never believed before she was entitled to do. It is also to include the family in the home so that she does not spend her life in the kitchen and they don't spend their lives out of it. It is the struggle for the entire family to take responsibility for work and thought on where they live and the woman, mothers and wives, they live with. It is to break the isolation and boredom of housework by being able to do things with her family. It is to raise her from the level of a house servant, a personal attendant on the breadwinner, who is old and drained at forty, to the level of a full member of the family. Thus her personal rebellion takes the profoundly important form of a struggle for the creation of the family on a new basis.

The battle is at times sporadic, breaking out over incidental things like why the dishes weren't done by some member of the family, or why clothes were not put where they belonged, instead of waiting on the woman of the house to do it. At times, it is done campaign style. A woman sets her mind to the fact that one sphere, dish-washing, a night out, big shopping, or certain parts of the meals, will be done by the husband or the kids. But no matter what the issue, the basic cause for what men call the complaint is almost always the same. It is to break the traditional division of labor between men and women which has no place in the modern world. Built on this traditional division of labor are the traditional privileges of men and the traditional subordination of women to these privileges, no less than the exploitation of men.

This woman, in her battle to involve her family in a new kind of family life, is immediately confronted with the facts which come to her on all sides, from her husband, from the papers, and from her own experience in the working class, that her husband is being drained daily and hourly by his work in the factory. This fact is his constant weapon in refusing further responsibility for the home and in retaining the privileges that society has given him. Though she lives outside the plant her life is shaped by the angers, bitternesses, frustrations and spiritual exhaustions of life in the factory.

A man working 8, 9 or 10 hours a day has little time or energy to spend with his children, little time to know even where their clothes are kept, and little time to maintain a personal life with his wife. He hasn't the money to offer her the compensations the well-to-do can offer. So that very often, a worker militantly progressive in industrial and political life in sheer self-defence, falls back in his personal life to the most reactionary prejudices of the society he is fighting outside the home. Thus, here it is the woman who, in her personal struggles, fights a social cause.

The working class woman must not only fight the prejudices of her husband which tell him it is feminine to wash dishes or to walk the baby. Much of that prejudice in the last few years she has totally routed. In struggling for a greater participation in the home by her husband, she is fighting the entire pattern of her life and his.

For this woman, paradoxically, the family is the thing above all that she instinctively wishes to preserve. It is the working class family and the working class community which, during social catastrophes as well as during the normal catastrophe of routine exploitation, provides stability, unity and sustenance. The great conflict which is placed before her is that every time she demands a family which is genuinely cooperative and which takes her into account as a separate human being, the framework of the old family crumbles from the shock. In order to preserve the family, it must be completely reorganized. And in order for it to be reorganized, the woman finds herself the instrument of destruction of an institution which all her class instinct and training impel her to preserve when she can see no immediate substitute.

This is the old society confronting the new, head-on. No one dares to claim openly that women are not entitled to play a full role in every sphere of society. Some do claim that women are destroying the family while there is no other family in view. But only the "higher standard of living" philosophers can fail to see that the irrepressible determination to negate the old is an inseparable part of the creation of the new. Woman cannot single-handedly create a new family. They are, however, paving the way for it. They are attacking, proving false, destroying all habits, psychological, social and political, which are the basis of the old family. They are solely responsible for the mistrust of the family which permeates all levels of society. But they have not dug the grave for the modern family in any conscious attempt to do so. They have done so because they have found it no longer tolerable. These are the new forces, passions, ideals which grow up within an old society, and finally, in combination with other new forces and needs, shatter the old shell to pieces.

And yet the need for the family is so apparent, the relations between men, women and children so deeply rooted in human feeling that, uncertain of the future, and in the face of the barrage of propaganda attacking women for not knowing what they want, working women at times falter in the struggle. But here, too, the faltering and hesitancy is, by the very nature of the conflict, temporary. Every advance creates the basis for a new family, a new society, and a clarification of women's role in it. Neglected as they are by liberal writers, abused by reactionary ones, working women are finding out who and what they are, and where they belong in relation to the whole world. They are so enmeshed in the fundamental relations and basic movement of society that their vision is shaped by the great concrete realities. These do not flatter but they do not deceive. Nowhere, not in divorce statistics or in progressive legislation favoring women, have their lives moved forward dynamically more than with the exit of women from their home for 8 or 9 hours a day to enter modern industry.

Women In Industry

The pull by women of the man into the home and away from a life which centers outside of it has been accompanied by the pull of women away from a life totally lived inside their homes. Women went to work during the war and they remained at work after. It has brought a great transformation in the minds, the relations and the actual status of women, and the conflict of women and modern society which takes the form of a conflict with men, has reached a new intensity, yet bringing at the same time greater confidence and wider perspectives.

It was during the war, when the government needed women in industry, that a campaign was opened in the public press and in magazines showing the natural abilities of women for industrial work. With the end of the government's need for women in industry, the campaign ended. The need now was for women to return to their homes, and a new campaign to that end began. As usual these campaigns, pro and con, were not concerned with people but with industry. This time, however, as so often in these transitional days, the campaigners had bitten off more than they could chew.

Women before had been told that they needed the protection of their homes, that they could not manage without it. In industry they managed their own affairs and their relations with men and other women. They became familiar with an aspect of life which their husbands had always clouded in secrecy and mystery — something which women could not understand and were better off not understanding in any case. The ignorance of women of the world outside could no longer be held as a weapon against them. Now they knew what their husbands were doing and a basis for understanding was opened up between them.

The reason women went out to work during the war was that their families would be broken up for the duration. They were putting some money aside for the new post-war life and keeping themselves busy during the long wait. But they stayed in industry and in offices because they had tasted too much independence to return ever again to the isolation and boredom of the home. A whole new world of social life and material things which could be gotten if a woman worked was opened to them. They could buy without financial crisis not only what was necessary, but, at times more important, what was not absolutely necessary. The second paycheck relieved the tension of the budget, and this tension had been just another of the women's jobs to cope with. The second paycheck made it easier to demand joint decisions in the house between husband and wife: "we" instead of "he." When it was the man's paycheck, it was the man's right to give orders and he was entitled to special consideration. The economic basis of the subordination of women is now cracked wide open, and the economic foundation for total equality is laid. Once this has happened, actual equality is merely a matter of time.*

Now that the woman was working, men found that they not only had to share the responsibility of the shopping and cleaning, but when they came home they had to take care of themselves. Some men couldn't take it. Women

---

* When this was written, there seemed no word other than "equality" to express what in the Postscript I call, after Marx, the "free association of individuals." This breaks with the bourgeois conception of equating one human being (and his or her labor) with another. It returns to the Marxist conception of freedom based on the uniqueness of each individual.

in plants will tell stories which amount to heroism of how they took on the jobs of working in and working out despite a continuous sabotage campaign on the part of their husbands to wear them down and demoralize them in order to get them back into the home for good.

With some men, it was not that they did not want their wives to have freedom. It was that they knew for each bit of freedom she gained, they would have to lose special consideration. But other men, with some prodding, began to understand that their wives were going to work and that they had to help to make it easier for them. After a few years of women working, when the country had settled down to the tendency having become a fact with big figures, men talked continuously about women working, one always taking the point of view that everything was better before women worked and others taking the point of view that housework does get tiring and boring. They knew, because since *their* wives had been working, they had done quite a bit of it, they began to understand and they were sympathetic, sometimes even proud of their wives. The task is not by any means easy, even for the woman who gets the cooperation of her husband. They cut corners and managed unmanageable schedules. Those people, however, who were surprised and expressed amazement at the skill, thought, resource that women showed to this new and difficult burden, were not only underestimating women. They were underestimating the human capacity to cope with any new situation and come triumphantly through it.

Women proved themselves in industry and jobs are permanently open to them. Except for the very highly organized industries where men and women work side by side, women are paid much less than men. But, characteristic of all modern workers, the fight in these plants, big and small, is not primarily for equal pay with men. It is for control of the production, so as, first, to ensure necessities which women feel it is their right to have: to go to the restroom more often, to refuse overtime work on the grounds that they have family duties, to lie down for an hour when they suffer from menstrual cramps. Though many women are totally dependent on their jobs for the support of their families, yet they continually try to establish that their families, not their jobs, come first. Companies have replied by taking women from the line and putting them in supervisory jobs, not top management, but just one step above the rest of the women. These women are the working class counterparts of the exceptional women of the middle-class. Women have embarrassed foremen in plants to the point where they could not come out of their offices. They cannot do the same with foreladies.

But with their entry into industry and their segregation in certain industries, the problem of the modern family has been taken right into the plant.

There is no doubt that women are in industry to stay. They are part of what the statistics call the labor force. What can statistics tell of these vast social changes where new patterns of family life are being work out? New women are constantly coming into industry and women who have not worked for some time are cóming back to it, while others are dropping away for a while. Statistics cannot report that the very number of women who work gives new encouragement to those who do not. Statistics cannot deal with the new social status which has come of age in the U.S., the status of the housewife who works. She does not work all the time, and remains basically a housewife. But for a few months out of every year, or a year out of every two or three, this housewife goes to work. The very fact that she can go out to work is sometimes enough to keep her going in the periods of isolation at home. And even for the woman who has never worked, there is the possibility that if relations in the home become unbearable she will join the "labor force" and realize herself in a new social milieu.

That women can go out to work, and that for some periods in their lives so many women have worked, has created in women a new awareness of themselves, and expanded their own conceptions of their capacities. Whence arise new problems of a totally unexpected kind. Women have become boldly aggressive and personal force has been added to their almost instinctive knowledge of how to deal with personal relations, the job for which they have been trained for centuries. Men, however, have been trained to be masters to docile women. In the face of this new aggressiveness and confidence on the part of women, neither men nor women know how to act to each other. Masculinity has in the past been identified with domination, femininity with subordination. These categories are no longer valid. Men, particularly young men, who have been trained to exercise domination, but have had little opportunity to do so, find themselves lost in their relations with these new women. They know no other expression for their masculinity other than domination, and they can no longer dominate. Their role is as much in question as is women's.

Women, with this combination of old instinct and new strength, having destroyed the position of men in relation to them, find around them men who are defeated. They go from the extreme of the complete defeat of the man they live with to that of once more trying to make him feel that he is "ruling the roost," in order to give him back some of his old self-confidence. In fact, many women today say there are no real men around. They do not want men who will dominate them, but men who will have strength without domination, who will not collapse in the face of the new strength of women, but who will *not* try to tell them what to do.

Chaos? Only on the surface. Now that so many women are able to hold their own in every sphere of life, fundamental questions have been raised that only a normal society can answer, namely, what exactly is masculine and what is feminine. But that masculinity means domination and femininity subordination, that conception has been shattered.

There are losses. Even those women who do not work and may never work have given up a women's trade, housewifery, as it was once known — a skill which took a lifetime to learn and which came easily to women. Women still have the knack in the kitchens, but they use the bakeries, the laundries, they buy food in cans and cook the easy way. The can-opener cooks will always tell you how it is cheaper to buy cakes than to make them, how it is cheaper to buy clothes than make them, and then they will add, "it's cheaper, it's faster, but it's a shame, isn't it?" They are referring to the fact that nothing bought is as good as something homemade, and they are also referring to the fact that they are sorry the housewife's motives and her pleasure of doing by hand and creating and using skills has virtually disappeared from the home. They are on the one hand, regretfully given up, but on the other cast willingly aside. And until a new family is created where the incentive for these skills will once again arise in both sexes, they will remain buried, with regret, but buried deep nevertheless.

The Institution of Divorce

What people expect from marriage has radically changed, particularly for women, but for men as well. The high percentage of divorce in the United States is proof enough that this is true. What women accepted as a burden they had to bear, they now reject as burdens they refuse to bear.

Today a women who leaves her husband puts her children in a nursery or with her parents, finds a job, finds an apartment and may in time find another man. She makes a new life for herself because she is not afraid of the world. Though her leaving is not encouraged, the attitude she most generally meets is: if two people can't get along, it is best that they break up rather than ruin two lives and the lives of the children as well. She is encouraged to "try again," but it is useless to ask her to "make the best of it." Society is not on her side, but it is no longer against her. Divorce is now as established an institution as marriage.* But the very fact that it is accompanied with hostility, bitterness and even violence is testimony to the shock of the breakup of the family, insufficient and stifling as it is, to human beings. It is always accompanied by a sense of guilt and personal failure on the part of the woman who has been taught to believe that the success or failure of a marriage is *her* responsibility.

Divorce itself is still expensive, but that expense can be managed. Even more expensive for the working class is maintaining support for two households, when it is hard enough to support one. This very harsh economic reality keeps many marriages together that would otherwise be instantly dissolved.

Many of these divorced women establish relations outside of marriage which come closest to what they believe marriage should be like. There is often both mutual respect and independence between themselves and their male friends. Money, like the home, is not usually shared between them, but gaps in either's paycheck are made up for by the other person. Traditional sexual morality is ignored.

Yet it is obvious that these relations are no solution to creating a new kind of family. After some years, both the men and women get tired of this half-nomad life and either marry or break it up, destroying the particular values of this kind of relationship either way.

We will not here go into the crisis in sexual relations which is such common knowledge in the United States. There, as everywhere else, the balance of forces is either delicately maintained or violently disrupted. For the woman of the working class, whose husband does not have the time or energy to talk to her across the dinner table, and whose nerves are at the breaking point after a day of monotonous work and two, three or four children, sexual relations can be sometimes the last straw in a series of unpleasant and bitter and frustrating straws. The sexual question is, of course, a far more complicated matter, as all human matters are, than we have stated here, but here is where it begins.

In accordance with the modern tendency to bureaucracy, the social workers and the experts are there always with free advice for the individual case, if the case is properly numbered in their files and if you are willing to wait your turn. No matter what the variations of their machine-made solutions are, they are variations on the same theme. They invariably tell a woman to

---

* We accept this so easily today that it is hard to believe how new it is. During the lifetime of women who are middle-aged today divorce, particularly in the working class, required great boldness and revolutionary determination and daring. Women would tell their crying daughters and sisters, yes, he beats you, but you can't leave him. Don't think of yourself, think of the children. It is not that the children would be fatherless but that they might be starving, even if they and their mothers were not ostracized.

go home, re-examine herself and find out what she can do to patch things up, to ask herself what it is in her personality which is creating family conflicts and what hobby she should take up to distract her all-too distracted mind.

Perhaps the decisive groups of women in the coming years will be the young people who are at every point tempted into marriage by the gauze of a white wedding-gown and the dream-like enchantments of being a bride as pictured in the magazines. The young people read and admire but are not fooled. They are surrounded by older women talking cynically or unhappily about married life. They have seen the examples of their mothers who so often are either worn old-fashioned women or rebellious, sometimes divorced new-fashioned ones. These young women have both the advantage and the disadvantage of never having seen the order and stability of marriage 25 years ago. They want a home, they want children, but they do not want for themselves any of the relationships they see around them. They are self-supporting. They are self-sustaining. They like men and are freer with them than any women ever before in history. But they hesitate about getting married. They do not become cynical about marriage after they have been married. They enter marriage with this cynicism. For those who wish to maintain society as it is today, these young women are lost causes. Most of them finally accept marriage because that is the only way they see to have children. But they are not prepared to reconcile themselves to any indignities.

These, then, are our conclusions:

The general demands for new family relations are sufficiently clear to destroy any illusion that the old society can satisfy them.

It cannot satisfy the new requirements because the new family cannot possibly be established except on the basis of the creation of entirely new relations in production itself, and a new unity between being a producer, man, woman, child, and being a member of a family. Working class women in their millions know that the man will never be fit for the profoundly serious responsibilities of modern family life until he has in his place of work such human relations as satisfy and develop his needs as a modern human being.

The present society cannot satisfy the new requirements because production is organized for the sake of production and not for human needs. A primary aim of a production organized by workers themselves will be to recognize the joint responsibility of men and women for the family and the household, and to organize itself accordingly. These two spheres can no longer be separate. Women today in the home are fighting a battle which is essentially a battle against the existing mode of production which is responsible for this separation, and the battle will gain in intensity until that mode of production is destroyed and replaced. Now, with their experience in the plant they are ideally fitted to carry out their share of that great constructive task.

The "higher standard of living" economists see society as improving (if it can improve) by means of greater increases in consumption. But the great masses of the people, taught by experience, are learning that a rational society begins in the process of production itself and they all share the confidence that once the relations of production are made human, and with them family relations, then the problems of consumption will be a joy and an adventure, rather than, as they are today, a palliative and a drug.

This change must inevitably draw with it an altered place for the children, both in the home and in production. If the man and woman share equally in the responsibilities and privileges of production relations, and of family relations, it will inevitably follow that the lives of the children will be shaped accordingly and there will arise for the first time the possibility of correcting one of the most dangerous abuses of modern civilization — the indescribable confusion as to aims, purposes, and methods which masquerades under the title of "modern education."

We stated it earlier, abstractly, but now we are able to repeat it concretely. No schools, no state control or intervention can substitute for the education of children by their parents. There is no reason why kindergartens and even elementary education cannot be carried on co-operatively within the community by both men and women, and there is every reason for it. For the first time children will begin to get a balanced view of the sexes and an end will be put to the one-sided femininity which they must now endure for all of their early years. This is not only for the education of the children, but for the education of the parents, particularly the father who for the first time for generations will begin to know and understand his children. Strong biological ties will not be in conflict with social relationships, but strengthened by them, and the personality of the younger generation will be liberated to fit the needs of modern social relations. It is then for the first time in many years that the family, whatever forms it takes, will fulfil its role in society, that of the educator, the preparer of the younger generation and the perpetuator of the standards, morals, attitudes and behavior of a society, but a new society. The physical structure of social life, the building pattern of the factory, the building patterns of the home, their distance from each other, transportation, times of work and shifts, merely to list them is to see how brutal, how inhuman, and how totally destructive to the modern personality and therefore to production itself, are the present arrangements under which people are forced to constrict and mutilate themselves to fit into a mode of life which places rock-like obstacles in the way to realization of themselves as creative producers and as builders of a family life.

What we are moving towards is a *community* of labor in the factory, a *community* of labor in the home, a community established between both, and children growing up in that community. But the total reorganization of the lives of millions can come from no social worker's blueprint. It is there in embryo already, all around us, being worked out every day.

There is not the slightest element of Utopianism in this. It is what millions of American working women want, the result of the continuing experiences of their daily lives. The Utopianism rather lies with those who believe that somehow or other the present system can continue, or with the Socialists, Communists and others who, recognizing that the old-fashioned family is obsolete, propose to abolish the family altogether and organize personal relations under that treacherous trap known as "planned economy." In reality it is this movement towards the integration of production relations and family relations on a new basis, and not any bureaucratic plan, which alone can bring into being that mastery of all social conditions which will rescue modern society.

What Can We Do?

And here it is legitimate to ask: what can those of us who are not workers do? There is one thing that all of us can do, and that is to think correctly about these problems. For serious and rewarding thinking, the first requirement is to see what the great millions are aiming at in their day to day living, to see the future already existent in the turbulent present. The second requirement is to recognize that this is coming, and can only come, from below. The third, and this is the function of all worker ideologists and politicians who see clearly what the people are doing, is to record what is happening and rid themselves of the mental limitations which the existing society has placed upon such conceptions as production, the family, the community, to help the people by clearing away the accumulated intellectual rubbish of centuries. We shall give here one or two examples. Together they will indicate the possible outlines of the society of tomorrow.

People write reams about the "modern" family. In truth, the typical modern family is no family at all. The implication of all those who defend the existing society is that modern people *want* to live this way because they are modern. Neither they nor anyone else knows any such thing.

In practically all previous societies, the family consisted of grandparents, uncles and aunts, parents and children. The extended family unit meant, despite the subjugation of the woman, a certain freedom for her. It gave her a community. There were aunts and cousins to look after the children and help to raise them. There were two or three generations of women to help in the house, and all household functions, though more physically taxing, without the use of washing machines and electric stoves, were communal affairs. Today a woman is isolated and alone in her little kitchen or kitchenette, using her vacuum cleaner or washing machine, if she can afford one, in a silence and loneliness which is only broken by the noise of the machine itself, the ringing of the telephone, salesmen at the door, or the day-time soap operas.

The family unit has decreased in number, among other reasons because people's confidence in society has decreased. They do not want to add to their already overburdened lives the responsibility of too many children.

Many families today are crowded into two and three room apartments where the children sleep in the bedroom and the parents in a bed that is the living room couch by day. There is no privacy. There is no closet space. There is only a two burner stove on which to cook. There is no place for the children to play where they will not be a constant annoyance to their mother. There is no place to entertain without disturbing the children after eight o'clock and the neighbours after ten. These are not slums and yet there is no room for anything but the bare necessities of life, the people and the walls, decorated with the not-too-expensive ivy plants from Woolworth's and other replaceable and inexpensive items. Everything is movable. These houses give no sign of past living and less sign that they will last into the future. In five years, they look old and worn.

They are furnished on the installment plan with a "compact" living room set, the "compact" bedroom suite, the "compact" dining room table. Modern, streamlined, useless after three years wear, but "compact," the absolute antithesis of comfort, ease, space, expansive living. And it fits the house, which fits the family, which fits the needs of modern, cramped, "compact" living. To us it seems unbelievable that people *want* to live in this way. But they assume that there is no alternative. At every single moment on every issue we must undermine this assumption.

In time we shall learn to look with astonishment at the impertinence of the common view that a woman having to bear and rear a child, or three or four children, lessens her opportunities in her competition for equality with men in the affairs of the outside world. What kind of work does any man do (and what is the sense of this competitiveness) in comparison with the bearing of children? The whole conception is a monstrous stupidity which still moves around, first because it has been around for so many generations, and, secondly, because it can serve the purpose of those reactionary elements who wish to maintain things as they are. It is not impossible that the large family, not only in the sense of the actual children in the household, but a family based on numerous relations, may so enlarge the family until it is expanded to a new social, educational and productive unit, the special contribution of modern technology to the long and changing history of the family in the development of society. At one stroke, individually and collectively, such family units could rid society of the monstrous bureaucratic growths which now strangle society.

All this is mere dreaming (or dangerously subversive doctrines) to the bleaters of a "higher standard of living." They have no conception that it is *their* organization of society which has forced millions of people into the contemporary mold. The list of their crimes is long, but not yet complete. Only the freedom which is being fought for will tell us whether these burdens and limitations which modern people have borne were not in direct contradiction not merely to the social, but the very biological needs of human beings.

Postscript

When the preceding was written in 1956, there was no Women's Liberation Movement. Those of us who belonged to the small Marxist organization from which this essay and other earlier work on this question emerged, worked on the assumption that the way things actually are can be seen and understood only on the basis of where they have come from and where they are going. Through study and analysis, we concluded that the U.S. was moving inevitably to great social upheaval. At that time this was a somewhat unique view of the United States, then still in the aftermath of McCarthyism. Particularly unique was the view that women were an integral part of that movement to revolutionary social change. With these as our premises,

1. we tried to analyze how women are exploited and degraded and how their condition impels them into activity on their own behalf.
2. we tried to describe the ways women rebelled which were invisible (as women were invisible), the effect of their action on their view of themselves and how they undermined the premises of their rulers, at that time the most successful ruling class in the world. We did not begin with their "level of consciousness" but with their activity. And since women were on the whole isolated in the home, this activity was seldom formally organized and had never been identified as political or revolutionary.
3. we tried to put forward, however tentatively, the perspective of a totally

new society and a new relationship between the sexes and generations. This appeared even then to emerge inevitably from the rejection by women of the institutions and relations in which they were imprisoned. We did not put forward a program, transitional or otherwise.

Fourteen years later, the inevitability of great social upheaval in the United States is not in question, though the outcome seems uncertain. But the blindness on the Left then to the revolutionary potential of the millions of exploited in the United States remains to stunt the living movement today. In England we hear that Women's Liberation is "not politics." In the States, from what one can gather at this distance, women are always faced with the decision: whether to support actions by the Left which thinks of you as less than human (and does not even know it thinks this), or to refuse to join with it in fighting the Establishment.

The collapse of a serious revolutionary perspective on the Left also means that the tasks which were once performed by organizations calling themselves Marxist now must be undertaken by the Women's Movement itself. It must provide its own theoretical foundations, again, as long ago, directly linked to the needs of people in the struggle. After the first wave of discovery, when a movement begins, it sits back for a moment (though it does not stop *acting*) and wants to know how it relates in some total and cohesive way to everything else that is happening and has ever happened in the whole world. On both sides of the Atlantic, in varying degrees, this is where we seem to have reached.

The question of what kind of society we are in painful process of building is crucial for dealing with all theoretical matters. The essay itself was unclear on the question of what is to replace the family as we know it under capitalism. We have to make this analysis now, and if we dig into the past of the revolutionary movement of which we are a vital part, we can, I believe, find help. The job is made easier because we have a movement that whittles away incessantly at the assumptions of our society which limit us all, so that we take less and less of what is socially given as natural and immutable. The way the movement came together, what it rejected to establish itself, indicates also the seed of the new society restless in the womb of the old.

It was white-middle class women who formed the Movement. Working class women, black and white, did not. If those from the Left who believe this fact alone is enough to condemn the Movement were really interested in workers, they would ask why. Unless of course they believe that working class women love the special degradations which they daily undergo.

The working class woman lives within a dilemma. The family can only exist if she denies her independent existence. Yet, when she undermines her family, she undercuts her own struggle for survival as a member of that class. The obvious parallel is the worker in relation to his or her trade union. Without the union, you are at the mercy of capital; with it, you are betrayed in every attempt to get capital once and for all off your back. Your struggle as a woman, therefore, distinct though it is from the general struggle of your class, nevertheless in your own interest, remains integral to that struggle. So, the tendency is to become independently active in struggles in which the class interest is at stake, if possible bringing the family along. Black workers are continually in the dilemma of having to support white racist workers against management. Working class women are faced with this *kind* of decision all the time: when you go on strike for equal pay the men stay inside; when the men come out for their demands, should you support them? And women too are called backward if they insist the union does not represent them and do not attend union meetings.

The middle-class family also consolidates a class interest, but it is the interest of the ruling class. Middle-class women traditionally shared the assumptions of this class with their men. That is, you have to keep the system going. The middle-class which performs ruling functions — doctors, lawyers, architects, sociologists, psychologists, psychiatrists, educators, petty officers in the industrial hierarchy — is paid well and seemed wedded to a successful and all-powerful ruling class. Middle-class women are either at the lowest rung in the hierarchy or, more often, merely adjuncts to the men who rule. The assumptions of the social need for their rule and of its permanence have been shattering everywhere around them. Movement people risking their lives in the streets make it impossible for those who perform ruling functions to hide from themselves any longer whose ideology they actually propagate and whose interests they actually defend. Young women, liberating themselves from the assumptions of their class, discovered how they, oppressed themselves, were used to oppress others.

Many women came to the revolutionary movement only to find there the elitism of the class they were leaving behind. In a world where mass movements put on the order of the day, every day, a total reorganization of political thinking, they refused to bear the consequences for them as women of the elitism of the Left. A separate movement had to be created, and it was.

The strength of a middle-class movement is that it identifies and actively confronts the degradations from which women suffer in common, irrespective of class. What all men and women think of themselves and each other is thereby changed. Even those who are hostile cannot resist its influence.

But the barriers of class remain, especially in England, where class divisions are the framework of all political thinking and where people identify each other immediately by class. A working woman from the audience in a British television program dismissed (though she did not condemn) the idea of fighting against sex discrimination in the professions. Working class women would never be professionals anyway, she said. Her problem was that her husband's pay packet was so small that she had to work, and she saw her family disintegrating because she wasn't at home. (This question dates from the Industrial Revolution when women in some areas of England constituted the work force and the family disintegrated, "liberating" only the infants, who died, often from neglect, of wage slavery.)

So though a section of the Movement may concern itself with the right to join the Establishment on equal terms with men, these can easily become the new "exceptional women" selling out for power at the expense of other women. Working class women can never have such an orientation, and this is a major strength in the struggle. Even if they do not join the Women's Liberation Movement, the Movement must join them.

The question is how. A working class woman will listen only if she is convinced the speaker is no longer the class enemy. (And those who perform ruling functions *are* the class enemy, a fact which being in the Movement does not change.) It will take longer in England for middle-class women from the Movement to become telephonists and factory workers, as is already happening in the States, to demonstrate solidarity by putting a middle-class life where theirs is, to learn what class means from the other side. It is absurd to expect or even suggest that the whole Movement should go into factories. Some women, nevertheless, feel that this is the logic of Women's Liberation which they betray unless they break with all inherited or acquired privileges.

There are other ways of making contact, most especially with the most degraded section of the working class, the housewife. But first we have to stop judging women by whether they are organized in the traditional sense. In England some women's groups are already leafleting council estates (public housing), but they are breaking up beauty contests too. Both kinds of action *together* ensure that when working class women participate *(as they always have)* in the struggles of their own class, their authority this time is assured. For too long they have been auxiliary. But they are more likely to come into the struggle as they are doing already, as active and independent members of movements, which represent their class or special national group interest, than to join a specifically women's movement. In England the West Indian community has already begun to attract and to develop, militant and talented women to the struggle against racism. They are Women's Liberation personified, although they may be scornful of the Women's Liberation Movement. The tenants' movement among English workers has attracted similar types of English women. One or two rise to prominence, the rest do the work that is needed and still keep their mouths shut. The Movement must create the climate for the inevitable move against male chauvinism.

And what will we put in place of the family that our Movement and this new level of participation inevitably destroys? We are asked for blueprints; we have none. (As a matter of fact the blueprints we are made to live by are killing us.) But we cannot live without a perspective even if it remains somewhat abstract. We have to begin with what we are rejecting.

We are all institutionalized. The roles, that is, the division of labor on which the family is based, the woman, the home, the man, the world, permeate our relations in every area of life, whether or not we are in a family relation or even doing characteristically women's work. Until the roles themselves are destroyed, we can never escape the domination of men. This means that in any relation between men and women, women must compromise their humanity or destroy the possibility of a functioning relationship. To discover this is devastating. Once you become aware of yourself, self-conscious, and glimpse your own possibilities, you confront men or utterly reject them; the alternative is to consciously deny whom you have discovered yourself to be.

Some women have already made it clear that they cannot compromise and must repudiate relationships with men. They have come to the conclusion that men and women will never make it together. This view of incompatibility is not unique to women; many blacks believe that racism is a permanent feature of life on this planet. It is a recognition of the depths of the schism, and a recognition also of self: the kind of people they will live with we can no longer be, and the kind of people we will live with they can never become. At least, they say, not for centuries.

There is nothing new in women being far beyond men in their perception of the opposite sex. The slave after all is always superior to the master: he or she must know the master to survive; while the master must remain ignorant of the slave's human capacity to justify his rule. (What nonsense that the exploited must achieve "equality" with those who are corrupted by being rulers.) What is new is that women no longer study men only in order to more easily endure. They study themselves and the totality of their relations in the society in order to move beyond endurance. By a most painfull process women are at last forced to face their real conditions of life and their relations with their kind, a terrifying and liberating confrontation.

This is the end of bourgeois society and of the bourgeois family with it. It is in this society and this family that the tendencies to division between men and women over centuries have reached their absolute. The biological relations and the social functions of the sexes are, under capitalism, totally alienated from each other. That is why our society is so dominated by a sexuality removed from every other aspect of social being. So that a woman sleeps with a man and is more intimate with the woman she works next to; and a man may sleep with many women and be intimate with no one.†

It is precisely at the moment when the alienation of the sexes is most acute that, on the basis of modern technology and the expansion of the modern individual personality, for the first time in history new relations between men, women and the generations are possible. The movement for the liberation of women can only be seen as the conflict between this expanding personality in mortal combat with the social institutions and production relations these personalities inherit. Women's Liberation, according to some, "isn't politics." If this isn't politics, then what is politics? Voting?

Millions of women are finding it more intolerable every day to live this antagonism. Men are bewildered and devastated, especially those who discover they do not know the women they married. Marx, over 100 years ago, gave in abstract terms what the relation of women to men must inevitably become if we are, both men and women, ever to be free. After referring to women as "the spoil and handmaid of communal lust" [our phrase is "sex objects"], he goes on to say: "The direct, natural, and necessary relation of person to person is the *relation of man to woman* . . . it therefore reveals the extent to which man's *natural* behavior has become *human*, or the extent to which the *human* essence in him [or her] has become a *natural* essence — the extent to which his *human nature* has come to be *nature to him*. In this relationship is revealed, too, the extent to which man's *need* has become a *human* need; the extent to which, therefore, the *other* person as a person has become for him a need — the extent to which he in his individual existence is at the same time a social being." We must release the basic biological relation, debased in the social relations and institutions which sustained class society, from these strangleholds.

Women have for centuries been economically socially, politically, even

---

† Those who would like to accuse the Movement of intrinsic lesbianism are obviously ignorant of the fact that when men and women who sleep together look to their own sex for the satisfaction of their social needs, as is common in our society, then heterosexuality is undermined.

physically dependent on men. The trouble was that the dependence was not mutual. More accurately, woman's dependence on man made her less than human, degrading her in the act of giving; while man's inability to be interdependent robbed him also of his humanity. What the sexes depended on each other for was determined not by individual or biological need but by apparently natural and unalterable divisions in economic and social function. Capitalist society may provide communal kitchens (for those who are not starving) or family hotels (for those who are not homeless); we will be more efficiently exploited if they do. It takes more than a mechanical reorganization of society to fundamentally alter degraded human relations, especially the most profound relation of human being to human being. To alter that, we must ourselves have created a society of individuals who freely associate themselves, men, women and children, and through that association consciously reconstruct society.

Will that association be a family? It can only be so different from what humanity has known before that we may find a new name for it. The very fact that a socialist society demands that we *consciously* create the relations we participate in demolishes our whole concept of institutions: received habits and practices which freeze humanity in molds suitable only to rigid and fragmenting economic structures.

Women in the Movement have found that, in the course of confronting male chauvinism, they uncover ever deeper layers of oppression. What we all are experiencing here is *the liberating process,* and the energy increasingly released makes the Movement bolder, drives it forward and broadens its scope. Men, as the instruments of an oppressive structure, submit us physically and psychologically to their will. We act as they direct us to act. When we do not understand what is happening, and even when we do, it drives us crazy. Liberation reverses this: we act on our own direction in a chosen unity with others, and we find out who are *not* and, by degrees, who we *are.* Our dilemma is that the relationships women are already capable of just cannot happen under capitalism. It is the most frustrating and painful part of the liberation struggle. Now and then you have a victory and seem to penetrate into the consciousness of the man what garbage in his head prevents him from seeing you and breaking out of his emotional self-involvement. But by the time he has caught up with that, you have moved miles ahead again, and the battle is renewed, in fact has never stopped. For what is happening is that in the painful process of destroying what has defined us, restrained us, and debased our most intimate needs, *we are transforming ourselves into self-acting individuals* who are capable of full participation in the contruction of a free society.

That some women can conceive of a socialist world which would be just a continuation of this grinding battle speaks by itself for the perverted concept of socialism which we inherit and which falls to us in Women's Liberation in particular to revise. The "reorganization of the economy" does not equal socialism, as if only a rearrangement of existing material furniture, what you do with *things*, will change the world. It is not only the division of labor between men and women which must be destroyed but the nature of that labor itself. Freedom for women can only be based on creative labor which gives full scope to their "natural and acquired powers." Thus the struggle to release ourselves from a dominating male society is inseparable from the struggle against the domination of machines and the whole productive process over men and women. Women cannot be free without a revolution by the working class in production, but the working class will not be free until women are, not only because women are part of that class but because workers, men and women, are more than units of production. The concept of freedom and the reintegrated human personality which the Women's Movement sharply poses has already gone beyond narrow and sterile formulations. It is the tip of the iceberg. Ultimately, socialism is dependent not on those who define it in words, but on those who in their millions cannot any longer live without it.

Meanwhile, since it is a middle-class movement let us take advantage of it by doing the work for which working class women are deprived of training.

Women's Liberation needs:

— to explore the economic, social and political basis for the exploitation of women as women and as members of different classes.

— to uncover the stage of the rebellion of the mass of women, particularly working class housewives, whose lives and struggles have rarely found their reflection in revolutionary thought.

— to write the history of that rebellion on an international scale *so that any woman can understand* and claim her own revolutionary past.†

— to destroy sociology as the ideology of the social services which bases itself on the proposition that this society is "the norm;" if you are a person in rebellion, you are a deviant.

— to destroy psychology and psychiatry which spend their time convincing us that our "problems" are personal hang-ups and that we must adjust to a lunatic world. These so-called "disciplines" and "sciences" will increasingly

† Women of the Third World have not yet spoken of the effect of colonial rule and industrialization on them and on the traditional family. When they do, the horrors we now associate with capitalism and imperialism will gain new dimensions. We need a woman's history of imperialism, and of division of labor between the industrial and agricultural world. This is bound to come.

incorporate our demands in order more efficiently to redirect our forces into safe channels under their stewardship. Unless we deal with them, they will deal with us.

— to discredit once and for all social workers, progressive educators, marriage guidance counsellors, and the whole army of experts whose function is to keep men, women and children functioning within the social framework, each by their special brand of social frontal lobotomy.

The garbage is piled very high. But women have been cleaning up for centuries.

The Political Economy
of Women's Liberation
Margaret Benston

Margaret Benston is a member of the
Chemistry Department faculty at Simon
Fraser University.

*The position of women rests, as everything
in our complex society, on an economic base.*
—*Eleanor Marx and
Edward Aveling*

The "woman question" is generally ignored in analyses of the class structure
of society. This is so because classes are generally defined by their relation
to the means of production, and women are not supposed to have any unique
relation to the means of production. The category seems instead to cut across
all classes; one speaks of working-class women, middle-class women, etc.
The status of women is clearly inferior to that of men,[1] but analysis of this
condition usually falls into discussing socialization, psychology, interper-
sonal relations, or the role of marriage as a social institution.[2] In arguing that
the roots of the secondary status of women are in fact economic, it can be
shown that women as a group do indeed have a definite relation to the
means of production and that this is different from that of men. The personal
and psychological factors then follow from this special relation to production, and a change in the latter will be a necessary (but not sufficient) condition for changing the former.[3] If this special relation of women to production is accepted, the analysis of the situation of women fits naturally into a
class analysis of society.

[1] Marlene Dixon, "Secondary Social Status of Women." An unpublished manuscript, University of Chicago, 1968.
[2] The biological argument is, of course, the first one used, but it is not usually
taken seriously by socialist writers. Margaret Mead's *Sex and Temperament* is an
early statement of the importance of culture instead of biology.
[3] This applies to the group or category as a whole. Women as individuals can and
do free themselves from their socialization to a great degree (and they can even
come to terms with the economic situation in favorable cases), but the majority of
women have no chance to do so.

The starting point for discussion of classes in a capitalist society is the distinction between those who own the means of production and those who sell their labor power for a wage. As Ernest Mandel says:

> "The proletarian condition is, in a nutshell, the lack of access to the means of production or means of subsistence which, in a society of generalized commodity production, forces the proletarian to sell his labor power. In exchange for this labor power he receives a wage which then enables him to acquire the means of consumption necessary for satisfying his own needs and those of his family.
>
> This is the structural definition of wage earner, the proletarian. From it necessarily flows a certain relationship to his work, to the products of his work, and to his overall situation in society, which can be summarized by the catchword "alienation." But there does not follow from this structural definition any necessary conclusions as to the level of his consumption . . . the extent of his needs, or the degree to which he can satisfy them."[4]

We lack a corresponding structural definition of women. What is needed first is not a complete examination of the symptoms of the secondary status of women, but instead a statement of the material conditions in capitalist (and other) societies which define the group "women." Upon these conditions are built the specific superstructures which we know. An interesting passage from Mandel points the way to such a definition:

> "The commodity . . . is a product created to be exchanged on the market, as opposed to one which has been made for direct consumption. *Every commodity must have both a use-value and an exchange-value.*
>
> It must have a use-value or else nobody would buy it. . . . A commodity without a use-value to anyone would consequently be unsalable, would constitute useless production, would have no exchange-value precisely because it had no use-value.
>
> On the other hand, every product which has use-value does not necessarily have exchange-value. It has an exchange-value only to the extent that the society itself, in which the commodity is produced, is founded on exchange, is a society where exchange is a common practice. . . .
>
> In capitalist society, commodity production, the production of exchange-values, has reached its greatest development. It is the first society in

---

[4] Ernest Mandel, "Workers Under Neocapitalism," paper delivered at Simon Fraser University. (Available through the Department of Political Science, Sociology and Anthropology, Simon Fraser University, Burnaby, B.C., Canada.)

human history where the major part of production consist of commodities. It is not true, however, that all production under capitalism is commodity production. Two classes of products still remain simple use-value.

The first group consist of all things produced by the peasantry for its own consumption, everything directly consumed on the farms where it is produced. . . .

The second group of products in capitalist society which are not commodities but remain simple use-value consists of all things produced in the home. Despite the fact that considerable human labor goes into this type of household production, it still remains a production of use-values and not of commodities. Every time a soup is made or a button sewn on a garment, it constitutes production, but it is not production for the market.

The appearance of commodity production and its subsequent regularization and generalization have radicaly transformed the way men labor and how they organize society."[5]

What Mandel may not have noticed is that his last paragraph is precisely correct. The appearance of commodity production has indeed transformed the way that *men* labor. As he points out, most household labor in capitalist society (and in the existing socialist societies, for that matter) remains in the pre-market stage. This is the work which is reserved for women and it is in this fact that we can find the basis for a definition of women.

In sheer quantity, household labor, including child care, constitutes a huge amount of socially necessary production. Nevertheless, in a society based on commodity production, it is not usually considered "real work" since it is outside of trade and the market place. It is pre-capitalist in a very real sense. This assignment of household work as the function of a special category "women" means that this group *does* stand in a different relation to production than the group "men." We will tentatively define women, then, as that group of people which is responsible for the production of simple use-values in those activities associated with the home and family.

Since men carry no responsibility for such production, the difference between the two groups lies here. Notice that women are not excluded from commodity production. Their participation in wage labor occurs but, as a group, they have no structural responsibility in this area and such participation is ordinarily regarded as transient. Men, on the other hand, are responsible for commodity production; they are not, in principle, given any

[5] Ernest Mandel, *An Introduction ot Marxist Economic Theory* (New York: Merit Publishers, 1967), pp. 10-11.

role in household labor. For example, when they do participate in household production, it is regarded as more than simply exceptional; it is demoralizing, emasculating, even harmful to health. (A story on the front page of the *Vancouver Sun* in January 1969 reported that men in Britain were having their health endangered because they had to do too much housework!)

The material basis for the inferior status of women is to be found in just this definition of women. In a society in which money determines value, women are a group which works outside the money economy. Their work is not worth money, is therefore valueless, is therefore not even real work. And women themselves, who do this valueless work, can hardly be expected to be worth as much as men, who work for money. In structural terms, the closest thing to the condition of women is the condition of others who are or were also outside of commodity production, i.e., serfs and peasants.

In her recent paper on women, Juliet Mitchell introduces the subject as follows: "In advanced industrial society, women's work is only marginal to the total economy. Yet it is through work that man changes natural conditions and thereby produces society. Until there is a revolution in production, the labor situation will prescribe women's situation within the world of men."[6] The statement of the marginality of women's work is an unanalyzed recognition that the work women do is *different* from the work that men do. Such work is not marginal, however; it is just not wage labor and so it is not counted. She even says later in the same article, "Domestic labor, even today, is enormous if quantified in terms of productive labor." She gives some figures to illustrate: In Sweden, 2,340 million hours a year are spent by women in housework compared with 1,290 million hours spent by women in industry. And the Chase Manhattan Bank estimates a woman's overall work week at 99.6 hours.

However, Mitchell gives little emphasis to the basic economic factors (in fact she condemns most Marxists for being "overly economist") and moves on hastily to superstructural factors, because she notices that "the advent of industrialization has not so far freed women." What she fails to see is that no society has thus far industrialized housework. Engels points out that the "first premise for the emancipation of women is the reintroduction of the entire female sex into public industry. . . . And this has become possible not only as a result of modern large-scale industry, which not only permits the participation of women in production in large numbers, but actually calls for it and, moreover, strives to convert private domestic work also into a

---

[6] Juliet Mitchell, "Women: The Longest Revolution," *New Left Review*, December 1966.

public industry."[7] And later in the same passage: "Here we see already that the emancipation of women and their equality with men are impossible and must remain so as long as women are excluded from socially productive work and restricted to housework, which is private." What Mitchell has not taken into account is that the problem is not simply one of getting women into *existing* industrial production but the more complex one of converting private production of household work into public production.

For most North Americans, domestic work as "public production" brings immediate images of Brave New World or of a vast institution — a cross between a home for orphans and an army barracks — where we would all be forced to live. For this reason, it is probably just as well to outline here, schematically and simplistically, the nature of industrialization.

A pre-industrial production unit is one in which production is small-scale and reduplicative; i.e., there are a great number of little units, each complete and just like all the others. Ordinarily such production units are in some way kin-based and they are multi-purpose, fulfilling religious, recreational, educational, and sexual functions along with the economic function. In such a situation, desirable attributes of an individual, those which give prestige, are judged by more than purely economic criteria: for example, among approved character traits is proper behavior to kin or readiness to fulfill obligations.

Such production is originally not for exchange. But if exchange of commodities becomes important enough, then increased efficiency of production becomes necessary. Such efficiency is provided by the transition to industrialized production which involves the elimination of the kin-based production unit. A large-scale, non-reduplicative production unit is substituted which has only one function, the economic one, and where prestige or status is attained by economic skills. Production is rationalized, made vastly more efficient, and becomes more and more public — part of an integrated social network. An enormous expansion of man's productive potential takes place. Under capitalism such social productive forces are utilized almost exclusively for private profit. These can be thought of as *capitalized* forms of production.

If we apply the above to housework and child rearing, it is evident that

---

[7] Frederick Engels, *Origin of the Family, Private Property and the State* (Moscow: Progress Publishers, 1968), Chapter IX, p. 158. The anthropological evidence known to Engels indicated primitive woman's dominance over man. Modern anthropology disputes this dominance but provides evidence for a more nearly equal position of woman in the matrilineal societies used by Engels as examples. The arguments in this work of Engels do not require the former dominance of women but merely the former equality, and so the conclusions remain unchanged.

each family, each household, constitutes an individual production unit, a pre-industrial entity, in the same way that peasant farmers or cottage weavers constitute pre-industrial production units. The main features are clear, with the reduplicative, kin-based, private nature of the work being the most important. (It is interesting to notice the other features: the multi-purpose functions of the family, the fact that desirable attributes for women do not center on economic prowess, etc.) The rationalization of production effected by a transition to large-scale production has not taken place in this area.

Industrialization is, in itself, a great force for human good; exploitation and dehumanization go with capitalism and not necessarily with industrialization. To advocate the conversion of private domestic labor into a public industry under capitalism is quite a different thing from advocating such conversion in a socialist society. In the latter case the forces of production would operate for human welfare, not private profit, and the result should be liberation, not dehumanization. In this case we can speak of *socialized* forms of production.

These definitions are not meant to be technical but rather to differentiate between two important aspects of industrialization. Thus the fear of the barracks-like result of introducing housekeeping into the public economy is most realistic under capitalism. With socialized production and the removal of the profit motive and its attendant alienated labor, there is no reason why, *in an industrialized society*, industrialization of housework should not result in better production, i.e., better food, more comfortable surroundings, more intelligent and loving child-care, etc., than in the present nuclear family.

The argument is often advanced that, under neocapitalism, the work in the home has been much reduced. Even if this is true, it is not structurally relevant. Except for the very rich, who can hire someone to do it, there is for most women, an irreducible minimum of necessary labor involved in caring for home, husband, and children. For a married woman without children this irreducible minimum of work probably takes fifteen to twenty hours a week; for a woman with small children the minimum is probably seventy or eighty hours a week.[8] (There is some resistance to regarding child-rearing as a job. That labor is involved, i.e., the production of use-value, can be clearly seen

---

[8] Such figures can easily be estimated. For example, a married woman without children is expected each week to cook and wash up (10 hours), clean house (4 hours), do laundry (1 hour), and shop for food (1 hour). The figures are *minimum* times required each week for such work. The total, 16 hours, is probably unrealistically low; even so, it is close to half of a regular work week. A mother with young children must spend at least six or seven days a week working close to 12 hours.

when exchange-value is also involved—when the work is done by baby sitters, nurses, child-care centers, or teachers. An economist has already pointed out the paradox that if a man marries his housekeeper, he reduces the national income, since the money he gives her is no longer counted as wages.) The reduction of housework to the minimums given is also expensive; for low-income families more labor is required. In any case, household work remains structurally the same—a matter of private production.

One function of the family, the one taught to us in school and the one which is popularly accepted, is the satisfaction of emotional needs: the needs for closeness, community, and warm, secure relationships. This society provides few other ways of satisfying such needs; for example, work relationships or friendships are not expected to be nearly as important as a man-woman-with-children relationship. Even other ties of kinship are increasingly secondary. This function of the family is important in stabilizing it so that it can fulfill the second, purely economic, function discussed above. The wage-earner, the husband-father, whose earnings support himself, also "pays for" the labor done by the mother-wife and supports the children. The wages of a man buy the labor of two people. The crucial importance of this second function of the family can be seen when the family unit breaks down in divorce. The continuation of the economic function is the major concern where children are involved; the man must continue to pay for the labor of the woman. His wage is very often insufficient to enable him to support a second family. In this case his emotional needs are sacrificed to the necessity to support his ex-wife and children. That is, when there is a conflict, the economic function of the family very often takes precedence over the emotional one. And this in a society which teaches that the major function of the family is the satisfaction of emotional needs.[9]

As an economic unit, the nuclear family is a valuable stabilizing force in capitalist society. Since the production which is done in the home is paid for by the husband-father's earnings, his ability to withhold his labor from the market is much reduced. Even his flexibility in changing jobs is limited. The woman, denied an active place in the market, has little control over the conditions that govern her life. Her economic dependence is reflected in emotional dependence, passivity, and other "typical" female personality traits. She is conservative, fearful, supportive of the status quo.

Furthermore, the structure of this family is such that it is an ideal consumption unit. But this fact, which is widely noted in Women's Liberation literature, should not be taken to mean that this is its primary function. If

---

[9] For evidence of such teaching, see any high school text on the family.

the above analysis is correct, the family should be seen primarily as a production unit for housework and child-rearing. *Everyone* in capitalist society is a consumer; the structure of the family simply means that it is particularly well suited to encourage consumption. Women in particular *are* good consumers; this follows naturally from their responsibility for matters in the home. Also, the inferior status of women, their general lack of a strong sense of worth and identity, make them more exploitable than men and hence better consumers.

The history of women in the industrialized sector of the economy has depended simply on the labor needs of that sector. Women function as a massive reserve army of labor. When labor is scarce (early industrialization, the two world wars, etc.) then women form an important part of the labor force. When there is less demand for labor (as now under neocapitalism) women become a surplus labor force—but one for which their husbands and not society are economically responsible. The "cult of the home" makes its reappearance during times of labor surplus and is used to channel women out of the market economy. This is relatively easy since the pervading ideology ensures that no one, man or woman, takes women's participation in the labor force very seriously. Women's real work, we are taught, is in the home; this holds whether or not they are married, single, or the heads of households.

At all times household work is the responsibilty of women. When they are working outside the home they must somehow manage to get both outside job and housework done (or they supervise a substitute for the housework). Women, particularly married women with children, who work outside the home simply do two jobs; their participation in the labor force is only allowed if they continue to fulfill their first responsibility in the home. This is particularly evident in countries like Russia and those in Eastern Europe where expanded opportunities for women in the labor force have not brought about a corresponding expansion in their liberty. Equal access to jobs outside the home, while one of the preconditions for women's liberation, will not in itself be sufficient to give equality for women; as long as work in the home remains a matter of private production and is the responsibility of women, they will simply carry a double work-load.

A second prerequisite for women's liberation which follows from the above analysis is the conversion of the work now done in the home as private production into work to be done in the public economy.[10] To be more specific, this means that child-rearing should no longer be the responsibility solely of

---

[10] This is stated clearly by early Marxist writers besides Engels. Relevant quotes from Engels have been given in the text; those from Lenin are included in the Appendix.

the parents. Society must begin to take responsibility for children; the economic dependence of women and children on the husband-father must be ended. The other work that goes on in the home must also be changed—communal eating places and laundries for example. When such work is moved into the public sector, then the material basis for discrimination against women will be gone.

These are only preconditions. The idea of the inferior status of women is deeply rooted in the society and will take a great deal of effort to eradicate. But once the structures which produce and support that idea are changed, then, and only then, can we hope to make progress. It is possible, for example, that a change to communal eating places would simply mean that women are moved from a home kitchen to a communal one, although this *would* be an advance, particularly in a socialist society where work would not have the inherently exploitative nature it does now. Once women are freed from private production in the home, it will probably be very difficult to maintain for any long period of time a rigid definition of jobs by sex. This illustrates the interrelation between the two preconditions given above: true equality in job opportunity is probably impossible without freedom from housework, and the industrialization of housework is unlikely unless women are leaving the home for jobs.

The changes in production necessary to get women out of the home might seem to be, in theory, possible under capitalism. One of the sources of women's liberation movements may be the fact that alternative capitalized forms of home production now exist. Day care is available, even if inadequate and perhaps expensive; convenience foods, home delivery of meals, and take-out meals are widespread; laundries and cleaners offer bulk rates. However, cost usually prohibits a complete dependence on such facilities, and they are not available everywhere, even in North America. These should probably then be regarded as embryonic forms rather than completed structures. However, they clearly stand as alternatives to the present system of getting such work done. Particularly in North America, where the growth of "service industries" is important in maintaining the growth of the economy, the contradictions between these alternatives and the need to keep women in the home will grow.

The need to keep women in the home arises from two major aspects of the present system. First, the amount of unpaid labor performed by women is very large and very profitable to those who own the means of production. To pay women for their work, even at minimum wage scales, would imply a massive redistribution of wealth. At present, the support of a family is a hidden tax on the wage earner—his wage buys the labor power of two people. And second, there is the problem of whether the economy can expand enough to put all women to work as a part of the normally employed labor force. The war economy has been adequate to draw women partially into the economy but not adequate to establish a need for all or most of them. If it is argued that the jobs created by the industrialization of housework will create this need, then one can counter by pointing to (1) the strong economic forces operating for the status quo and against industrialization discussed above, and (2) the fact that the present service industries, which somewhat counter these forces, have not been able to keep up with the growth of the labor force as presently constituted. The present trends in the service industries simply create "underemployment" in the home; they do not create new jobs for women. So long as this situation exists, women remain a very convenient and elastic part of the industrial reserve army. Their incorporation into the labor force on terms of equality—which would create pressure for capitalization of housework—is possible only with an economic expansion so far achieved by neocapitalism only under conditions of full-scale war mobilization.

In addition, such structural changes imply the complete breakdown of the present nuclear family. The stabilizing consuming functions of the family, plus the ability of the cult of the home to keep women out of the labor market, serve neocapitalism too well to be easily dispensed with. And, on a less fundamental level, even if these necessary changes in the nature of household production were achieved under capitalism it would have the unpleasant consequence of including *all* human relation in the cash nexus. The atomization and isolation of people in Western society is already sufficiently advanced to make it doubtful if such complete psychic isolation could be tolerated. It is likely in fact that one of the major negative emotional responses to women's liberation movements may be exactly such a fear. If this is the case, then possible alternatives—cooperatives, the kibbutz etc.—can be cited to show the psychic needs for community and warmth can in fact be better satisfied if other structures are substituted for the nuclear family.

At best the change to capitalization of housework would only give women the same limited freedom given most men in capitalist society. This does not mean, however, that women should wait to demand freedom from discrimination. There *is* a material basis for women's status; we are not merely discriminated against, we are exploited. At present, our unpaid labor in the home is necessary if the entire system is to function. Pressure created by women who challenge their role will reduce the effectiveness of this exploitation. In addition, such challenges will impede the functioning of the family and may make the channeling of women out of the labor force less effective.

All of these will hopefully make quicker the transition to a society in which the necessary structural changes in production can actually be made. That such a transition will require a revolution I have no doubt; our task is to make sure the revolutionary changes in the society do in fact end women's oppression.

APPENDIX

Passages from Lenin, *On The Emancipation of Women,*
Progress Publishers, Moscow.

Large-scale machine industry, which concentrates masses of workers who often come from various parts of the country, absolutely refuses to tolerate survivals of patriarchalism and personal dependence, and is marked by a truly "contemptuous attitude to the past." It is this break with obsolete tradition that is one of the substantial conditions which have created the possibility and evoked the necessity of regulating production and of public control over it. In particular, . . . it must be stated that the drawing of women and juveniles into production is, at bottom, progressive. It is undisputable that the capitalist factory places these categories of the working population in particularly hard conditions, but endeavors to completely ban the work of women and juveniles in industry, or to maintain the patriarchal manner of life that ruled out such work, would be reactionary and utopian. By destroying the patriarchal isolation of these categories of the population who formerly never emerged from the narrow circle of domestic family relationships, by drawing them into direct participation in social production, . . . industry stimulates their development and increases their independence (p. 15).

Notwithstanding all the laws emancipating woman, she continues to be a *domestic slave,* because *petty housework* crushes, strangles, stultifies, and degrades her, chains her to the kitchen and the nursery, and she wastes her labor on barbarously unproductive, petty, nerve-racking, stultifying and crushing drudgery. The real *emancipation of women,* real communism, will begin only where and when an all-out struggle begins (led by the proletariat wielding the state power) against this petty housekeeping, or rather when its *wholesale transformation* into a large-scale socialist economy begins.

Do we in practice pay sufficient attention to this question, which in theory every Communist considers indisputable? Of course not. Do we take proper care of the *shoots* of communism which already exist in this sphere? Again, the answer is *no.* Public catering establishments, nurseries, kindergartens— here we have examples of these shoots, here we have the simple, everyday means, involving nothing pompous, grandiloquent or ceremonial, which can *really emancipate women*, really lessen and abolish their inequality with man as regards their role in social production and public life. These means are not new, they (like all the material prerequisites for socialism) were created by large-scale capitalism. But under capitalism they remained, first, a rarity, and secondly—which is particularly important—either *profit-making* enterprises, with all the worst features of speculation, profiteering, cheating and fraud, or "acrobatics of bourgeois charity," which the best workers rightly hated and despised (pp. 61-62).

You all know that even when women have full rights, they still remain downtrodden because all housework is left to them. In most cases, housework is the most unproductive, the most savage, and the most arduous work a woman can do. It is exceptionally petty and does not include anything that would in any way promote the development of the woman (p. 67).

We are setting up model institutions, dining-rooms and nurseries, that will emancipate women from housework. . . .

We say that the emancipation of the workers must be effected by the workers themselves, and in exactly the same way the emancipation of working women is a matter for the working women themselves. The working women must themselves see to it that such institutions are developed, and this activity will bring about a complete change in their position as compared wth what it was under the old, capitalist society (p. 68).

A Woman's Work
is Never Done
Peggy Morton

*PEGGY MORTON is active in Toronto
Women's Liberation.*

There has been a great deal of debate in Women's Liberation over the
past few years about the function of the family in capitalist society. Discussion has generally focused on the role of the family as the primary unit of
socialization; the family is the basic unit in which authoritarian personality
structures are formed, particularly the development of authoritarian relationships between parents and children and between men and women; the family
is necessary to the maintenance of sexual repression in the sexuality is
allowed legitimate expression only in marriage; through the family men
can give vent to feelings of frustration, anger and resentment that are the
products of alienated labor, and can act out the powerlessness which they
experience in work by dominating the other members of the family; and
within the family little girls learn what is expected of them and how they
should act.
   This theoretical work has provided important insights and understanding
of the ways in which the family oppresses women, and the functions of the
family in alleviating tensions created within the society. It has also forced
the English-Canadian New Left to deal with the questions of cultural,
sexual and psychological oppression. But we have neglected to deal with the
family as an economic unit, and as a result the question of women and the
family has been divorced from our understanding of advanced capitalism,
and has failed to develop an understanding of the dialectic between the
economic and psychological functions of the family.
   One way the ruling class tries to control people is to mutilate their iden-
tities. But our task as organizers is not to tell women that they are oppressed
but first to understand the ways in which people rebel every day against
their oppression, to understand the mechanism by which this rebellion is
co-opted and contained, how people are kept separate so that they see their

"This is a revised and expanded version of an article printed in *Leviathan*, vol. 2,
no. 1 (May, 1970), pp. 32-7 by permission of the author."

oppression as individual and not sex and class oppression, and to provide revolutionary theory and practice which can give rise to new forms of struggle against that oppression. The greatest obstacle is not "false consciousness" but not knowing how to fight the family system, as for blacks 20 years ago the greatest obstacle was not knowing how to fight the racist system. Revolutionary movements are born out of the consciousness that people already have of their oppression and the transformation of individual understanding through collective action which produces a higher level of consciousness. The women's movement will grow out of this consciousness. It is our own chauvinism towards other women that keeps us from understanding how much women already understand about their own oppression.

A second problem with much of both the psychological and economic analysis of women's oppression is that it often has been developed out of the need to *justify* the importance of women's liberation rather than as a serious attempt to lay the basis for an understanding of the relationship of women to the capitalist system and a basis for strategy. Dixon mentions the "invisible participants" (movement men) in her article in *Radical America*, and she is right, but the problem goes even deeper. Even socialist women in women's liberation do not yet see analysis as a tool for the development of *strategy*, but only as a tool for increasing our individual and collective *understanding* of our oppression. This encourages a real liberalism among us about the way we look at the oppression of women, because lack of strategy means we don't have to act and so "analysis" serves instead to focus on our individual lives and the hope of changing them.

What Defines Women? or —
Does Lady Astor oppress her garbageman?

Maggie Benston's paper *What Defines Women?* (published in *Monthly Review* as *The Political Economy of Women's Liberation*) is very important as one of the first arguments that we must analyze the role of women in the family from the point of view of production rather than consumption. Benston argues that because the work of women in the home is based not on commodity production, which in capitalist society is the only kind of production considered to be real work, but on the production of use-values without exchange-value,† that the work that women perform is not considered to be real and valid work, and that, therefore, women are defined as inferior to men.

---

† By "use-value' we mean things produced which people find a use for; by "exchange-value" we mean things that have a value in the marketplace.

She sees the family, and women's production role within the family, as the material basis for the oppression of women. This argument is significant not only because it rejects the idea that the family is primarily a unit of consumption, but because it challenges the view that the only *economic* basis to the oppression of women is the super-exploitation of women in the labor market. Those who argue that the economic oppression of women exists only within the workplace conclude that, therefore, women need not organize either separately or differently from men, and that there is no need for an autonomous women's movement. And even Marxist women's liberationists often envisage organizing working women in the same terms as if they were organizing men, using the same analysis and the same strategy.

Benston correctly situates the oppression of women in their role in the family and correctly argues that real contradictions exist for women as women, and not only on the basis of their class position. But there are very serious problems with the structure of Benston's argument. The chief problem is that it does not provide any basis on which strategy for a women's movement can be based. Does it mean to say that women have a unique relationship to the means of production and are therefore a class? We know that despite this common relationship to production in the home women are nevertheless objectively, socially, culturally and economically defined, and subjectively define themselves, through the class position of their husband or their family and/or the class position derived from work outside the home. We know that upper class women gain very real privileges from their class position which override the oppression which they experience as women.

Secondly, to define women through their work as unpaid household laborers does not help us to understand how to organize women. The logical conclusion would be that women should be organized around their relationship to production, i.e., organized around their work in the home. Yet, the isolation of housewives, which is an important aspect of their oppression, is also a great barrier to their organization. Historically, women have begun to organize not when they were tied to the home, but when they entered the labor market.

There are some areas where Benston's analysis does bear fruit. The demand to socialize the care of children through day-care centers must clearly be part of our strategy. Another possibility is the demand for housing which does not isolate people in family units but provides space for people to live in other arrangements, with facilities for day-care, areas for children to play, common areas for women who are forced to live a prison-like existence in the "privacy" of their own homes, and communal eating facilities to relieve women of the task of preparing food daily for their families. But in a capitalist society, unless these demands are tied in with an attack on the private ownership of the means of production, the logical solution would be the capitalization, not the socialization of household labor. And probably women would be hired at low wages to perform these services. We need to integrate the demand for the socialization of household labor with the demand for the socialization of labor outside the home.

A third problem with Benston's analysis is that it does not provide the framework for understanding the changing nature of the family as an economic institution. Women do not play a peripheral role in the labor force, and the numbers of women working outside the home are growing very significantly. The sense in which women's role in the labor force is peripheral is that women's position in the family is used to facilitate the use of women as a reserve army of labor, to pay women half what men are paid, but women's work in the labor force is peripheral neither to the women's lives nor to the capitalist class.

One, Two, Three, Many Contradictions

We need an analysis of the family that will help us understand how and why these changes are taking place. I have been arguing that very little of the analysis of women's oppression that we have done in women's liberation has been strategic analysis and that the way we look at women's oppression reflects both the inner-directedness of the women's movement and our desire to provide to ourselves and to men that we are Marxists, that we have an economic analysis, and so on. We must now begin to examine the specific material and historical conditions out of which the present Women's Liberation Movement has arisen, and the contradictions which women experience that are increasing women's consciousness.

The essence of the position I want to argue in this paper is as follows: (a) as Benston argues, the primary material basis of women's oppression lies in the family system; (b) that particular structural changes are taking place in capitalism that affect and change the role of the family, are causing a crises in the family system and are raising the consciousness of women about their oppression; (c) that the key to understanding these changes is to see the family as a unit whose function is the *maintenance of and reproduction of labor power*, i.e., that the structure of the family is determined by the needs of the economic system, at any given time, for a certain *kind* of labor power; (d) that this conception of the family allows us to look at women's public role (in the labor force) and private role (in the family) in an integrated way. The position of women in the labor force will be determined by the needs of the family system, i.e., what the family needs to do in order to carry out the functions required of it, and by the general needs of the economy for specific kinds of labor power. (e) Strategy must be based on an understanding of the contradictions within the family, contradictions which are created by the needs that the family has to fulfill, of the contradictions within the work-force (contradictions between the social nature of production and the capitalist organization of work), and the contradictions created by the dual roles of women — work in the home and work in capitalist production. This paper will try to deal with the contradictions within the family, and the contradictions between public and private roles.

We are taught to view the family as a sacrosanct institution, as the foundation-stone of society and as constant and never-changing. But, as Juliet Mitchell says:

> "Like woman herself, the family appears as a natural object, but it is actually a cultural creation. There is nothing inevitable about the form or role of the family any more than there is about the character or role of women. It is the function of ideology to present these given social types as aspects of nature herself."

Particularly in times of social upheaval, the family is extolled as the "greatest good" — whether it be the *Kinder, Kirche, Küche* of the Nazis or the togetherness preached in America. Because the family is so clearly important in maintaining social stability, many women's liberationists see the family as the "lynch-pin" of the capitalist system, and see their major task as the "destruction of the family." The problem with this view is that it tends to become totally idealist — a declaration of war on the *ideology* of the family system and not its substance. Instead, our task is to formulate strategy from an understanding of the contradictions in the family system. To do this we must understand how the family has developed in different stages of capitalism as the requirements for the maintenance and reproduction of labor power change. Through this approach we can examine the size of families encouraged, the socialization of children in the home and in educational institutions, whether women are working or at home, the role of the wife in giving psychological support and playing a "tension-management" role for her husband. In short, we can study the economic, social, ideological and psychological functions of the family in an integrated way.

By "reproduction of labor power" we mean simply that the task of the family is to maintain the present work force and provide the next generation of workers, fitted with the skills and values necessary for them to be productive members of the work force. When we talk about the evolution of the family under capitalism, we have to understand both the changes in the family among the proletariat, and the changes that come from the increasing proletarianization of the labor force, and the urbanization of the society.

The pre-capitalist family functioned as an integrated economic unit; men, women and children took part in production — work in the fields, the cottage industry, and production for the use of the family. There was division of labor between men and women, but in essence all production took place within the family.

The Family in the First Stages of Capitalism

For those who became the urban proletariat, the function of the family in the reproduction of labor power was reduced to the most primitive level; instead of skilled artisans, the factories required only a steady flow of workers who required little or no training, learned what they needed on the job, and who were easily replaceable. Numbers were of primary importance, and the conditions under which people lived were irrelevant to the needs of capital. The labor of women and children took on new importance.

> "On what foundation is the present family, the bourgeois family, based? On capital, or private gain. In its completely developed form this family exists only among the bourgeoisie. But this state of things finds its complement in the practical absence of the family among the proletarians, and in public prostitution.... The bourgeois clap-trap about the family and education, about the hallowed correlation of parent and child, become all the more disgusting, the more, by the action of Modern Industry, all family ties among the proletarians are torn asunder and their children transformed into simple articles of commerce and instruments of labor." (*The Communist Manifesto*)

The need of capitalism in the stage of primitive accumulation of capital for a steady flow of cheap and unskilled labor primarily determined the structure of the family. In contrast, the prevailing ideology was used in turn to prepare the working class for the new drudgery. The repressive Victorian morality, brought to the working class through the Wesleyan sects, clamped down harder on the freedom of women, and perpetrated the ideology of hard work and discipline. The Victorian concept of the family was both a reflection of the bourgeois family, based on private property, and an ideal representing a status to which the proletarian would like to rise.

In North America, conditions were initially the same as in pre-capitalist Europe. The settling of the continent required a family structure, initially even stronger in form than in Europe, given the absence of other developed institutions to meet social and psychological needs. Industrial workers did experience conditions similar to those of Europe in the early stages of capitalist development. But, as in Europe, the evolution of capitalism called for a restructuring of the family.

A similar pattern emerges for groups within advanced capitalism who serve as a reserve army of unskilled labor. During slavery, the black family was systematically broken up and destroyed, and in many ways has never been reinstated. Because black people have been used as a reserve army of unskilled labor, there has been no need for a family structure that would ensure that the children received education and skills. And direct oppression and repression (racism) eliminated the need for more subtle social control through the socialization process in the family. Often the women were the breadwinners because they were the only ones who could find jobs, and when there were no jobs the welfare system further discouraged the maintenance of the family by making it more difficult to get welfare if the man was around.

A new kind of worker was required as the production process became more complex — workers who could read instructions and blueprints, equipped with skills that required considerable training. As the need for skilled labor increases, the labor of women and children tends to be replaced by that of men; workers involve a capital investment and therefore it makes more sense to employ those who can work steadily throughout their lives.

At the same time, the growth of trade unions and the increasing revolutionary consciousness of the working class forced the ruling class to meet some of their demands or face full-scale revolt. The rise in material standards of living accommodated both the need to restrain militancy, to provide a standard of living that would allow for the education of children as skilled workers, and the need for consumers to provide new markets for the goods produced. The abolition of child labor and the introduction of compulsory education were compelled by the need for a skilled labor force.

Reproduction of Labor Power in Advanced Capitalism

The transformation in the costs of educating and training the new generation of workers is fundamental to the changes that have taken place and are still taking place in the family structure. A fundamental law of capitalism is the need for constant expansion. Automation is required for the survival of the system. Workers are needed who are not only highly skilled but who have been trained to learn new skills. Profits depend more and more on the efficient organization of work and on the "self-discipline" of the workers rather than simply on speed-ups and other direct forms of increasing the exploitation of the workers. The family is therefore important both to shoulder the burden of the costs of education, and to carry out the repressive socialization of children. The family must raise children who have internalized hierarchical social relations, who will discipline themselves and work efficiently without constant supervision. The family also serves to repress the natural sexuality of its members — an essential process if people are to work at jobs which turn them into machines for eight or more hours a day. Women are responsible for implementing most of this socialization.

The pressure to stay in school and the growth in post-secondary education, which serves both to train skilled workers and managers and to absorb surplus manpower that cannot be employed, means that the earnings of married women begin to replace the earnings of unmarried children. In 1951, married women were only 8.9% of the labor force; by 1965, 18.5% of all workers were married women. In contrast, there has been a decline in the number of unmarried children in the labor force — from 20.7% of the labor force in 1951, to 17.2% in 1965. As young people tend more to move away from home when they start to earn money, fewer families have the income of older children to help make ends meet. And besides not having these extra wages, the family must often pay for tuition for the children's education.

The second paycheck often makes the difference between poverty and keeping your head above water. A study of data from the 1961 census found that only 43% of non-farm families had only one wage-earner. In 37% of all non-farm families, the wives had earned income, and in 20% income has been contributed by unmarried children. As the percentage of working women has risen from 28.7% in 1961 to 34.4% in 1968, the percentage of families having income from wives would now be still larger. Much of the "affluence" of working class, and even many "middle-class" families depends on the wages of women.

In this situation, women are indispensable to the maintenance of the family where the children are coerced into remaining at school, supported by their parents, or prone to unemployment if they have left school at an early age. They are, though, in another sense, superfluous, because the children whom they are supposed to mother are old enough to take care of themselves, resentful of parental authority and rebelling against the system's control over their lives.

The pressure to finish high school and the growth of community colleges for the children of the working class make this picture increasingly real even for the working class family.

The schizophrenia of living through other people becomes even more pronounced as those who one is supposed to live through rebel and demand their autonomy. It is little wonder that the largest group of "speed freaks" are women in their 40's and 50's, or that one half of the hospital beds are taken up by victims of mental-emotional disease, many of these middle-aged women.

The changes in the kind of labor needed are also reflected in the decline in the size of families. For a rural family, children mean hands to do chores as well as mouths to feed, and since food and housing are not such a major cost on a farm as in the city, large families are not a liability but are valued for the sense of security and companionship they provide. In the early stages of capitalism, large numbers of workers were needed and so large families were not discouraged. Even though large families meant hardships for working class urban families, the old social patterns were slow to change.

Only 40% of the Canadian population was living in towns and cities in 1911; in 1961 almost 70% of the population was urban. The high cost of housing, food, clothing and education and the easier access to birth control have all produced a tendency for smaller families. And because urbanization is a quite recent phenomenon, the gap between cultural values and economic necessity means that the trend to smaller families is relatively new.

The demands that women are now making for birth control and abortion will eventually be met, because they do not threaten the basic needs of the system. But we should see this as our first victory not as proof that these demands are "reformist" and that we should not organize around them. And the general reluctance of the ruling class to grant these demands should also make us aware of their double-edged nature. On the one hand, the family itself could function better if birth control and abortion on demand were readily available to all classes. On the other hand, the existence of the family itself is threatened by the introduction of measures which will further legitimize and make possible sex outside of marriage. As women have fewer children, to define themselves primarily as mothers will make less and less sense, and a whole pandora's box is opened. And part of the rationale for the exclusion of women from so many jobs requiring training disappears when women are capable of determining when they wish to have children.

The trend to smaller families is both a reflection of the family's need for the wages of women, and a further cause of the increases in the numbers of working women. Smaller families make it more possible for women to remain out of the labor market while the children are small and return when they are in school. This is precisely the pattern that is developing.

For young people themselves, the changes in the kind of labor power required also have an effect on the formation of families, how soon those who marry have children, and whether the young wives work. Prolonged schooling has reduced the percentage of young men in the labor force. In 1953, 51.7% of males 14-19 were in the labor force; in 1968, only 39.1%. Similarly, only 84.3% of males 20-24 were in the labor force in 1968 as compared to 92.9% in 1953.

For those who quit school, the picture is often bleak. Men 14-19 experience unemployment rates double the average unemployment for all men. And men 20-24 are also much more likely to be unemployed than older workers. For those who are working, there is an increasing gap between the wages paid to young workers and older workers. Young workers, male and female, are more concentrated in sectors in which employment is declining (especially where unskilled labor is being supplanted by increased automation), and in low-paid sectors like retail sales and clerical work.

Compare this situation with that after World War II which produced the baby boom. The baby boom was caused by a rise in the proportion of married women, not by women having larger numbers of children. One reason for the increases in the numbers of married women was that women were thrown out of the jobs that had fallen to them during the war, in sectors that were normally reserved for men. Just as important were the "opportunities" for young male workers. Low birth rates during the Depression meant that young workers were in short supply. The economy was in a period of boom and expansion due to the war, the growth of the permanent war economy, and the expansion of imperialism. Jobs were in good supply in heavy industry, and the average earnings for young workers were quite close to those of older workers. The demand for labor encouraged immigration on a large scale, and brought many rural youths to the cities. Many young people were alone in the city, uprooted from their communities and families, and in the absence of the kind of youth culture that now provides some alternatives to marriage, there were natural reasons why young people married and started their own families.

The 70's, in contrast, see a period of rising unemployment, wage freezes, coercion of youth to stay in school, and increasing distance between the wages of younger and older workers. In 1961 constant dollars, the average wages of a male wage-earner 35-44 rose $1481 between 1951 and 1961; while those of men 20-24 rose only $520 and those 14-19 only $20. So not only the cultural but the economic situation makes the stable family of the 50's an unlikely model for the 70's. Young people who do marry find that they desperately need the wages of the wife — 58% of women 20-24 were working in 1968, a rise of 10% from 1960, (and more were in school as well). In families where the "head" was under 25 (if there is a male in the family he is considered the head whether or not he supports the family) women contributed about one quarter of the total income for these families in 1965. Given the low wages paid to women, this indicates a high number of young working wives.

The trend to early marriage has abated, and fertility rates have hit an all-time low. More sexual freedom outside marriage, the availability of birth control, and the economic situation will probably mean that the trend to low birth rates that has been going on since 1959 will continue.

Women as Producers

It is clear that the way in which the family is evolving creates new contradictions that produce a higher level of consciousness of their oppression among women. But we cannot understand the contradictions within the family system unless we understand more clearly the other half of the coin — the situation of women in the labor force. For the same structural changes in capitalism which affect the family also affect women in their role as wage-laborers, and the contradictions between these two roles are an important source of the new consciousness.

Women's Liberationists have argued correctly that women are super-exploited in two senses: women who have jobs outside the home work not eight but sixteen hours a day for the capitalist, in the family, to maintain and reproduce the working class, and as members of the labor force; and women workers are paid only about half the wages that a man would receive. But we have treated this moralistically — to prove that women are more oppressed than men, rather than to analyze the structure of women's employment.

Questions about the importance of wage demands cannot be argued in the abstract. Do we want to organize women into the present male-dominated, sell-out unions (and in Canada into American-controlled unions)? Yet we know that no organizing in the work place can neglect the real needs of the people, which means, especially for women, the fact that meagre pay-checks cannot provide the essentials of life. And the possibility of economic independence is a pre-condition for women conceiving of their own autonomy and independence.

But we must also understand the specifics of the importance of women in the labor force if we are to be clearer about the importance of unions and wage demands. Those sectors of industry which are at the highest stage of capitalist development (a very high degree of monopolization and automation, huge investments in plant and equipment, etc.) do not have an absolute need to control wages. Their interests are not just in keeping wages down, but in keeping the unions out and, therefore, maintaining stability, avoiding strikes, and so on. In addition, in the highly monopolized industries in the goods-producing sectors, high wages are passed on to the consumer in the form of higher prices and do not affect profits.

In contrast, the type of industry where women are concentrated tends to be labor-intensive rather than capital-intensive, and wages form a relatively high percentage of total costs. Women constitute 75% of all clothing workers, 65% of workers in knitting mills, and 51% in leather products. (About 70% of all women workers are in the textile, clothing and related industries, in food and beverages, or in electrical apparatus and supplies.) Average weekly wages and salaries for clothing and related industries were, for September 1969, $78 in clothing and knitting mills, and $81 in leather products, as compared to $139 in chemicals, and $133 in non-metallic metal products, where women were 22% and 11% of the total workers, respectively. These are also the industries with the lowest rate of automation. The low wages of women in these sectors (and thus the lower wages of male workers as well) are not simply a matter of the capitalist making higher profits from employing women at low wages. Equal wages in this sector would not just mean less profit for the capitalist, but a transformation of the industry. (In textiles, it might force automation, or it might mean that the industry would not survive in competition with textile industry in the Third World.)

Moreover, within industries employing many women where average wages are high (like electrical products, where women are 31% of all workers, and average wages and salaries $132 a week), women generally work at labor-intensive jobs like assembling and packaging where low wages are important in keeping costs down and profits up.

Most women are not employed in manufacturing, but in the service sector. The employment of large numbers of women in the industrialized service sector is part of a general tendency for employment to grow fastest in this sector. In Canada, as early as 1961, the percentage of trade and service workers in the labor force (40.6%) equalled that in direct production of goods.

Of projected growth to 1980, over 40% of the net increase in the labor force is expected to be women and, in fact, the female labor force has been growing faster than projected.

Not only is the service sector growing, but the jobs within it are becoming more industrialized and thus more amenable to organization. Growth in this sector means both the creation of (a) more "professional and technical" or "new working class" jobs, which are reasonably well-paid, potentially creative, which require a considerable degree of training and education (such as teachers, technicians, nurses, engineers), some of which are proletarian in character, and (b) a whole sector of jobs that require little training, are badly paid, where the work is uncreative and unrewarding (although sometimes potentially creative) and where working conditions are very bad — store clerks, hospital workers, waitresses, clerks in government bureaucracies, etc.

A growing number of these jobs are in the state sector. Because of increasing economic demands on the state and growing pressure on government finances, there is a sizeable and continuing gap between the wages of public and private employees, and a tendency toward increasing discontent and attempts at unionization among government workers. Large numbers of women work as public employees and can be expected to be affected by these developments.

It is clear then, that when we say that women are used as a "reserve army of labor" (as, for example, black people in the United States are also used as a reserve army of labor), we are not talking about a group of workers that are peripheral to the economy, but a group which is central to the maintenance of labor-intensive manufacturing, and service and state sectors where low wages are a priority. A few simple wage comparisons will indicate clearly the importance of wage differentials on the basis of sex.

Average earnings for full-year workers, 1961, DBS — categories where few or no women have been excluded:

	male	female
managerial	$7920	$3351
professional & technical	7602	4226
clerical	4713	3263
sales	5287	2077
service	4120	2099
production workers	5290	2756

Even in the professional and technical sphere, where wages are highest for women, the average wages are over $1,000 a year less than those of male production workers and only in the service sector — a field where many women are employed — do men make less than the average for women in the highest field.

The unionization of women workers, which is already beginning to take place in previously unionized sectors, will clearly be a blow to the stability of the capitalist system. The vast majority of women workers have jobs which are, by any sensible definition, "working-class." Only about 15% of all women workers are professionals, and about 85% of these are found in those professions already beginning to unionize — nurses and teachers. Very few women have managerial jobs, and the vast majority are wage-earners.

Sisters, Let's Get It Together

Clearly, women works are strategic, but we should not conclude that we can bring down the system only by making wage demands and beginning to work for the unionization of women workers, as a strategy for a mass movement. Our revolutionary potential lies in the fact that most women are both oppressed as women and exploited as workers, and our strategy must reflect this duality. The demands of women strike both at an institution which is central to the system — the family — and at sectors of the economy which are ill-provided to meet even traditional demands of the labor movement. Because organizers in the past have refused to organize women as women, women have been viewed as "unorganizable" because they have little time, work in sectors that are hard to recognize, and they move in and out of the labor force. For example, all the structural reasons that make the textile industry the most exploitative, also make it harder to organize there — the workers can easily be replaced, the low investment in plant and equipment mean that management can hold out longer against strikes, the plants are small, and so on. Similarly, many women in the service sector are hard to organize in the traditional way because they work in such small establishments — waitresses, store clerks, etc. A strategy of work-place organizing alone cannot overcome these problems, but as we develop an analysis of the oppression of women, we can turn these same factors into a basis for organizing and an integral part of our strategy.

I have argued that the importance of the family as an economic unit, the importance of the cheap labor supply that women provide mean that the system must act to retain the family system. The breakdown of the family, besides meaning that women will demand jobs that don't exist, will make the struggle for equal access to jobs, equal pay, day care, maternity leave, job security, etc. even more militant. At the present time, one family in ten has a woman as its sole supporter. Neither the state nor the sectors where women

work will easily be able to meet the needs of women who must support themselves and often their children.

Yet most people, especially the working class, will continue to hold onto
the family as the only place where basic emotional needs for love, support
and companionship can be met at all; because there are no alternatives, as
things stand now, most women can't, and don't want to go it alone. If our
cry is "destroy the family," the woman's movement will be contained within
a small sector of professionals and younger women without families. The
masses of women will not relate to Women's Liberation because it is not relating to their needs. What we must do, instead, is to begin to organize
around demands which provide the pre-condition for autonomy for women
— economic independence. This struggle will, in fact, heighten the contradictions within the family system.

This means that our task is not to focus on initiating struggles around
basic needs of women that are essentially reformist. There is a fundamental
difference between waging a battle to get day-care for all women, and a
strategic perspective that looks to day-care organizing in terms of cadre-
building. For example, welfare mothers, who have none of the security of
the family, who in many ways have nothing to lose, and whose desperation
and anger will increase as the state becomes more and more hard-pressed to
provide welfare benefits that are even vaguely related to the amount needed
to sustain life, *cannot* act politically as long as they are unable to get out of
the house even for a few hours. Day-care organizing with welfare mothers is
not only a matter of relating to the needs of these women, but makes it possible to build revolutionary cadre. In addition, many of the forms of communal living which young women in the movement are developing to meet
their need for political and emotional support also speak to the needs of
women who now live alone with small children. Many of the gaps that we
see between our needs and those of other women exist only between our ears.

We must not fall prey to the chauvinism and arrogance that assumes that
"working class" women are capable of being organized only around "economist issues" and that they have no consciousness of their oppression as
women and no yearnings for freedom and independence. We must raise the
level of every issue — providing birth control information for young women
means we can talk about repressive sexuality and its functions in capitalist
society. Day-care can be an exemplary form of communal care of children
and other communal forms. The clear male domination of the present unions
makes it easier to talk about rank and file caucuses (women's caucuses) or
new unions to replace those controlled by male sell-out leadership. Abortion
laws and the oppressive treatment of women in hospitals can be put in the

perspective of struggle for community control of the hospitals. Many women work not only for money but to escape the isolation of their homes, and because they want to have an identity based on what they *do*. Thus the lack of creative work is a real and bitter disappointment when they do take a job. We can talk about work under socialism, about the difference between work for the Cubans and the Vietnamese, who are working to build socialism, and work for the man in capitalist society.

But even with this perspective we can easily become reformist if we lose sight of our political goals. All too often we forget why we are organizing women; the purpose of building a mass movement is not to build a mass movement, but to make revolution. The Panthers feed hungry children and so do the Salvation Army: the difference is that the Panther "serve the people" programs exist to gain the trust of the people in order that they can wage armed struggle, because they know that there will always be hungry children until imperialism is smashed. When we run abortion counselling services or start day-care centers, there is no difference between us and liberal reformers unless the basis of these programs is to win the confidence of women that we *can* win, that we can destroy the monster that is sucking our blood. To often we see the question of winning people's trust as a process where they come to like and trust us not for what we are, not because we are socialists, but because we pretend to be something else.

Our task is to consciously build a revolutionary cadre among women. To do this we have to figure out which sectors of women are going to move fastest. In all revolutions most of the cadre have come from the youth. "Hip" women who are learning to live off the streets and already have some of the toughness and desire to fight that is so often lacking in the women's movement, young women in the high schools and community colleges, young typists and file clerks and waitresses, welfare mothers, women who are raising children alone will move fastest. The job of the revolutionary women's movement is to build a cadre within these groups.

It is wrong to think that our task is to get a job in an office, which leaves us tired and unable to do political work outside the office, and spend two or three years hiding our politics and trying to organize a union. To the extent that we will be able to talk to women in offices and factories, this will happen if we are doing things we can rap about. What might make sense is to work at temporary jobs where in two or three weeks in an office we can find the women who have the most consciousness, build relationships with these women, rap a lot of politics, introduce them to other women's liberationists and so on. These women might well want to organize in their office, and our task will be to try to raise the level of this organizing. And unions of the traditional kind may not be the highest form of struggle possible: "working to rule" could almost shut down a bank, for example. Women who work in offices know hundreds of ways of gumming up the works. All power to the imagination!

The percentage of women aged 20-24 who are in the labor force is almost twice as high as in any other age group. And the post-war baby boom means that the percentage of young people in the society is very high. So the emphasis on young women when we are talking about work-place organizing is not an emphasis on a small minority of workers, but a significant and large sector.

It is not necessarily the most oppressed women who have the most potential for becoming revolutionaries. Young women are in many ways the least oppressed — they are not tied down for life to a family and husband and children, they have still some choices about how they are going to live. At the same time, the general proletarianization of youth means that we cannot be static about our understanding of oppression — increasingly there will be fewer and fewer choices available to us; conditions have forced us to go beyond the "existentialist" attitudes of the early sixties when we thought that making a commitment to be a revolutionary was an abstract moral decision. To become a revolutionary is to choose life over death, and our strength lies in this, that only by learning to fight this system can we become truly human.

Because objective conditions will force women to demand unions, day-care, equal pay, the right to control their own bodies, etc., we should not see our task as initiating and directing these struggles. We can give expression to the needs that women have and at the same time raise the level of these struggles through militant actions around some of these issues. But we cannot limit ourselves to responding to and organizing around only the spontaneous manifestations of women's consciousness of their oppression. We must become an exemplary force — a force that shows other women that we can fight, and that we intend to win. This means that we must take leadership not only in "women's organizing" but in anti-imperialist struggles as well.

The cutting edge which destroyed the possibility that the suffrage movement in the United States could become revolutionary was the aligning of the movement with racist Southern white women in order to win the vote. If we fail to see ourselves, in practice as well as theory, as part of a movement of all oppressed peoples, our movement will take the same road.

Project Company Day-Care

Helke Sander
Introduction by Enid Eckstein

> *Enid Eckstein has been active in Madison*
> *SDS and in women's liberation.*

The Women's Movement in the United States has become increasingly attracted to group care of children as a supplement or alternative to the rearing of young children by the individual parents—i.e., mother. The intent is that child care should become a community, a social affair, the proper work of both men and women. Successful day-care programs are seen as a way of removing a part of the material basis of woman's oppression, her inferior status in the labor force, and of alleviating her isolation in the home. Some experimental community controlled centers have been started in this country. The New York City Day Care Collective is an excellent model of an attempt to provide an alternative to existing day-care facilities. These new centers are staffed by parents and friends—both men and women. They are trying to develop new teaching methods that break down competition and provide a first step toward the elimination of the ideology of the child as property.

The awareness of the need and potential of group day-care within the Movement coincides with a growing recognition of *other* interest groups of the uses and benefits to *them* of day-care centers. The Nixon administration has taken a step in this direction with its new welfare program, the Family Assistance Plan. The administration plan is eventually to set up enough federally funded day-care centers to *force* welfare mothers out of the home and into work training programs.

Day-care has also become big business. Many companies are developing models of day-care centers which they intend to put on the market. One example of this trend is the development of the twenty-state chain of Mary Moppet's Day Nursery Schools. These centers work on a franchise basis, according to which almost anyone can set them up if they adhere to the codes determined by the individual state. However, there centers are *geared* for a *middle-class clientele.*

Working class women and their children are to be serviced by the large

229

corporations themselves. In December of 1969, a conference was held in New York City which studied the advantages and uses of day-care centers. Attending this conference were representatives of some of the largest corporations in the world, including Con Edison, Standard Oil Company, United States Steel, Bankers Trust Company, the Chase Manhattan Bank Foundation, and the United Fruit Company. The businessmen heard one speaker state that day-care was relevant to them since an early socialization of children would catch America's youth before they become drop-outs, hippies and rebels and turn them into people who will instead build, and not burn down, buildings.

West German Women's Liberation and groups in that country's Extra-Parliamentary-Oppostition (New Left) have been able to sustain many "anti-authoritarian" day-care centers in major cities for several years. It is with this background of experience that Helke Sander is able to evaluate industrial day-care and related programs. Intent upon viewing the company day-care situation within the broader context of women in West Berlin, Sander also focuses upon the dilemma of the isolated housewife and the demands of kindergarten teachers in West Berlin. We will have to study our situation more closely before we will know if we can in any way take up her proposals for linking the day-care issue with other women's demands. The one element we do miss in Helke Sander's analysis is that the day-care issue is also important in the struggle to break down, wherever possible, the existing divison of sex-roles which types child-care as woman's work and inferior to "real" (paid) work—man's work. However, Sander's reservations about company day-care centers where parental control is likely to be scant are clearly very relevant to the situation in the United States, as are her criticisms of short-sighted and short-lived attempts by people on the Left to *use* the need for day-care as a way to reach and "politicize" women workers.

Project Company Kindergarten
Helke Sander
translated by Christel Koppel

Helke Sander is a member of the Action Council for Women's Liberation in West Berlin. She has been active in a workshop for highschool students.

The concept of company day-care center has been circulating among many groups on the Left recently; such centers seem to be the "in" cause for those who want to agitate in factories. 30.7% of all employees in West Berlin's industry are women, and this number will increase in the near future. Therefore, it is mandatory for us to evaluate such organizing attempts in order to see if this age-old demand of unions should once again be picked up. We must get some clarity on the needs of women and on how to work politically among our sisters.

The organizing collective in Wedding (a working class district of West Berlin) has been planning for some time to establish a company day-care center as part of their political work; however, up until now there has been little open discussion on the goals and strategy of such day-care centers. Because they will effect the lives of many women and children and because they are seen as an important part of socialist strategy, I intend to discuss the company day-care center more critically than one might consider necessary at first glance.

The term "company day-care center" must first be explained. Ordinarily it means a center established and maintained by a company for the young children of its blue and white collar workers. The company day-care center does not exist for pedagogical reasons but follows from industry's need to attract and hold female employees.

The collective in Wedding, however, which sees this project as their main political work, has an entirely different concept of company day-care centers.

Note: We have tried to find English equivalents to the various terms in this article. The German terms in the original article for "company day-care center," "children's shop of the organizing collective," and "organizing collective" were respectively, "Betriebskindergarten," "Basiskinderladen," and "Basisgruppe."

Reprinted from *Radical America*, vol. IV, no. 2, February, 1970, pp. 68-79, by permission of the author and *Radical America*.

Through agitation they hope to interest a portion of the women workers in a particular firm in such a center. These women, with the help of other female comrades, would then set up a day-care center for their own children. The costs would be paid by the parents, by comrades from the organizing collective, or by leftist organizations.

It should be clear that the company and the collective have two entirely different things in mind when they speak of day-care centers. Since the structure of the group, the distribution of costs and the conceptual content are so different in each case, I shall henceforth refer to the day-care center of the organizing collective as the *children's shop;* the term "company day-care center" will be used according to the common definition. Inaccuracies in language, however, reflect vague objectives; this vagueness must be eliminated as far as is possible.

It will be necessary to formulate some possible goals for such a children's shop project. One might be to set up a model for other children's shops as a way of working toward the foundation of socialist mass education in cooperation with the parents and children. This, however, seems an unrealistic goal since the specific financial circumstances which made possible the first children's shop will not repeat themselves indefinitely. The establishment of a children's shop alone is not proof of organizational power. This power must come from knowing the sources for funds and from the consciousness that we ourselves must determine the education of our children according to our own goals. We do not have this consciousness yet; if we did, we would be looking for the means to make possible a socialist education for all children, regardless of the working conditions of their parents. That is, we would not restrict our efforts to the women employed in one firm.

Although it is inevitable that the whole question of socialist mass education will arise as a secondary problem for the people working in such children's shops, we must conclude that the comrades in the collective have some other goal in mind with this project. If the intention were to free a few women employees who would then be able to do political work on the conflicts existing within the company, this would be elitist. Nor would this children's shop have anything to do with the formation of cadres, since the same barriers to political work (children, husbands, home) would continue to exist for other women. It is even conceivable—although undesirable—that this collective merely would like the prestige of having started a women's group which can talk about workers' control (while a female comrade takes care of the children). If we eliminate these as possible intentions, however, it would seem that the immediate group to be won is the women with young children working in the particular company. The goal of the first children's shop could be to reach all the working mothers in the company through those whe send their children to the initial children's shop. Together, then, these women could demand and fight for a company day-care center, supported and maintained by the company. Supposedly, a day-care center with certain amenities would allow the women to gain the necessary time and consciousness and would be an indirct way to lead them to the so-called primary problems, i.e. those which develop out of the process of production. It is unclear to me whether those who are fighting for the children's shop want to politicize only a few women or all of them. It is also unclear, as we shall discuss later, whether the children's shop will be able to give the women the time and energy necessary for pursuing the mainstay of agitational work, i.e., the provocation of conflicts between workers and the company bosses and the achievement of solidarity through struggle.

Before we can determine whether we should seek to develop political consciousness among these women within or outside the sphere of production, we will have to know certain facts. Thirty-six percent of all workers and employees in West Berlin are women. According to the metal workers' union 43.4% of them are married and 11.7% are widowed or divorced. In other words, more than fifty percent of all working women have family responsibilities. This number is going to increase in the coming years, because the need for female workers is also increasing.

Another salient factor is the dearth of day-care centers, nursery schools and kindergartens in the city. Parents have great difficulty gaining admission for children, and when they succeed in doing so, they (and the children) often have to put up with such severe inconveniences as long commuting distances, loss of wages, and very early rising. Therefore, almost any attempt to establish any sort of center for young children will find the support of working mothers.

Reacting to this need, industry has seized upon the day-care center as a means of attracting the female workers they need into the labor force. According to a study made by the Berlin State Commission, by the end of 1966, there were 350,000 women of working age in Berlin who were willing but unable to work (and who were neither invalids nor in training programs). Their reasons lay primarily in their family duties. "Most of the young mothers are particularly good workers, because they very often surpass their unmarried colleagues in interest in the job and in a sense of responsibility." Therefore, the Commission concludes that new and unconventional ways of utilizing this reserve labor force must be found—which would mean above all the establishment of company day-care centers. "The reserves of 350,000 presently non-working women is of prime importance in our attempts to increase the size of the labor force in West Berlin without having to recruit people from outside Berlin."

Thus, demands for company day-care centers do not meet the same resistance today that they have for the past fifty years. On the contrary, some of the advertising campaigns are using the existence of day-care for children of female employees as an attraction for women. Kreuzberg, another working class district of West Berlin, already has two company day-care centers, and several other companies have volunteered to set up such centers. In a few years, company day-care centers may well be as standard a practice as the two weeks of vacation, both designed to extract higher production rates from the worker.

Since industrial day-care centers will soon multiply, we must now ask whether at this point we should use our energies in hurrying their arrival or whether we should rather work to prevent this. Should we work to politicize these working mothers in order to mobilize them to fight, as an example, for the limitation of group size to fifteen instead of twenty or more children? For the answers we must analyze what a company day-care center will mean for those involved.

The Effects on Mother and Child

At first glance, the benefits to both parties seem self-evident. The company day-care center can provide the mother with reliable and perhaps inexpensive care for her child at her place of work. The child is assured of playmates—which is not always the case in some individual babysitting arrangements. The family might also gain an extra half hour or so of sleep in the morning. And, if the child was formerly being cared for by a relative, the mother is relieved of her guilty conscience for having to impose.

How real are these benefits to mother and child? The existence of a company day-care center does not alter the times of the work shifts in the factory. The mother must still get to work on time; life may simply be a little less hectic in the early morning for the working mother and her family. During the day, the mother may be expected to spend the few minutes during her coffee break with her child, though she may desparately need that time for herself. Then, at half-past-four, the child leaves with the mother, is dragged along on shopping errands, and supervised until it is time for bed. There are probably other children of the same age living in the neighborhood who are in the same situation. But this child meets them only when the mother has the time to supervise their play, unless the child is old enough—and the street safe enough—to play without parental supervision. Because the mother has had to tend to the child immediately after her exhausting work day, there will be ample opportunity for aggressions to arise between mother and child.

Our demands must be applicable to all working mothers and all working conditions. Therefore, how will we insure that even the many small companies which employ women set aside large, sunny rooms and outside play area for the children, as the large and wealthy firms can easily do? These centers could easily prove to be a repressive situation for the children. Another important disadvantage could accompany the company day-care center: Under present conditions, if the job is too strenuous or frustrating, the woman at least has the option of changing jobs. However, if her child is enrolled in the company's day-care center, she will think long and hard before changing jobs, for it is unlikely that she will readily find another day-care arrangement for her child. Even if more company day-care centers are established, there will not be enough to meet the demand. Moreover, a company might decide that its day-care center is a useful means of keeping female employees in line. Women might be required to earn places for their children in the day-care center through special merit. Thus, the company would be able to prevent them from achieving solidarity.

What is the alternative? Clearly the women need day-care for their children, but they need day-care which will really help them to cope with their problems. They do *not* need the kind that will in the final analysis make them more dependent and immobile. It has been proven that it is extremely difficult to organize women in factories and firms. Even interested women are afraid that their husbands or friends would oppose such political work. Or, if they have children, they have no time or energy to spare for such organizational work. Lack of free time is the main problem for most working mothers. Those people who know the luxury of sleeping until mid-morning on occasion will have difficulty in comprehending what it means to work a sixteen-hour day, every day. Nor can we overlook overbearing husbands or demanding children, for both are very real considerations in the lives of working women.

In general, women do the most simple-minded kind of work, work which allows not even a remnant of self-identity. The work has a dulling effect that stifles any imagination, such as thinking of ways to earn more money or ways to reorganize their work or work shifts. The work is so bad that it should really be abolished, but it cannot be abolished. These workers depend upon such work; the idea that stupid work should be automated to make room for more meaningful work is unrealistic for people who are used to getting only the kind of jobs which others shun. In the event of automation, these women would be left jobless; this is a truly realistic evaluation, since most women are untrained in any skilled labor.

To elicit their support, any work conflict would have to let these women envision a change in their situation outside of work as well. Outside of work they may still have hopes, they may not have become hardened yet. Thus, this is precisely the area in which they are prepared to fight. In other words, we must find ways of relieving the burdens in other spheres of working women's lives before they will be free to organize for better conditions at work.

There may be another approach for political work which may be more effective not only in helping working mothers and their children but also in integrating the company day-care issue with the needs and demands of other groups of women—nursery school and kindergarten teachers, elementary school teachers *and* isolated housewives.

Demands of the Teachers

Nursery school and kindergarten teachers in the regular school system are obviously quite a relevant group for the company day-care centers.

Having organized for nearly two years, these teachers tried to prepare a strike with political content. (I will not go into the details here as to why the strike could not take place and what errors were made.) However, in their struggle, these teachers at the bottom of the school hierarchy had a qualitatively different target than would the women in the company day-care struggle, as now envisioned. The target in the teachers' struggle is the Senate of Berlin; their demands are for substantive reforms in their work. Primarily they demand to be allowed to fulfill their true pedagogical task. They refuse to go on turning the children into the broken, disciplined creatures found among the mass of today's population. For this reason, one of their demands was that the Senate not open additional day-care centers until the present centers had enough trained personnel and until the size of the groups were reduced to numbers which would make meaningful pedagogical work possible.

The negative response to their demands showed them that their demands would not be met within the present structure of society but that they would have to fight the system. The teachers know who their real opponent is. They have recognized their potential for breaking the system. They are correct in fearing that the establishment of new company day-care centers would obscure the situation and destroy the new solidarity which has slowly developed within their ranks. More day-care centers at this point would mean that trained nursery school and kindergarten teachers would migrate into industry for better salaries, and the questions of teacher education and state control of education would remain untouched. Thus, the demand for further company day-care centers would amount to a stab in the back to those teachers who are now organizing themselves, and that according to socialist principles.

These teachers have gained experiences which could be of great importance to teachers in elementary schools. The nursery school and kindergarten teachers have realized the impossibility of doing anything for the individual child under present conditions. So far, politicized elementary school teachers have continued to try to make improvements for their children under the old conditions or to experiment with new forms through which to achieve a degree of politicization — for example, by giving the children permission to eat in class, by allowing them to remain seated while giving an answer, or even by talking to them about Vietnam. These teachers do, of course, face immense obstacles, without being rewarded by any concrete success. Moreover, the classes in the elementary schools are bigger than those in the younger grades, and, thus, the necessity for discipline is greater, making pedagogical work nearly impossible.

Almost all teachers are very dissatisfied with these conditions. We must ask ourselves whether this discontent should not be taken up in an effort to politicize and organize the teachers. In that case the nursery school and kindergarten teachers would have to coordinate their efforts with other groups of teachers. However, at this point in time the kindergarten teachers are the only ones organizing.

Teachers and Mothers Must Organize as Women

These, then, are the problems: working women need their work load at home and on the job reduced to a bearable level before they can proceed. The kindergarten teachers demand small groups, better teacher training and changes in the content of the education. Lastly, there is the situation of those women not in the production process. Because of their isolation at home they become neurotic, experiencing the world only through their husbands and children. Any woman who rebels against this situation is condemned by society as a sick outcast, since these women are, after all, "getting what they have coming to them."

It must now be shown that kindergarten teachers, female workers, and mothers in the home must organize as women, since the demands for smaller groups, more teacher training facilities and less repressive education have direct bearing on the overload of work upon women in industry and on the isolation of women at home. This is not immediately apparent.

At first glance, it seems that kindergarten teachers and mothers have a conflict of interests. This, of course, was immediately picked up by the press at the time the strike was under preparation. By defining the issues in this way, they tried to mobilize the mothers against the kindergarten teachers: The kindergarten teachers call for the immediate halt to the admission of children, for a delay in the establishment of new day-care centers, and they demand that in the event a kindergarten teacher is sick her class be cancelled if no trained substitute is available. The mothers, on the other hand, demand more day-care centers and kindergartens for their children. They are often even willing to send their children to a bad kindergarten since that is the precondition for their being able to go out and work. And they depend upon this work for financial reasons or because it seems the only way for them to break out of their isolation.

However, the kindergarten teachers do not wish to exclude these children who need to be looked after and educated. They are working on a concept of education which would, on the contrary, prevent all children from becoming mental cripples. The teachers no longer want to contribute to the psychological destruction of children who will then later have very little motivation to defend themselves.

If the kindergarten teachers succeed in preventing the opening of new day-care centers, the general question of teacher training must be attacked; at the kindergarten level this involves the training of women. Today kindergarten teaching is a middle-class profession. For a socialist education, however, we need working class teachers.

The militantly activated desire of women for more and different types of centers for their young children will raise the whole problem of education of girls and work opportunity for women to a new level. As it stands now, women are divided and kept in a state of ignorance and are thus suppressed and made dependent upon official protection. Naturally, they then become the backbone of reaction; but few wish to see this backbone destroyed.

The hysterical reaction of unions and Senate to the preparations for the strike of the kindergarten teachers shows that the powers that be see the teachers as a key group. At the same time, however, it is obvious that the teachers themselves are not yet aware of their full power because they lack the theory behind it. They will sink into reformism without the cooperation and control of the female workers. It seems that bureaucracy is one step ahead of us in its theoretical evaluation, for it realizes the significance of the development of solidarity among teachers, working women and mothers. The political work of these groups of women will to a great extent determine whether the 350,000 potential female workers in Berlin will remain oppressed women open to exploitation.

Again, what do the demands of the kindergarten teachers have in common with the interests of the mothers? The mothers would readily agree that it is better for the children not to be crowded into small rooms. They might also realize that because children become more stable in smaller groups, the children would not need to work out repression they were exposed to during the day by provoking their parents in the evening. However, this demand by itself will not get the mothers to join the kindergarten teachers on the barricades.

Let us return to the small groups. Much space is necessary to allow for small classes; however, if we became more flexible and imaginative in our ideas on what constitutes proper space and location for day-care centers and kindergartens, we could utilize space in apartment buildings, stores and office buildings. The advantages of centers in residential neighborhoods are obvious. Involving the children in the area would have the advantage that social contacts either already exist or would be possible because the families live in the same vicinity.

When a mother realizes that it would be feasible to establish a kindergarten for her own and the neighbor's children right in their own apartment building and she then finds out that the Senate refuses to give them funds to run such a day-care center or kindergarten, she will begin wondering why money is available for land speculators but not for the children. Or, if she is told that there are no kindergarten teachers she will ask why so many girls with a junior high school education or less *(Volksschule)* who are interested in becoming teachers are barred from the profession because of their educational and social background. She will also want to know why it is that those people who have had but eight years of schooling and who may have many children of their own are not permitted to learn how to take care of an equal number of other children — i.e., to become teachers.

In order to activate and coordinate these desires, needs and demands we must continually examine and compare the situation of the teachers and the mothers, so that we may learn to demand from society as a whole what it denies us. However, for that purpose we must first learn *as women* to realize our oppression in its full extent, so that we can fight against it. We have to see the point where specific feminist interests coincide with specific class interests.

The Work Which Lies Ahead

We cannot permit conflicts to be picked up hastily and solutions offered which once again would leave us and the other women we work with as diminished human beings. It is for this reason that I have subjected the company day-care project to such critical scrutiny. In order to learn how to fight for true socialism, we have to learn to articulate what we understand by it and to transfer this knowledge to other women. Our strategy must develop from this common understanding and not out of the men's perception of the position of women; men make less radical demands because they lack the experience of certain oppressions.

We are, however, still only stuttering. We still have trouble formulating our own demands and standing up for them without retreating before the supposed theoretical superiority of the men. Despite the Action Council* (for Women's Liberation) we still are in danger of vacillating as individuals and doing things we have not really thought through independently — all because we wish to defend ourselves in front of the men and prove to them that we can work politically. One dangerous symptom of this attitude leads some female comrades to say they want to work in factories in order "to reach the women," when they are at the same time extremely bored when other female comrades talk to them about their own child-raising problems. These are problems which these childless comrades will also have to face when they begin to work with the women in the factories. I also know comrades who refuse to move into communal apartments where there are children for fear that the children would disturb their political work. This kind of political work seems to follow the pleasure principle rather than necessity.

We need to develop the confidence to draw from our knowledge of what oppresses us as women and of how our oppression relates to that of other women. We must overcome fears about whether our work will be political enough for our male comrades and whether our work will be recognized as worthwhile. I think we will be strong only when all theoreticians can call us inflexible, rigid, unbending and emancipationist and we no longer regard these words as attacks, but rather as an expression of insecurity in the men.

(This article first appeared as "Projekt Betriebskindergarten," *Rote Presse Korrespondenz* No. 27-28 (August 29, 1969), pp. 19-23.
*This is the name of the umbrella organization for Women's Liberation in West Berlin.

ABORTION LAW REPEAL (Sort of): A Warning to Women

Lucinda Cisler

Lucinda Cisler is one of the foremost experts on abortion in the Women's Liberation Movement. She has fought for years for women's right to control their own bodies.

One of the few things everyone in the women's movement seems to agree on is that we have to get rid of the abortion laws and make sure that any woman who wants an abortion can get one. We all recognize how basic this demand is; it sounds like a pretty clear and simple demand, too — hard to achieve, of course, but obviously a fundamental right just like any other method of birth control.

But just because it *sounds* so simple and so obvious and is such a great point of unity, a lot of us haven't really looked below the surface of the abortion fight and seen how complicated it may be to get what we want. The most important thing feminists have done and have to keep doing is to insist that the basic reason for repealing the laws and making abortions available is JUSTICE: women's right to abortion.

Everyone recognizes the cruder forms of opposition to abortion traditionally used by the forces of sexism and religious reaction. But a feminist philosophy must be able to deal with *all* the stumbling blocks that keep us from reaching our goal, and must develop a consciousness about the far more subtle dangers we face from many who honestly believe they are our friends.

In our disgust with the extreme oppression women experience under the present abortion laws, many of us are understandably tempted to accept insulting token changes that we would angrily shout down if they were offered to us in any other field of the struggle for women's liberation. We've waited so long for anything to happen that when we see our demands having any effect at all we're sorely tempted to convince ourselves that everything that sounds good in the short run will turn out to be good for women in the long run. And a lot of us are so fed up with "the system" that we don't even bother to find out what it's doing so we can fight it and demand what *we* want. This is the measure of our present oppression; a chain of aluminum *does* feel lighter around our necks than one made of iron, but it's still a chain, and our task is still to burst entirely free.

The abortion issue is one of the very few issues vital to the women's movement that well-meaning people outside the movement were dealing with on an organized basis even before the new feminism began to explode a couple of years ago. Whatever we may like to think, there *is* quite definitely an abortion movement that is distinct from the feminist movement, and the good intentions of most of the people in it can turn out to be either a tremendous source of support for our goals or the most tragic barrier to our ever achieving them. The choice is up to us: we must subject every proposal for change and every tactic to the clearest feminist scrutiny, demand only what is good for *all* women, and not let some of us be bought off at the expense of the rest.

Until just a couple of years ago the abortion movement was a tiny handful of good people who were still having to concentrate just on getting the taboo lifted from public discussions of the topic. They dared not even think about any proposals for legal change *beyond* "reform" (in which abortion is grudgingly parceled out by hospital committee fiat to the few women who can "prove" they've been raped, or who are crazy, or are in danger of bearing a defective baby). They spent a lot of time debating with priests about When Life Begins, and Which Abortions Are Justified. They were mostly doctors, lawyers, social workers, clergymen, professors, writers, and a few were just plain women — usually not particularly feminist.

Part of the reason the reform movement was very small was that it appealed mostly to altruism and very little to people's self-interest: the circumstances covered by "reform" *are* tragic but they affect very few women's lives, whereas repeal is compelling because most women know the fear of unwanted pregnancy and in fact get abortions for that reason.

Some people were involved with "reform" — and are in the abortion movement today — for very good reasons: they are concerned with important issues like the public health problem presented by illegal abortions, the doctor's right to provide patients with good medical care, the suffering of unwanted children and unhappy families, and the burgeoning of our population at a rate too high for *any* economic system to handle.

But all these good reasons are, in the final analysis, based on simple expediency. Such reasons are peripheral to the central rationale for making abortion available: justice for women. And unless a well-thought-out feminism underlies the dedication of these people, they will accept all kinds of token gains from legislators and judges and the medical establishment in the name of "getting something done NOW"— never mind what that is, or how much it cuts the chances for real changes later by lulling the public into a false sense of accomplishment.

These people do deserve a lot of credit for their lonely and dogged insistence on raising the issue when everybody else wanted to pretend it didn't exist. But because they invested so much energy earlier in working for "reform" (and got it in ten states), they have an important stake in believing that their approach is the "realistic" one — that one must accept the small, so-called "steps in the right direction" that can be wrested from reluctant politicians, that it isn't quite dignified to demonstrate or shout what you want, that raising the women's rights issue will "alienate" politicians, and so on.

Others, however (especially in centers of stylish liberalism like New York City), are interested in abortion because they are essentially political fashion-mongers: Some of them aspire to public office and some just like to play around the pool. For them, it's "groovy" to be for something racy like abortion. You can make a name for yourself faster in a small movement, such as this one still is, than in something huge like the peace movement, and it's sexier than supporting the grape strikers in their struggle.

Unfortunately, the "good people" share with these pseudo-militants an overawed attitude toward politicians, doctors, lawyers, and traditional "experts" of all kinds; they tend to view the women's movement as rather eccentric troops they can call upon to help them with colorful things like unavoidable demonstrations, rather than as the grassroots force whose feminist philosophy should be leading *them* in the right direction. Even those who have begun to say that the woman's right to abortion *is* the central issue show a good deal of half-concealed condescension toward the very movement that has brought this issue to the fore and inspired the fantastic change in public opinion witnessed in the last year or so.

Because of course, it *is* the women's movement whose demand for *repeal* — rather than "reform" — of the abortion laws has spurred the general acceleration in the abortion movement and its influence. Unfortunately, and ironically, the very rapidity of the change for which we are responsible is threatening to bring us to the point where we are offered something so close to what we want that our demands for true radical change may never be achieved.

Most of us recognize that "reforms" of the old rape-incest-fetal deformity variety are not in women's interest and in fact, in their very specificity, are almost more of an insult to our dignity as active, self-determining humans than are the old laws that simply forbid us to have abortions unless we are about to die. But the *new* reform legislation now being proposed all over the country is not in our interest either: it looks pretty good, and the improvements it seems to promise (at least for middle-class women) are almost irresistible to those who haven't informed themselves about the complexities of the abortion situation or developed a feminist critique of abortion that goes beyond "it's our right." And the courts are now handing down decisions that look good at a glance but that contain the same restrictions as the legislation.

All of the restrictions are of the kind that would be extremely difficult to get judges and legislators to throw out later (unlike the obvious grotesqueries in the old "reform" laws, which are already being challenged successfully in some courts and legislatures). A lot of people are being seriously misled because the legislation and the court decisions that incorporate these insidious limitations are being called abortion law "repeal" by the media.

It's true that the media are not particularly interested in accuracy when they report news of interest to women, but the chief reason for this dangerous misuse of language is that media people are getting their information from the established abortion movement, which wants very badly to think that these laws and decisions *are* somehow repeal. (It seems pretty clear that when you repeal an abortion law you just get rid of it; you do not put things back into the statutes or make special rules that apply to abortion but not to other medical procedures.)

The following are the four major restrictions that have been cropping up lately in "repeal" bills, and some highly condensed reasons why feminists (and indeed anyone) must oppose them. No one can say for sure whether sexist ill-will, political horse-trading, or simple ignorance played the largest part in the lawmakers' decision to include them, but all of them codify outmoded notions about medical technology, religion, or women's "role":

1. Abortions may only be performed in licensed hospitals. Abortion is almost always a simple procedure that can be carried out in a clinic or a doctor's office. Most women do need a place to lie down and rest for a while after a D&C or even a vacuum aspiration abortion, but they hardly need to occupy scarce hospital beds and go through all the hospital rigmarole that ties up the woman's money and the time of overworked staff people.

Hospital boards are extremely conservative and have always wanted to minimize the number of abortions performed within their walls: the "abortion committees" we now have were not invented by lawmakers but by hospital administrators. New laws that insure a hospital monopoly will hardly change this attitude. (The same committees regulate which women will be able to get the sterilizations they seek — even though voluntary sterilization is perfectly legal in all but one or two states.) The hospitals and accreditation agencies set up their own controls on who will get medical care, and doctors who want to retain their attending status are quite careful not to do "too many" abortions or sterilizations.

Hawaii's new law has this kind of restriction, and hospitals there are already busy setting up a new catechism of "guidelines," none of which insure that women will get more abortions and all of which insure that they will have to ask a lot of strangers for "permission" before they are allowed to spend the considerable amount of money that hospitalization inevitably costs. Maryland's recent bill and the legislation and "guidelines" proposed in several other states — like New York — contain the same provisions that essentially shift the locus of control over women's decisions from the state to the hospital bureaucracies and their quasi-legal "regulations."

2. *Abortions may only be performed by licensed physicians.* This restriction sounds almost reasonable to most women who have always been fairly healthy and fairly prosperous, who are caught up in the medical mystique so many doctors have cultivated, and who accept the myth that abortion is incredibly risky and thus should cost a lot. But it is one of the most insidious restrictions of all, and is most oppressive to poor women.

Most doctors are not at all interested in performing abortions: even the ones who don't think it's dirty and who favor increasing the availability of abortion generally consider it a pretty boring procedure that they don't especially want to do. One reason they do find it tedious is that it is basically quite a simple operation, especially when the new vacuum aspiration technique is used, rather than the old dilation and curettage. The physicians who would like to see paramedical specialists trained to perform abortions with the aspirator (or who would like to perfect other promising new methods, such as hormone injections) would be completely thwarted by this restriction in their desire to provide efficient, inexpensive care on a mass basis. The general crisis in the medical delivery system in fact demands that paramedical people be trained to do a great many things that physicians do now.

If physicians themselves were to try to perform all the abortions that are needed, they would be swamped with requests and would have to charge a great deal for their specialized training. Childbirth is statistically eight or ten times more dangerous than abortion, and yet nurses are now being trained as midwives in many medical centers. Why can't they and other medical personnel also be specially trained to use the aspirator so that five or six of them can perform clinic abortions under the general supervision of one physician? Only if paramedicals are allowed to do abortions can we expect to have truly inexpensive (and eventually free) abortions available to all women.

In the fall of 1969 a Washington, D.C. court threw out the District's limitations on a doctor's right to perform abortions — but upheld the conviction of a paramedical aide who said she had wanted to help poor women. Anyone who knows what the present situation in D.C. is will know that abortion is *not* readily available when its performance is limited to doctors only. The public hospital where poor women go had to be forced by court order to provide this service; private hospitals that serve middle-class women still operate restrictively and charge a lot; a few doctors willing to brave the stigma of being "abortionists" are performing abortions in their offices for $300 or so. Although they work long hours, they are inundated with patients (one has a backlog of five weeks). Another is so swamped, partly because he continues to muddle through with D&C, that he does not even take the time to give the women an anesthetic (although they are assured before they arrive that they will get one).

Several attempts have been made to get D.C. doctors to devote a few volunteer hours each week to a free clinic for the poor; doctors have refused, expressing either indifference or fear of professional censure.

Some women insist that because *they* would prefer to go to a doctor, *all* women must be compelled by law to go to one. It is each woman's right to choose to spend $300 for an abortion from a doctor, but she is obviously oppressing other women when she insists that all must do as she does. An abortion performed by a paramedical person with special training in a given modern procedure could easily, in fact, be safer than a D&C performed by a physician who hasn't done many abortions before.

In any case, it is only when doctors have the right to train the people they need to help them meet the demand, and women have the right to get medical care at a price they can afford, that butchers and quacks will be put out of business. Existing medical practice codes provide for the punishment of quacks, but as long as poor women cannot find good abortions at a price they can pay, so long will butchers elude the law and women continue to die from their ministrations as they still do in states that have "reform."

Looking not so far into the future, this restriction would also deny women themselves the right to use self-abortifacients when they are developed — and who is to say they will not be developed soon? The laws regulating contraception that still exist in thirty-one states were made before contraceptive foam was invented, at a time when all effective female contraception involved a visit to the doctor. That visit was frozen into a legal requirement in some states, and we still have the sad and ludicrous example of Massachusetts, where non-prescriptive foam cannot legally be bought without a prescription.

The "doctors only" clause is a favorite in legislation that masquerades as repeal. New York, Hawaii, Maryland, Alaska, and Washington State, are among the important states where this restriction was (rather quietly) included.

3. *Abortions may not be performed beyond a certain time in pregnancy, unless the woman's life is at stake.* Significantly enough, the magic time limit varies from bill to bill, from court decision to court decision, but this kind of restriction essentially says two things to women: (a) at a certain stage, your body suddenly belongs to the state and it can force you to have a child, whatever your own reasons for wanting an abortion late in pregnancy; (b) because late abortion entails more risk to you than early abortion the state must "protect" you even if your considered decision is that you want to run that risk and your doctor is willing to help you. This restriction insults women in the same way the present "preservation-of-life" laws do: it assumes that we must be in a state of tutelage and cannot assume responsibility for our own acts. Even many women's liberation writers are guilty of repeating the paternalistic explanation given to excuse the original passage of U.S. laws against abortion: in the nineteenth century abortion was more dangerous than childbirth, and women had to be protected against it. Was it somehow less dangerous in the eighteenth century? Were other kinds of surgery safe then? And, most important, weren't women wanting and getting abortions, even though they knew how much they were risking? "Protection" has often turned out to be but another means of control over the protected; labor law offers many examples. When childbirth becomes as safe as it should be, perhaps it will be safer than abortion: will we put back our abortion laws, to "protect women?"

And basically, of course, no one can ever know exactly when *any* stage of pregnancy is reached until birth itself. Conception can take place at any time within about three days of intercourse, so that any legal time limit reckoned from "conception" is, meaningless because it cannot be determined precisely. All the talk about "quickening," "viability," and so on, is based on old religious myths (if the woman believes in them, of course, she won't look for an abortion) or tied to ever-shifting technology (who knows how soon a three-day-old fertilized egg may be considered "viable" because heroic mechanical devices allow it to survive and grow outside the woman's uterus?) To listen to judges and legislators play with the ghostly arithmetic of months and weeks is to hear the music by which angels used to dance on the head of a pin.

There are many reasons why a woman might seek a late abortion, and she should be able to find one legally if she wants it. She may suddenly discover that she had German measles in early pregnancy and that her fetus is deformed; she may have had a sudden mental breakdown; or some calamity may have changed the circumstances of her life: whatever her reasons, *she belongs to herself and not to the state.*

This limitation speaks to the hangups many people have, and it would be almost impossible to erase from a law once it were enacted — despite its possible constitutional vulnerability on the grounds of vagueness. It is incorporated in New York State's amended abortion law, among many others, and in a recent Federal court decision in Wisconsin that has been gravely misrepresented as judicial "repeal." The Washington, D.C. decision discussed the "issue," and concluded that Congress should probably enact new laws for different stages of pregnancy. This is not repeal, it is a last-ditch attempt at retaining a little of the state ownership of pregnant women provided for under the worst laws we have now.

4. Abortions may only be performed when the married woman's husband or the young single woman's parents give their consent. The feminist objection to vesting a veto power in anyone other than the pregnant woman is too obvious to need any elaboration. It is utterly fantastic, then, to hear that some women's liberation groups in Washington State have actually been *supporting* an abortion bill with a consent provision. Although such a debasing restriction is written into law in most of the states that have "reform," some legal writers consider it of such little consequence that they fail to mention it in otherwise accurate summaries of U.S. abortion laws.

This may be the easiest of these restrictions to challenge constitutionally, but why should we have to? Instead we could prevent its enactment and fight to eradicate the hospital regulations that frequently imposed it even where the law does not.

All women are oppressed by the present abortion laws, by old-style "reforms," and by seductive new fake-repeal bills and court decisions. But the possibility of fake repeal — if it becomes reality — is the most dangerous: it will divide women from each other. It can buy off most middle-class women and make them believe things have really changed, while it leaves poor women to suffer and keeps us all saddled with abortion laws for many more years to come. There are many nice people who would like to see abortion made more or less legal, but their reasons are fuzzy and their tactics acquiescent. Because no one else except the women's movement is going to cry out against these restrictions, it is up to feminists to make the strongest and most precise demands upon the lawmakers — who ostensibly exist to serve *us.* We will not accept insults and call them "steps in the right direction."

Only if we know what we *don't* want, and why, and say so over and over again, will we able to recognize and reject all the clever plastic imitations of our goal.

AN ABORTION WARNING

DANGER

There are only 4 methods of abortion which can be considered safe. Competent, medically trained abortionists, whether they are acting legally or not, NEVER USE METHODS DESCRIBED BELOW. THESE METHODS INVOLVE EXTREME PAIN AND CAN LEAD TO PERMANENT DISABILITY, INFECTION, OR DEATH:

Oral Means:

Ergot compounds — overdose is poison — can cause fatal kidney damage
Quinine Sulphate — can cause deformities in fetus or death to mother
(Estrogen — useless)
(Castor oil — useless)

NOTHING THAT IS SWALLOWED CAN CAUSE ABORTION WITHOUT ALSO CAUSING DEATH OR SEVERE DISABILITY TO THE MOTHER

Solids inserted into uterus: DANGER DEADLY:

Knitting needles
Coat hangers
Slippery Elm bark
Chop sticks
Ballpoint Pen
Pastes

Catheters
Gauze (packing)
Artists Paintbrushes
Curtain Rods
Telephone wire

COMMON DANGER OF PERFORATION (bursting) OF WOMB AND BLADDER — DEATH FROM INFECTION OR HAEMORRHAGE

Fluids inserted into uterus:

Soap suds, Alcohol, Potassium Permanganate
Lye, Lysol, Pine Oil

SEVERE BURNING OF TISSUES — HAEMORRHAGE-SHOCK-DEATH

Air pumped into uterus:

COLLAPSE FROM GAS EMBOLI INTO THE BLOOD STREAM. SUDDEN
VIOLENT DEATH.

Injections into Uterine Wall:

Ergot, Pitocin — poison
Sodium Pentothal — overdose causes death

Other Means:

Vacuum Cleaner — connected to uterus — not to be confused with vacuum aspiration — is fatal almost immediately — extracts uterus from pelvic cavity.

Physical exertion such as lifting heavy objects, running, etc. is useless

Falling down stairs — severe injury to mother but no abortion

BUTCHER ABORTIONS ARE DEADLY — ONLY DOCTORS OR OTHER SPECIALLY TRAINED PERSONNEL CAN SAFELY USE ONE OF THE 4 METHODS OF ABORTION — ALL OTHER METHODS CAN CAUSE DEATH BUT RARELY INDUCE ABORTION

If you have used on yourself or have allowed to be used, any of the above methods of abortion GO TO THE NEAREST HOSPITAL IMMEDIATELY. THERE IS NO LEGAL DANGER TO YOU.

LIKE BONE TO THE GROUND

Not till he started to feel her
first her wrist then suddenly under
her coat ramming her against the wall
starting to but she couldn't scream
the knife in his hand
groin up against her
his thigh splitting her knees till
she cracked like bone to the ground
flesh ripped silk in his teeth
once more
her screams gurgled blood
then it was over

next day she didn't show up for work
or any day after.

Lyn Lifshin

Reprinted from *Why is the House Dissolving?* Poems by Lyn Lifshin, open skull press, San Francisco, 1968.

BIBLIOGRAPHIC NOTES:
FROM FEMINISM TO LIBERATION
FROM FEMINISM TO LIBERATION

From Feminism to Liberation
Edith Hoshino Altbach

Edith Hoshino Altbach is a graduate student at the University of Wisconsin. She edited the Radical America *(Feb. 1970) issue on Women's Liberation.*

Women and History

Looking at the history of women, one is struck above all by the continuity of their inferior status. At points of transition from one technological or socio-economic period to another, when they might have expected to gain a lasting measure of liberation, they have not been able to do so. If there has been progress in any sphere for women, it has been accompanied by regression in others. Moreover, it is proving very difficult for women to study the history of their sex, for such a history has yet to be written. Scholars, scientists, and writers have given a marginal and distorted treatment of women.[1]

Recently, the various inadequate and invalid theories of women have come under attack. Simone de Beauvoir's *The Second Sex*,[2] is probably the best general summary of the limitations of the existing theoretical systems used to define woman,[2] although accuracy in some few areas is sacrificed to comprehensive coverage.

In *Life Against Death*, Norman O. Brown shows how Freud revealed the Kantian "schemata of rationality" to be "schemata of repression."[3] People are now looking with the same critical eye at Freud himself, among others. Herbert Marcuse and Norman O. Brown do try to push beyond Freud's theory of patricidal-castration-guilt complex to a primal "maternal reality principle," but we should beware lest those who would save us from the old familiar myths bring us only reinterpretations or new ones in their stead.[4]

---

[1] Well documented by Mary R. Beard. *Woman as Force in History.* New York: Macmillan Co., 1946, pp. 47-76.
[2] Simone de Beauvoir. *The Second Sex.* New York: Bantam Books, 1961.
[3] Norman O. Brown. *Life Against Death.* New York: Random House, 1959, p. 95.
[4] Herbert Marcuse, *Eros and Civilization.* New York: Vintage Books, p. 210, and Brown, *op. cit.*, p. 126.

Yet, these various critiques have contributed to a trend away from a view of women as a part of the "natural phenomena" which form a constant backdrop for history. Aileen Kraditor analyzes this trend as a parallel development to the growing respectability of social and cultural history alongside constitutional, diplomatic and economic history.[5] Kraditor, however, warns elsewhere that women have been premature before in predicting a change for the better in their affairs.

Ultimately too, the above critiques remain critiques. To repeat, there are no histories of women, there is no substantial body of literature pertinent to women. Thus, this article on the literature about women must inevitably be limited and fragmentary. First, it will review some early writings on women, particularly important to the Women's Rights Movement of 1848-1920, but also relevant today. Then, it will discuss writings on the subject of women's role in the family and at work, considering first socialist and feminist views and then establishment views. Finally, it will analyze some of the commentary (both sympathetic and hostile) on women's liberation movements, past and present.

Beginnings

The present movement for the liberation of women refers back to the pioneering works written on women, some 100 years old. These works were influential in the Women's Rights Movement which ran its uneven course from 1848-1920. Historians have defined this movement as the suffrage movement, thereby obscuring or ignoring its radical strain. They pass over the contribution of the women who considered the suffrage movement a vehicle for greater social change. But today women are rediscovering the more radical strain of this older movement.

Many of the pioneering works on women are based on early anthropological research. In the last decades, however, anthropology has been permeated with a cultural relativism.[6] Radicals generally distrust anthropological research of this variety because it tends to glorify the "wonderful diversity of human behavior," overlooking forces of domination or oppression. Out of the Women's Liberation movement there have recently come some critical appraisals of cultural relativism.[7] Moreover, throughout

---

[5] Aileen S. Kraditor. *Up From the Pedestal. Selected Writings in the History of American Feminism.* Chicago: Quadrangle Books, 1968, p. 3.

[6] Norman O. Brown, *op. cit.*, p. 245.

[7] The most critical type of appraisal is exemplified in Evelyn Reed. "Problems of Women's Liberation." New York: Merit Publishers, 1969.

history chauvinists of one sort or another have bandied about such an assortment of theories on the natural woman in her savage, barbarian and primitive stages that caution seems the better part of wisdom in the anthropological area. However, we remain faced with the fact that many important early works make forays into anthropology.

Friedrich Engels' *The Origin of the Family, Private Property and the State*[8] must have had enormous impact in the early "natural rights" period of the feminist movement; it is widely cited even today in the current Women's Liberation movement. To summarize very briefly, Marx and Engels recognize that the family system and the position of women, involved as they were in that original production — reproduction of the species — had much to do with the development of society and social institutions. Engels based his book on the work of Bachofen, McLennan and Morgan.[9] The enduring contribution of their work was to shake the unquestioned belief in the correctness of the male-dominated nuclear family with all the corresponding limitations on sexuality and sex roles. But their anthropological material has proven to be the weakest point in Engels' book. However, as Margaret Benston points out, Engels' arguments on the inextricable connection between the development of private ownership and the subjugation of women are still valid if one postulates a more nearly equal position of women instead of the gynecocracy which Engels describes.[10]

Freud's depiction of prehistory is even more dubious than Engels'. Freud reconstructed a life and death struggle within the primal horde between the father-despot and the sons over the possession of the women (the mothers) in the horde. Fears of castration and death kept the sons under control until they rebelled and killed the father. However, the brothers' sense of guilt at having killed the sustainer and orderer of the horde insured that the restraints and denials imposed earlier by the father become internalized in each brother clan, providing the basis for civilization. Discussing Freud's description, Marcuse says: "If Freud's hypothesis is not corroborated by any anthropological evidence, it would have to be discarded altogether except for the fact that it telescopes, in a sequence of catastrophic events, the historical dialectic of domination and thereby elucidates aspects of civilization hitherto unexplained. We use Freud's anthropological specula-

---

[8] First published in 1884.

[9] J. J. Bachofen. *Mother Right.* 1861. S. F. MacLennan. *Primitive Marriages,* 1865. Lewis H. Morgan. *Systems of Consanguinity and Affinity of the Human Family* and *Ancient Society,* 1877.

[10] Margaret Benston. "The Political Economy of Women's Liberation," see this volume, p. 203.

tion only in this sense: for its symbolic value."[11] Marcuse's argument is in part very persuasive; however, a history of the dialectic of domination based upon a "symbolic anthropology" has a way of spiralling off in tangent, missing our subject: woman.

A brief summary of Veblen's ideas on women may also be of interest. His work is undeniably problematic and contradictory, his psychology fragmentary and erratic; these inadequacies were some of the reasons for his fall into oblivion within the social sciences. David Riesman provides a good discussion of Veblen's radical views regarding masculinity and femininity: "Much of his work can be seen as a passionate defense of women; Veblen regarded women as the great oppressed cadre, whether they were slaves of marauding tribes and thus the first 'private property' or the 19th century slaves of fashion who bore the brunt of male emulation; intrinsically freer than men of such superstitions as nationalism, the women were the core carriers of social decency and simplicity underneath the perversions and rituals created and dominated by men."[12] More specifically, Veblen analyzed "the close connection, particularly in point of psychological derivation, between individual ownership, the system of status, and the paternal household, as they appear in this culture."[13] Like Engels, Veblen felt that warfare and slavery arose at that level of technology which made possible the production of a surplus. Prior to this stage, Veblen postulated a form of non-coercive monogamic marriage terminable at will by either party. He called it the "household of the unattached woman." The type of marriage replacing this older form originated from the new custom of securing women from other tribes as trophies of battle. Through this custom, marriage based upon coercion and ownership was introduced. Because of the growing prestige of the warriors and consequently of "ownership-marriage," all other forms of marriage lost status; the independent, unattached woman especially lost caste. In the minds of all men and women, the relationship between the sexes based upon capture and ownership by the man became the standard for "beauty and honor." When a group's increase in size made it difficult to secure enough wives by capture, marriage rites involving "mock capture" were introduced to make it possible to find wives within the group. "Hence," Veblen concludes, "the formal profession of fealty and submission on the part of the woman in the marriage rites of peoples among whom the house-

---

[11] Marcuse, *op.cit.*, p. 54.

[12] David Riesman. *Thorstein Veblan, A Critical Interpretation.* New York: Charles Scribner's Sons, 1953, p. 41.

[13] Thorstein Veblen. "The Barbarian Status of Women," *American Journal of Sociology* Vol. 4, No. 4 (Jan. 1899), pp. 503-14.

hold with a male head prevails. . . . In the words of the formula, even after it has been appropriately softened under the latter-day decay of the sense of status, it is the woman's place to love, honor and obey."[14]

J. J. Bachofen, using as sources ancient classical literature, postulated the existence of a religion of the Great Mother.[15] However, mother worship does not necessarily mean rule by women: "Myth is not so crassly tied to reality."[16] Simone de Beauvoir discusses the ambiguities of being enshrined in this way. Her central criticism of Engels in *The Second Sex* is that he reduces woman to an economic being in his analysis. Engels does give an overly simplified outline of how woman's supposed economic disadvantage was basic to the subsequent growth of exploitative and male-dominated social institutions, but this may not be sufficient reason to discount his work. Marx and Engels did not seek to explain all of social life as but a reflex of economic life.[17] Significantly, in a later criticism of her own book, de Beauvoir says she should have used a more materialist analysis: "I should base the notion of woman as *other* and the Manichean argument it entails not on an idealistic and *a priori* struggle of consciences, but on the facts of supply and demand."[18] In a general discussion on "stereotypes of woman's place," a veteran in the struggle for women's rights sums it up in this way: " . . . the state of the economy affects the limits of personal range. Then the persuaders take over and make those limits attractive. The rewards are certified, the penalties suppressed. Nor is the pattern limited to the design for making a living. Every cultural process has its corresponding caveat."[19] Another approach to a reevaluation of Marx and Engels on archaic society sees power as essentially psychological in derivation: Norman O. Brown writes, "Marxian anthropology, with its assumption of the economic derivation of power and its correlative assumption that the psychology of economics is universally the psychology of appropriation, is committed to deny or belittle the existence of power in the archaic society."[20]

---

[14] *Ibid.*

[15] Bachofen, *op. cit.*

[16] Brown, *op. cit.*, p. 126.

[17] Melville J. Herskovits, *Economic Anthropology*, New York: Alfred A. Knopf, p. 494.

[18] de Beauvoir, *Force of Circumstances*, 1965, p. 192; cited and discussed in Juliet Mitchell, "Women: the Longest Revolution," see this volume, p. 99.

[19] Nancy Reeves, "A Moratorium on Marriage," a paper presented at the 1969 UCLA Conference on Stereotypes of Woman's Place.

[20] Brown, *op. cit.*, p. 251.

Marcuse's critique of the book, while not naming it specifically: "All talk about the abolition of repression, about life against death, etc., has to place itself in the

Slave or idol, it is not of woman's choice. . . . L. H. Morgan worked with kinship systems among American Indian tribes in formulating his view of archaic society as a peaceable gynecocracy run along the lines of a primitive communism. But here we should beware of creating new myths to conquer the old. Norman O. Brown, in searching for a theory of dynamic interrelations between family structure, religion, and natural culture says: "If the emergence of social privilege marks the Fall of Man, the Fall took place not in the transition from 'primitive communism' to 'private property' but in the transition from ape to man."[21] A more cautious statement, of Lawrence Ludovici, reads: "Yet the burden of the theory put forward by Bachofen and others seems incontrovertible. If we scratch hard enough to reach beneath the benevolent Jovinian patriarchy of ancient Greece, we discover surely all the signs of the earlier matriarchal cultures."[22] August Bebel, in referring to criticisms of his own book, saw in them attempts to "prove that neither the natural sciences nor anthropology provide any material for showing the necessity and usefulness of socialism."[23]

There have been doubts cast upon the matriarchy theory which cannot entirely be passed off as male chauvinism. Simone de Beauvoir shows the problems in lumping together matriolatry, matriarchy and matrillineage. She refers to Claude Levi-Strauss, who analyzes marriage as a bond not between men and women but between men by means of women.[24] Woman herself is but the symbol of her line. True authority rests with her father or brother. Moreover, the persistence of the custom of residence after marriage among the man's kin takes away from our picture of autonomous women under matrilineal systems. Malinowski goes so far as to say that, in view of the universal pattern of legitimacy with regard to children, it can be thus said that "the group consisting of a woman and her offspring is not a sociologically complete unit."[25] With the same "bias" he goes on to interpret the matrilineal family as did Levi-Strauss later as permitting a

---

actual framework of enslavement and destruction. Within this framework, even the liberties and gratifications of the individual partake of the general suppression. Their liberation, instinctual as well as intellectual, is a political matter, and a theory of the chances and preconditions of such liberation must be a theory of social change." From the Preface, to *Eros and Civilization, op. cit.,* p. xi.

[21] *Ibid.*

[22] Lawrence Ludovici. *The Final Inequality. A critical assessment of woman's sexual role in society.* New York: W. W. Norton & Co., 1965.

[23] August Bebel. Preface to the 25th Edition of *Woman and Socialism.*

[24] Claude Levi-Strauss. *The Elementary Structures of Kinship.* Boston: Beacon Press, 1969, p. 116.

[25] Bronislaw Malinowski. *Sex and Repression in Savage Society.* New York: Harcourt, Brace and Co., 1927, p. 213.

freer relationship between parents and child but retaining the stern authority figure and model for social ideals and ambition in the mother's brother. Furthermore, in the course of looking for a variant explanation of the incest taboo, Levi-Strauss defines woman in archaic society as the original and most precious form of goods for gift and barter. Yet, after defining woman as a piece of merchandise, Levi-Strauss can still say that in spite of centuries of abuse as an object, she retains something of her innate subjective value, "thus explaining that richness, that fervor and mystery which the relations between the sexes have preserved."[26] In a similar attempt to "soften the blow," Herskovits takes issue with the designation of woman as "property object" or "profitable capital" and says that as supposed "living property," (livestock?) women "must be cared for in a special manner, they arouse especially strong sentiments of affection or antipathy, etc." Therefore he would modify the claim of ownership a man has over a woman as "authority and responsibility" over her. These are very fine distinctions indeed.

Family vs. Work for Women: Socialist and Feminist Views

Engels, and August Bebel after him, saw in the family institution the embryo form of slavery and serfdom: "in miniature all the antagonisms which later develop on a wide scale within the society and its state."[27] Consequently, Engels thought that the contradictions inherent in the capitalist system were destroying the nuclear, male-dominated family. With full employment of women in industry, he predicted the removal of both the raison d'etre and the material foundation of "male-dominated monogamy." This belief led him to avow that only in the proletarian marriage, where the husband had no economic power over his wife and where she was herself employed, could there be any possibility of true "sex love." This, in turn, led to his statement, far less male chauvinistic than many another writer but irritating nonetheless, that "the last remnants of male domination in the proletarian home have lost all foundation — except, perhaps, for some of that brutality toward women which became firmly rooted in the establishment of monogamy."

In their organizational and educational work, socialist women did not carry further this sharp critique on the origins and functions of the family.[28]

---

[26] Levi-Strauss. *op. cit.*, p. 496.
[27] Marx, quoted in Engels, *The Origin of the Family, Private Property and the State*. Moscow: Progress Publishers, 1968, p. 96, possibly taken from Marx's "Abstract of Morgan's *Ancient Society*," *Marx-Engels Archive*, Vol. IX.
[28] For a discussion of women in socialist theory, see Juliet Mitchell, in this volume.

Mari Jo Buhle's paper on "Women in the Socialist Party, 1901-1914" shows how sporadic were the attempts to organize American women around distinctly women's causes. The German women's movement, which seems to have suffered from the same lack of ideology as did the American movement, nevertheless did have a number of very charismatic leaders on the socialist side, in the proletarian women's movement. Clara Zetkin and Lily Braun were active for many decades working for women's rights within the labor and socialist movements. Zetkin had close ties to Lenin, resulting in a number of interesting interchanges between the two on women. Once Lenin, while agreeing that women had to be freed from the home, proposed that women try to achieve an "extension and exaltation of motherliness from the individual to the social sphere,"[29] ie., women comrades should work within the youth movement. However, among socialist women one seldom finds any objection to their limitation to a child-bearing and nurturing role. At the end of her militant pamphlet on the awakening of political consciousness among women workers, Lily Braun says social and economic conditions "hit women in the hallowed center of their nature," i.e. their mother love, and that "only intellectually free, strong women can bear and raise a generation of free men capable of leading socialism on to victory."[30] This emphasis on the protection of motherhood in socialist programs was praised by the internationally known Swedish feminist, Ellen Key, who wrote and spoke against the "amaternalism" of much of the women's movement.[31] Miss Key proposed that the "service of the mother" be given equal status as military service. The woman whose work was in all likelihood being so described was Charlotte Perkins Gilman. A non-Marxian socialist, Darwinist, she has been called the "Marx and Veblen of the movement."[32] A comparison with Marx and Engels works in so far as she relates the subjugation of women to their exclusion from recognized social production and calls for the organization and industrialization of housework. However, she felt that the labor movement as well as the women's movement had mistakenly made a class issue of what she termed "social evolution." Furthermore, whereas she may have agreed with Engels and Bebel that woman was the first being to taste of bondage, she believed the centuries of woman's subjugation a necessary step in racial evolution. Woman is the "bearer of the life principle"

---

[29] Clara Zetkin. "Lenin on the Woman Question," New York: International Publishers, 1934.

[30] Lily Braun. *Die Frauen und die Politik*. Berlin: Expedition der Buchhandlung Vorwärts, 1903, p. 38.

[31] Ellen Key. *The Woman's Movement*. New York: G. P. Putnam's Sons, 1912.

[32] Charlotte Perkins Gilman. *Women and Economics*. New York: Harper and Row, 1966, p. 171. (first appeared 1898)

whose innate ability toward sustaining and preserving functions has civilized the man, her master. For, once subjugated by the man, she became his responsibility and in the process he was forced to take on some maternal traits of protecting and caring. "Love makes the world go round," she said.

The major criticism which Perkins Gilman directs against this unhealthy "sexuo-economic" imbalance[33] (not to be confused with Wilhelm Reich's sex-economic morality) is its socially and radically counter-evolutionary effects on women. "Half the human race is forced to confine its productive human energies to the same channels as its reproductive sex-energies."[34] Woman becomes a parasite and a "Priestess of the Temple of Consumption."[35] Olive Schreiner made many of the same points in her book on *Woman and Labor*.[36] However, as Schreiner points out in discussing male attitudes toward woman and labor, "it is not the labor, or the amount of labor, so much as the amount of reward that interferes with his ideal of the eternal womanly."[37]

In a sense, the tendency of many feminists to stress the economic powerlessness of women obliterated their indispensable economic functions in the past. The 1848 Declaration of Sentiments and Resolutions adopted at the Seneca Falls Women's Rights Convention stressed the civil and legal death of the married woman. This misinformed view of the legal position of women has been traced by many observers to the infamous and influential *Commentaries on the Laws of England* by Sir William Blackstone, which obliterated and distorted the body of laws which, in practice, gave women far more leeway than the slogan of "civil and legal death" of the married woman implied. (M. R. Beard also has a good discussion of this in her book.) Under these conditions it is understandable, says Perkins Gilman, that the attitude of the married woman toward the prostitute is like "the hatred of the tradeunionist for scab labor."[38]

Perkins Gilman hints at relationships later taken up by Marcuse. In *Woman and Economics* she says: "The false economic position of women . . . sexualizes our industrial relation and commercializes our sex relation. And, in the external effect upon the market, the over-sexed woman, in her unintelligent and ceaseless demands, hinders and perverts the economic development of the world."[39] She expressed her disdain for women caught in this

---

[33] *Ibid.*, p. 23.
[34] *Ibid.*, p. 117.
[35] *Ibid.*, p. 117.
[36] Olive Schreiner. *Woman and Labor*, New York: Frederick A. Stokes, Co., 1911.
[37] *Ibid.*, p. 213.
[38] Perkins Gilman. *op. cit.*, p. 110.
[39] *Ibid.*, p. 120.

parasitic existence elsewhere when she referred to society as filled with a legacy of "innumerable weak and little women, with the aspirations of an affectionate guinea pig."[40] Yet, she was radical as an ideologue for the movement, especially in view of the arguments of expediency then rampant in the literature of suffragism. Viewed together, the works of Thorstein Veblen, Charlotte Perkins Gilman and Elizabeth Cady Stanton, to name but three, were also valuable in counteracting the pernicious theories on women put forth by other Social Darwinists around the turn of the century.[41] However, as a means of legitimizing the women's movement, scientific arguments on the innate biological equality or superiority of womankind proved as risky for the movement as the earlier citations of chapter and verse to show Biblical support for the equality of the sexes.

The work of Charlotte Perkins Gilman and Elizabeth Cady Stanton, the only comparable figure in the women's movement, shows the radical potential which has been until recently obliterated. Their views on organized religion are close. Many people had criticized and ridiculed women's preoccupation with religious observances. Veblen, for instance, explained this preoccupation by the fact that women "stand in no such direct organic relation to the industrial process at large as would tend strongly to break down those habits of thought which, for the modern industrial purpose, are obsolete."[42] However, Stanton believed that women would never be emancipated until the pernicious influences of organized religion were thrown off; in 1895 she reinterpreted the Bible from a feminist point of view. Responding to one of the many critics of her *Woman's Bible*, Mrs. Stanton summarized the image of woman in the Bible:

> "Reading the Book with our own unassisted common sense, we do not find that the Mother of the race is exalted and dignified in the Pentateuch. The female half of humanity rests under the ban of general uncleanness. Even a female kid is not fit for a burnt offering to the gods. Women are denied the consecrated bread and meat, and not allowed to enter the holy places in the temples. Woman is made the author of sin, cursed in her maternity, subordinated in marriage, and a mere afterthought in creation."[43]

---

[40] *Ibid.*, p. 168.

[41] Riesman, *op. cit.*, p. 64.

[42] Veblen. *The Theory of the Leisure Class.* New York: B. W. Huebsch, 1918, p. 323.

[43] Letter to the Editor," *The Critic*, March 28, 1896, pp. 218-19; as quoted in Kraditor, *op. cit.*, p. 118-19.

Perhaps in keeping with her own view of woman as "bearer of the life principle," Perkins Gilman in her attack on religious institutions expressed the belief that modern religion would show less preoccupation with death and damnation, if women had more to do with its origin and development."[44] Both Stanton and Perkins Gilman had a far more comprehensive view of woman's condition than did their contemporaries in the Women's Rights and Suffrage movements.

Perkins Gilman's most radical proposals were not, however, that women could reform religious institutions, nor that women combine home with work, something that was then in fact taking place, but that domestic industries be made public services and that child-rearing also be removed from the private sphere. "Simply to bear children is a personal matter — an animal function. Education is collective, human, a social function."[45] She outlined the liberating benefits to child and mother if both were freed at least partially from the isolation of the home and the intensely personal relationship it created between parent and child.

One well-known modern example of successful transformation of the family along these lines is provided by the Israeli Kibbutzim. The Kibbutz movement has tried to place the rearing of children and household tasks in the responsibility of the community. The children are raised from infancy in small groups which live separate from the parents. Adults live in furnished rooms; however, all household tasks which otherwise fall to the woman are part of the communal work sphere. The founders of the Kibbutz movement, strongly influenced by the European women's movement, considered the bourgeois woman to be little more than a kept slave; they believed that the role of the husband as patriarch could only be destroyed by changing the legal, social and economic status of women.[46]

Much of the literature on the Kibbutz concentrates on more general matters or on its contribution to theories of human development. Consequently, there has been no concentrated investigation into woman and the Kibbutz.[47] The experience of Kibbutz education has strikingly refuted studies by Rene

---

[44] Quoted from Perkins Gilman. *His Religion and Hers*, 1923, by Carl Degler in the "Introduction" to Perkins Gilman. *Women and Economics, op. cit.*, p. vii.

[45] Perkins Gilman, *op. cit.*, p. 283.

[46] Melford E. Spiro. *Kibbutz: Venture in Utopia*. New York: Schocken Books, 1963, p. 115.

[47] Spiro. *op. cit.* Spiro. *Children of the Kibbutz*. New York: Schocken Books, 1965. Bruno Bettelheim. *The Children of the Dream*. New York: Macmillan Co., 1969. David Rapaport. "The Study of Kibbutz Education and its Bearing on the Theory of Development," *American Journal of Orthopsychiatry*, XXVIII (1958), pp. 587-97.

Spitz, John Bowlby[48] and others who claimed that a continuous uninter-
rupted intimate relationship to the mother was necessary for the emotional
and physical well-being of the child. The bonds of affection and responsibility which grow within the child peer groups have proven more than
adequate as replacements of the traditional mother-child relationship. Of
course, this is not to say that first generation Kibbutz parents do not have
ambivalent feelings about their more detached relationship to their children.

Yet, Kibbutz life does seem to present problems perculiar to women.
However, it is difficult to evaluate this syndrome of women's problems because so much of the success or failure of these settlements is determined by
their economic, political and social relationship to the State of Israel. Largely
because of the physical and economic realities of Kibbutz life, there is a
strong work ethic and a real need to meet production rates and schedules.
Consequently, in these agricultural communes, women have often found
themselves unable to compete with the men in those jobs requiring physically
strenuous labor or in those jobs where leaves of absence for childbirth and
nursing of infants would be a hazard to production. The result is that women
are concentrated in the "service" jobs. Spiro describes the situation in which
woman becomes a "specialist in one aspect of housekeeping" without the
compensation of variety which the traditional housewife has. The combination of "low prestige, difficult working conditions and monotony" have
meant that many women in the Kibbutz find little happiness in their work.[49]

In his book, *The Children of the Dream*, Bruno Bettelheim admires the
success of the Kibbutz in creating "a viable personality type wholly different
from that of the parents, in a single generation" (he specifically suggests
such a radical cure as a solution to our "slum problem").[50] Nevertheless he
describes the Kibbutz today as a "static society," characterized by a "modern
monasticism" which seeks to preserve rather than to change. Therefore, as
a model of how communal life could liberate women, the Kibbutz Movement
is not without its problems.

Family vs. Work For Women: Establishment Literature

In contrast, the huge corpus of establishment research on women, family,

[48] Rene Spitz. *The First Year of Life*. New York: International Univ rsities Press,
1965. Spitz has also written many articles, some dealing with the phenomenon of
"hospitalism."
John Bowlby. "The Nature of the Child's Tie to His Mother," *International Journal of Psycho-Analysis*, XXXIX (1958), pp. 350-73. Between 1950 and 1960 Bowlby
wrote many articles on this subject.
[49] Spiro, *Kibbutz: Venture in Utopia. op. cit.*, p. 229.
[50] Bettelheim. *op. cit.*, p. 49.

and marriage reinforces the central position of the family. The key words here are socialization and stability; or in the language of the social sciences: "The family serves as an agent of social placement for the new members of society, and by acting as an agent of control of marital relations, it regulates social alliances between family units and helps to place individuals into a patterned network of interweaving social relationships. The first of these features is known as the Principle of Legitimacy, the second as the Principle of Reciprocity."[51]

An encyclopaedic book, *The Family and Democratic Society*, by Joseph K. Folsom, provides a mass of data bewildering in its detail out of which some few references stand out which we may find relevant to the present Women's Movement. Folsom found family systems of primitive and complex societies readily comparable and concluded that "civilization does not elaborate the family system as it does the material culture and the economic organization."[52] Folsom attempts to make correlations from the huge amount of data he covers: the tendency to give consideration to the bride increases "as we go up the cultural scale." Yet, he finds no correlation between marital stability and stage of economic or cultural development. He notes the fact that throughout much of the modern period in the West the state has used the family to strengthen itself, most conspicuously through laws of inheritance. Folsom finds no qualitive difference in the treatment of women in matrilineal and patrilineal societies, nor does he find evidence of the existence of a genuine matriarchate. However, he does mention briefly the hypothesis that patrilineal societies taboo female orgasm of the clitoris, whereas matrilineal societies permit it and encourage sexual foreplay for that purpose.[53]

Great numbers of books and special issues of scholarly journals and newspaper articles concerned with the threatened stability or transition in the institutions of family and marriage in the United States and Europe were printed in the late Forties and Fifties. Folsom's book was part of that group, and in a section on trends in the American family, he calls for major reforms toward specialization and industrialization in the domestic sphere. He then went on to say, with less subtlety than most, that such steps were necessary for "the salvation of democratic society." A 1950 example states

[51] Rose L. Coser, ed. *The Family: Its Structure and Functions.* New York: St. Martin's Press, 1964, p. xiv.
[52] Joseph K. Folsom. *The Family and Democratic Society.* New York: John Wiley and Sons, 1934.
[53] Reo F. Fortune. "Social Forms and Their Biological Basis," *American Sociological Review*, Vol. 6 (1941), p. 571 and 725.

in consternation that not only was there never a Golden Age of the family in the United States but that there have been periods of dissatisfaction and rebellion against the values, restraints and objectives of family life throughout the history of the country.[54]

Viola Klein's widely cited book, *The Feminine Character, History of an ideology*,[55] lists as factors which sway research on women: the prevailing status and ideology assigned to women in a particular society as well as the author's personal, perhaps unconscious, attitudes toward women. In her introduction, one of the few places in the book where she admits that women are a subjugated group, she describes women as an " 'out-group' distinguished from the dominant strata by physical characteristics, historical tradition and social role." She examines Mathilde and Mathias Vaerting's book, *The Dominant Sex*, which collects attributes of subordination (in either sex) from the ancient "matriarchal" civilizations of Egypt, Libya and Sparta. The subordinated sex showed these traits: a passive role in love-making, obedience and submission, dependence on spouse, fearfulness, modesty, chastity, love of home, restricted interests, tenderness toward babies, relatively greater monogamous inclinations, interest in bodily adornment, finery.[56]

In her historical section on women's social and economic roles and the women's movement, she is careful to stress that women were not kept in submission by men but rather that "cultural lag" was operating. Whereas Bebel, as noted earlier, described woman as the first slave, V. Klein merely sees that woman remained a serf "after men had already outgrown the state of serfdom." She rightly counters the viewpoint that women were throughout history excluded from the economic life of society; yet she is forced to admit that, in all periods, woman's work was dependent upon and subservient to man's work, meagerly reimbursed and largely unskilled. In this section her historical sketch corrects the overly positive portrayal of woman's influence in Mary Beard's book.

Ten years after *The Feminine Character*, V. Klein collaborated with Alva Myrdal on *Women's Two Roles, Home and Work*.[57] It is a competent work

---

[54] Ray H. Abrams. "The Concept of Family Stability." *The Annals of the American Academy of Political and Social Sciences* Vol. 272 (Nov. 1950).

[55] Viola Klein. *The Feminine Character. History of an Ideology.* New York: International Universities Press, 1946.

[56] Mathilde and Mathias Vaerting. *The Dominant Sex. A Study in the Sociology of Sex Differentiation.* London: Allen & Unwin, 1923.

[57] Alva Myrdal and Viola Klein. *Women's Two Roles. Home and Work.* London: Routledge and Kegan Paul, 1956.

but refuses to allow a radical critique of the problem and consequently has no radical proposals for change. They see the main problem confronting women as their uncertain position between two conflicting ideals: the hardworking housewife and the lady of leisure. The general explanation for this phenomenon is, according to Klein and Myrdal, that women have in all spheres lagged one step behind men in the process of social evolution. In her paper "The Roots of Ambivalence in American Women,"[58] Alice Rossi questions the irrational, dysfunctional maintenance of traditional marital and fertility customs. (Recent women's liberation literature has tried to analyze ways in which the nuclear family is indeed quite functional, with periodic reforms, within the system.)

The practical effect of so-called labor-saving devices has been, Klein and Myrdal explain, "to decentralize services which had in an earlier stage moved from the home into the factory. . . . The concentration of production, which was the governing principle of industrialization, had come to a standstill in the sphere of the home."[59] While the authors do state after 161 pages that there must be a change in the "minds and habits of men" and that the patriarchal family has outlived its day, the main thrust of their book places the blame of inferior status with women themselves: "This is the price women have to pay for their uncertainty as regards their occupational future."[60] Their assessment of women's occupational opportunities in the course of the book shows — unintentionally perhaps — that a middle-class reliance on Right-to-Work and Equal Opportunity reforms can lead full circle. Women's entrance into the labor force, they write, amounts to the recovery of positions lost to women when they were "squeezed out of the economic process." However, they note, as is well known, that women generally remain in the lowest positions regarding skill and earnings. They further note that the "emancipation" of women has replaced "amateurs by professionals in the 'feminine' occupations rather than men by women in the 'masculine' spheres." Their solution to the conflict in women's roles is to structure a woman's life into three successive phases: education, family and social service. And lest this seem too radical, they are careful to add that their plan need not entail a new sexual division of labor. While not abandoning the feminist call for equality, they say "there is no use shutting our eyes to the facts of life in pursuit of an abstract ideal."[61]

---

[58] Alice S. Rossi. "The Roots of Ambivalence in American Women," unpublished manuscript.
[59] Myrdal and Klein. *op. cit.*, p. 80.
[60] *Ibid.*, p. 74.
[61] *Ibid.*, p. 156.

Even Joseph Folsom was more innovative in his unequivocal plea for industrialization of housework. With some variation in emphasis and tone, most establishment literature on American women in the past 15 years holds out as *future* steps a drive to bring social values more completely up to date with changes in economy and development, to educate the public to accept wider, more flexible roles for both sexes, and to establish cooperative or public arrangements for household tasks and child care. A little adjustment is deemed sufficient for the present to restore peace and tranquility.

Betty Friedan has a good section attacking the "functional freeze" effects of social science research on women. One of the sociologists bitterly criticized by Friedan, Mirra Komarovsky, has in her own book pointed to another branch of science, psychoanalysis, as the intellectual basis of neo-anti-feminism.[62] This criticism refers to the work of Freud and Helene Deutsch as opposed to the "dissident" psychoanalysts (also known as the "neo-Freudian revisionist school"[63]) who, she says, take into account social causes for feminine character. But perhaps the work of such "dissident" psychoanalysts as Fromn, Bettelheim and Erikson with their discovery of "motherly and fatherly principles"[64] and "inner and outer spaces,"[65] has also had detrimental effects on women. Much of psychoanalytic writing in the recent past, though having cast off the more blatantly patriarchal, as well as other dialectically more penetrating sections of Freud, continue to give scientific credibility to the image of women projected in the mass media.

Another general problem with most analysis of women is that, on the one hand, woman is examined out of historical context without consideration for social factors or, on the other hand, she is measured and judged within the confines of the institution of the family. Juliet Mitchell also makes this criticism in regard to Socialist theory on women. "In Marx's early writings woman becomes an anthropological entity, an ontological category, of a highly abstract kind. . . . (Later) the problem of women has been submerged in an analysis of the family."[66] She mentions as one error resulting from this approach Marx's premature prediction of the imminent disolution of the bourgeois family and his idea that the traditional family no longer existed in the working-class.

[62] Mirra Komarovsky, *Women in the Modern World.* Boston: Little, Brown & Co., 1953.

[63] Marcuse, *op. cit.,* p. 217.

[64] Erich Fromm. *The Art of Loving.* London: George Allen & Unwin, 1957.

[65] Erik Erikson. "Reflections on Womanhood, *"Woman in America,* Robert Jay Lifton, ed., Boston: Beacon Press, 1967. Also, Bruno Bettelheim, in *Women and the Scientific Professions.* Cambridge: M.I.T. Press, 1965.

[66] Juliet Mitchell, "Women: the Longest Revolution," see this volume, p. 95-96.

We have seen that some of the most incisive feminist and socialist analysis of women was done some time ago; both are badly in need of up- dating, correction and expanding. In socialist literature, the commitment to the woman question has often been little more than rhetorical. Establish- ment literature on women suffers from its need to reinforce and suggest ad- justments in the status quo and from its acceptance of certain myths about women as empirical truths. Much work lies ahead.

Observations on Movements for Women's Liberation

The first American women's movement has received scant attention from social analysts in view of the fact that it stretched over the better part of a century. The few books on the movement show the injurious effects of a tendency to rely on the biographical approach when the subject is woman. This tendency has perhaps led historians and others to discredit ideological convictions in favor of personal psychological motivation on the part of activists in the women's movement.[67]

Recently a number of books have dealt with ideological trends within the women's movement, taking into account the relationship to the broader social and political climate. The Kraditor book and William L. O'Neill's recent book, subtitled "The Rise and Fall of Feminism in America,"[68] stress the early radicalism in parts of the movement. Kraditor calls this the "Natural Rights" period, during which women, fresh from the Abolition Movement redefined woman as human being, citizen, women, wife, in that order. Kraditor and Andrew Sinclair[69] credit the anti-slavery movement with having radicalized the active women into an awareness of their own oppression: Kraditor discusses further steps in this process:

"When the woman suffrage was a radical cause, a handful of pioneers who were willing to brave public censure were its leaders. . . . The

---

[67] Example: Andrew Sinclair: "Yet, whatever the cause—her early infatuation with her brother-in-law, her differences with her husband, or her sympathy with her own sex—Elizabeth Stanton was fired throughout her life with indignation against woman's wrongs." On Susan B. Anthony: "She was a living example of how much good a public life does for a single woman." (see reference #69 also)
[68] William L. O'Neill. *Everyone was Brave. The Rise and Fall of Feminism in America.* Chicago: Quadrangle Books, 1969.
[69] Andrew Sinclair. *The Better Half.* New York, 1965. It is pointless to refute every instance of ("lively") male chauvinistic writing, but Sinclair's reference to the woman of the 1848 Seneca Falls Convention as "[William Lloyd] Garrison's group of women" deserves special notice.

treatment they received in turn encouraged their tendency to question all that their society held sacred in the realm of religion as well as in the field of politics. But, by the last decade of the nineteenth century, woman suffrage had become respectable, and women who held orthodox opinions on every other issue could now join a suffrage organization without fear of ostracism."[70]

O'Neil does not quite agree with the analysis of the origin of the movement which links it so closely with the radicalizing effect of Abolitionism. He explains the emergence of the movement in the 1830's as women's rebellion against their confining, male-dictated sex-role within the Victorian conjugal family.[71] Christopher Lasch speaks of the movement as one of "emancipated neurasthenic women." "aliens" to their own class. For him the movement, "the feminine impulse," is nothing more than one "aspect of a more general development — the revolt of intellectuals against the middle-class.[72] In any case, there is wide agreement that the movement was reacting against oppressive domesticity.

The Women's Movement, however, developed out of more material and tangible sources than the discontent of disoriented female intellectuals at the cultural limitations placed upon women's roles. Veblen in *Theory of the Leisure Class* and V. Klein et al. have examined the fact that revolt was not possible until industrialization freed some women from the drudgery of housework, concretely in the sense of providing them with maids from among the masses who came to the cities looking for jobs. Alice Rossi, underlining the fact that marriage itself hinders the growth of solidarity among women, finds that "the size of a woman's rights movement has been responsive to the proportion of 'unattached' women in a population."[73] She links the lull in women's rights activism in the Fifties to early age at marriage and the all time high proportion of married vs. single women. Likewise, she relates the rise in activism in the mid-Sixties to a reversal of trends in the Fifties.[74]

[70] Aileen Kraditor. *The Ideas of the Woman Suffrage Movement 1890-1920.* New York: Columbia University Press, 1965, p. 84.
[71] Cited in O'Neill: Philippe Ariès. *Centuries of Childhood: A Social History of Family Life.* New York: Vintage Books, 1962. Shows that the tightly knit nuclear family is a relatively modern creature.
[72] Christopher Lasch. *The New Radicalism in America* 1889-1963. New York: Alfred A. Knopf, 1965, p. 62.
[73] Alice S. Rossi. "Sex Equality: the Beginnings of Ideology." *The Humanist,* Vol. XXIX, No. 5 (Sept./Oct., 1969), p. 5.
[74] *Ibid.*

Whatever the basic causes underlying the emergence of the movement in the 1830's, they are all related to its middle-class origins. Feminists were demanding equal rights and opportunities when women in the labor and socialist movements were demanding differential and protective treatment and legislation. Ellen Key phrased it in this way: "Nothing so clearly elucidates in what stage of feminism the upper-class movement was than its obstinate adherence to 'the principle of personal freedom,' in the face of the atrocious actual conditions which resulted from 'the freedom of work' of the women factory hands."[75] Only when the women's movement identified with the working-women as workers did organized women workers begin to actively support the major goal of the movement — suffrage.

Kraditor points out that the egalitarianism of the early stage of the suffrage movement, with its origins in the anti-slavery struggle, returned at the end of the century in the form of social concern for the poor immigrant, for instance Jane Addams' work. But this time the social concern for another oppressed group did not have a radicalizing effect on the women. The movement had in its latter stages become broad, moderate, and opportunistic, willing to form alliances with any group in its drive for the vote. The vote itself was no longer demanded as an inalienable right. Some sections of the suffrage movement began to court the support of conservative groups — normally anti-feminist — by claiming that enfranchizing the women would insure more educated middle and upper class voters to counteract Negro and foreign-born voters. Later in the suffrage movement much stress was laid on the uniquely salutary benefits to the country of "feminine character" which would supposedly come once women had the vote.[76] In the end, movement women redirected support to the very idealized roles as wives and mothers from which they had originally sought freedom.[77]

Any movement which strives for the liberation of women must also concern itself with the sphere of sexuality. This is proving a necessary concern in the present Women's Movement, and it has been the subject of much debate in the commentary on earlier movements. Indeed, to many, the term "emancipated woman" has only the sexual connotation.

Lenin believed that a proletarian revolution would create the basis for "real renovation in marriage and sexual matters." Consequently, he chastised Clara Zetkin for allowing questions of sex and marriage to be the main topics in discussion groups of women comrades. He did not consider the enlighten-

---

[75] Ellen Key. *op. cit.*, p. 35.
[76] Aileen Kraditor. *Ideas of . . ., op. cit.* is the source for this discussion of the various stages in the suffrage movement.
[77] O'Neill's book has a good discussion on this topic.

ment of proletarian women on these subjects of very high priority. More specifically, Lenin was critical of Rosa Luxemburg's efforts in organizing and supporting prostitutes, even though he realized tthey were doubly oppressed by the property system and moral hypocrisy. Zetkin's reply to his admonishments is similar to arguments in Women's Liberation today: "The questions of sex and marriage in a bourgeois society of private property, involve many problems, conflicts and much suffering for women of all social classes and ranks. . . . A critical, historical attitude to these problems must lead to a ruthless examination of bourgeois society, to a disclosure of its real nature and effects, including condemnation of its sexual morality and falseness. All roads lead to Rome."[78]

Speaking of experiments in new sexuality, Lenin said, "However wild and revolutionary the behavior may be, it is still really quite bourgeois. It is, mainly, the hobby of the intellectuals . . . ."[79] Marx characterized such experiments as being carried on "behind society's back."[80] Herbert Marcuse also rejects a reliance on the supposed revolutionary power of a liberated adult sexuality as proposed by Wilhelm Reich. This rejection is very obvious from an interesting interview with Marcuse in Germany on the emancipation of women done in 1962 prior to the publication of *One-Dimensional Man*.[81] Marcuse criticized feminist efforts as effectively obtaining for women an equal share in the repression to which the man is exposed in the work sector. The point was then raised that parts of past women's movements had seen themselves as the last prop holding up a repressive society; they believed that society might undergo major change if men, coerced and manipulated in the production process, were unable to compensate by having a woman at home to dominate. To this Marcuse replied that the entry of women in to the work sphere would not emancipate the woman as woman but transform her into an instrument of work. Furthermore, he believed that society could successfully absorb the full employment of women. Today in Women's Liberation there is little disagreement that women have spent much of their history as precisely that — an instrument of work, a beast of burden. One remembers the arguments of the anti-

[78] Zetkin. *op. cit.*, p. 14.

[79] *Ibid.*, p. 7.

[80] This reference to Marx appears in Elisabeth Busse-Wilson. *Die Frau und die Jugendbewegung*. Hamburg: Freideutscher Jugendverlag Adolf Saal, 1920, p. 77. This book also gives an excellent analysis of the oppression of women by a youth movement which thought it was one of liberation.

[81] "Herbert Marcuse und Peter Furth—Emanzipation der Frau," *Das Argument* Vol. 4, No. 23 (Oct./Nov., 1962).

suffragists, arguing that participation in politics would diminish the innate purity of women. Marcuse goes on to relate Sartre's theory in *Being and Nothingness* that the woman's capacity for joy, not as an instrument of labor but as a giver of pleasure, lies precisely in her distance from direct participation in the production process. Statre becomes very specific: those parts of the body which have the least to do with work are the most erogenous zones and as the woman becomes more involved in the production process, physically as well as psychologically, her capacity for joy and pleasure also decreases. S. de Beauvoir herself, after spending much of her book describing the dulling effects of woman's sphere of "immanence," makes a telling distinction between "white collar" work and housework.

"Cooking, washing, managing her house, bringing up children, woman shows more initiative and independence than men slaving under orders. . . . The woman gets more deeply into reality. The baby fed and in his cradle, clean linen, the roast, constitute more tangible assets; yet just because, in the concrete pursuit of these aims, she feels their contingence — and accordingly her own — it often happens that woman does not identify with them and she has something left of herself. Man's enterprises are at once projects and evasions: he lets himself be smothered by his career and his 'front.' "[82]

Implicit in these reservations is a question as to whether the woman is a freer less co-opted being than the man.

Marcuse also doubted whether the expansion of public services to ease housework or child care responsibilities of the woman would be a progressive step, for the reason that any intervention of the apparatus of social production into the private sphere becomes in turn a means of further social conformism and repression. In a repressive society the good becomes bad.

This small sampling of commentary on Women's Liberation shows the extent to which the revolutionary potential of the movement is judged by impressions of the failure of previous movements. The present Movement must study the mistakes and errors as well as the successes of earlier women's movements. A critical study of the mass of written material on women is one necessary step in developing both a theoretical and a strategic analysis of women's oppression and human liberation.

---

[82] de Beauvoir, *op. cit.*, p. 588.